Singing
FOR
DUMMIES®
2ND EDITION

by Pamelia S. Phillips, DMA

WILEY

Wiley Publishing, Inc.

Singing For Dummies®, 2nd Edition

Published by
Wiley Publishing, Inc.
111 River St.
Hoboken, NJ 07030-5774
www.wiley.com

Copyright © 2011 by Wiley Publishing, Inc., Indianapolis, Indiana

Published by Wiley Publishing, Inc., Indianapolis, Indiana

Published simultaneously in Canada

For general information on our other products and services, please contact our Customer Care Department within the U.S. at 877-762-2974, outside the U.S. at 317-572-3993, or fax 317-572-4002.

For technical support, please visit www.wiley.com/techsupport.

Wiley also publishes its books in a variety of electronic formats. Some content that appears in print may not be available in electronic books.

Library of Congress Control Number: 2010937161

ISBN: 978-0-470-64020-3

Manufactured in the United States of America

10 9 8 7 6 5 4 3 2

WILEY

About the Author

Dr. Pamelia S. Phillips is the Professional Program Director and Chair of Voice and Music at CAP21 (Collaborative Arts Project 21). Dr. Phillips earned her Doctorate of Musical Arts and Master of Music in Vocal Performance from Arizona State University and her Bachelor of Music Education from Arkansas State University. Her performances range from contemporary American Opera premieres to guest performances with major symphonies.

Dr. Phillips has also taught at Wagner College, Arizona State University, Scottsdale Community College, and South Mountain Community College.

Performances include title roles in *Carmen, Tragedy of Carmen, Dido and Aeneas,* and *Lizzie Borden;* the Witch in *Hansel and Gretel;* Giulietta in *Tales of Hoffmann;* Dorabella in *Cosi fan tutte;* Mum in *Albert Herring;* Constance in the world premiere of *She Stoops to Conquer;* Lady with a Hat Box in *Postcard from Morocco;* Frau Bauer in *Dora;* Beatrice in the stage premiere of *Garden of Mystery;* Mrs. Cornett in *Tobermory;* staged performance of *From The Diary of Virginia Woolf;* Gloria Thorpe in *Damn Yankees;* Gymnasia in *A Funny Thing Happened on the Way to the Forum;* Liebeslieder singer in *A Little Night Music;* and Lady Thiang in *King and I.* Symphonic performances include Berlioz's *Le mort de Cléopâtra* with the Bronx Symphony, Mahler's *Fourth Symphony* with the Centré Symphony, and *Das Lied von der Erde* and Mahler's *Third Symphony* with the New York Symphonic Arts Ensemble. Dr. Phillips has also been a guest artist with the Phoenix Chamber Symphony, the Scottsdale Fine Arts Orchestra, the Putnam County Chorale, and the National Chorale.

Dedication

In memory of my sister, Debbie Griggs (d. 2003).

Author's Acknowledgments

I gratefully acknowledge Project Editor Sarah Faulkner for her amazing attention to detail and endless supply of encouragement, Acquisitions Editor Michael Lewis for the invitation to write a second edition, Technical Editor David Kelso for sharing his wealth of knowledge, and Copy Editor Krista Hansing for always looking out for the reader. I was so fortunate to work with this amazing team.

Thank you to my parents, Holmes and Darlene, for all the lessons you paid for, the hours you had to listen to me practice, and the many miles you drove to attend my concerts.

Thank you to George, for your encouragement and for tolerating all the late nights and weekends I spent writing.

Eternal thanks to my students (and a few colleagues) who sang so beautifully on the CD and to my students and colleagues who offered advice and support. You inspire me.

Special thanks to my voice teachers, Julia Lansford, Jerry Doan, Norma Newton, and Judith Natalucci.

Publisher's Acknowledgments

We're proud of this book; please send us your comments at http://dummies.custhelp.com. For other comments, please contact our Customer Care Department within the U.S. at 877-762-2974, outside the U.S. at 317-572-3993, or fax 317-572-4002.

Some of the people who helped bring this book to market include the following:

Acquisitions, Editorial, and Media Development

Project Editor: Sarah Faulkner

(Previous Edition: Jennifer Connolly)

Acquisitions Editor: Michael Lewis

Copy Editor: Krista Hansing

(Previous Edition: Esmeralda St. Clair)

Assistant Editor: David Lutton

Technical Editor: David Kelso

Media Development Associate Producer: Shawn Patrick

Media Development Assistant Project Manager: Jenny Swisher

Editorial Manager: Christine Meloy Beck

Editorial Assistants: Jennette ElNaggar, Rachelle S. Amick

Art Coordinator: Alicia B. South

Cover Photos: © iStockphoto.com/ Chris Hutchison

Cartoons: Rich Tennant (www.the5thwave.com)

Composition Services

Project Coordinator: Sheree Montgomery

Layout and Graphics: Carl Byers, Joyce Haughey, Mark Pinto

Proofreader: Bonnie Mikkelson

Indexer: Sharon Shock

Publishing and Editorial for Consumer Dummies

Diane Graves Steele, Vice President and Publisher, Consumer Dummies

Kristin Ferguson-Wagstaffe, Product Development Director, Consumer Dummies

Ensley Eikenburg, Associate Publisher, Travel

Kelly Regan, Editorial Director, Travel

Publishing for Technology Dummies

Andy Cummings, Vice President and Publisher, Dummies Technology/General User

Composition Services

Debbie Stailey, Director of Composition Services

Contents at a Glance

Table of Contents

Introduction

1'm so happy you chose this book! Whether you're a shower singer or you secretly desire to sing on a stage, this book is for you. The book is full of helpful information covering all aspects of singing, from posture and breathing to vocal health and techniques for increasing your range. Absolutely no experience is necessary! Even if you know zero about singing, you're going to have a great time exploring your singing voice.

You can't develop your singing voice overnight; it takes time. Some people are born with a voice ready to sing at the Hollywood Bowl, but most people who like to sing have to work on their voice to prepare it for the first performance. Whichever category you fit into, this book has some valuable information for you.

Exercising the singing voice is the ticket to improving your technique. The exercises in the book are similar to what you may encounter in a voice lesson or a class about singing. By working on exercises, you give your body a chance to figure out exactly how to make the sounds. After you get the technical details cooking, you can apply that information to your songs and sound even better.

You may not have someone there listening to you as you practice, but you find suggestions throughout the book on how to listen to your voice and critique it for yourself so that you can improve every time you practice.

About This Book

This book is designed as a reference guide, not as a tutorial, and includes exercises to help you improve your singing. Flip through and look for parts that interest you. (For that matter, I recommend that you also go through the parts that don't interest you — who knows what you may discover about your voice?) What's important to remember is that you don't have to read this book from cover to cover to improve your singing; look for the topics you need and use both the exercises and the CD to develop your best voice.

The CD is an important partner to your book. The CD exercises work the technical info that you read about in the book. You hear a pattern played for you on the piano, a singer demonstrates the pattern for you, and the pattern is repeated several times for you to sing along. Just singing songs is cool, but you want to work on technique to get your songs to sound great. If you work on the articulation exercises on the CD and then apply that information and skill to songs, you can sing with great skill and be understood. If you've never had lessons, you may not see the benefit of the exercises in the beginning, or they may seem difficult. Keep trying them during your practice sessions, and you may see how quickly the exercises can help you to sing.

Chapter 10 gives you ideas on developing a practice routine to coordinate all the information that you read in the book with what you hear on the CD. After you plot out your practice routine, keep the CD handy so you can choose which tracks to practice. Storing the CD in the back of the book in the plastic cover is best. Or you may want to put the CD in your car to sing along with as you drive. That's cool, as long as you pay attention to your driving.

Because many people respond quickly to imagery, I include ways to use imagery to help you improve your singing. Knowing the mechanics works well for some singers, and others prefer knowing what to think about or visualize as they sing. If you want to know what to listen for, I give you that information as well. I also explain the exercises by having you do something physical. Sometimes just feeling the movement in your body gets the idea across. Whatever way you prefer to use, you can find it in this book.

Conventions Used in This Book

To help you navigate this book with ease, I set the following conventions:

- I use **bold** text to highlight key words in bulleted lists.

- When I introduce a new term that you may not be familiar with, I use *italic* and define the term within the text.

- Web addresses appear in `monofont` so they're easy to find on the page.

- When this book was printed, some Web addresses may have needed to break across two lines of text. If that happened, rest assured that I didn't put in any extra characters (such as hyphens) to indicate the break. So when using one of these Web addresses, just type in exactly what you see in this book, as though the line break doesn't exist.

- I spell out the vowel sound for you or use symbols found in *Webster's* dictionary, because that's most common to new singers and nonsingers.

- Throughout the book you have opportunities to sing specific vowel sounds. One vowel sound may need a little explanation. I use the shape "a" for the vowel sound in the words cat, hat, or Matt. For the vowel sound in the words father, plaza, or blah, I use "*ah*." You can practice these sounds in Chapter 8 so you know what to do when you see them in other places in the book.

  ✔ Musical styles continue to change and the terms used to describe the styles also continue to change. If you read the history of pop or rock music, you'll see a long list of titles to describe each era. I use the term *pop-rock* for songs that can cross over into both styles. It's common to see a great song listed on the hit-song list for different styles of music. In Chapter 14 you can read about the sounds used in different styles, but know that *pop-rock* refers to a song that could fit in either style.

  ✔ I use musical examples throughout the book to give you a visual explanation of the exercises on the CD. You can read an explanation about musical notation in Chapter 1. There you find information about how the little circles on the page correspond with the notes on the piano and the notes you'll sing in specific parts of your range.

What You're Not to Read

This book is full of great information about singing. If you're new to singing, you'll have a great time exploring all the details and exercises designed specifically for you. Feel free to start anywhere in the book that interests you, and know that the Technical Stuff icon is for singers who are ready for more detailed information. The same is true for the sidebars. The info in these gray-shaded boxes is interesting and fun, but not crucial to read the first time through. You can read it the first time, if you like, or come back to it later.

Foolish Assumptions

Because you're reading this book, I assume that you have an interest in singing and discovering how to improve your singing. You don't need any previous knowledge about singing. You can find information for beginners, as well as advanced information for singers who have some experience.

How This Book Is Organized

The book is organized into six parts, with each part containing specific types of information about singing. You explore the mechanics of singing before you work on your technique. If you have no experience singing, you may find the first part especially helpful.

Part 1: Exploring Singing Basics

I cover the three huge singing topics — posture, breathing, and tone — in Part I. You want these skills to be rock solid. If you have a grasp on these three important topics, you can increase your singing capability. You may find yourself coming back to these chapters often to solidify these skills. Take your time as you work through the first four chapters. You may want to add the exercises you find in this part to your practice journal. By working on these skills every day, you can see steady improvement. Another interesting topic in this part is voice types. If you've always wanted to know the difference between a soprano and a mezzo, Chapter 2 is waiting for you.

Part II: Improving Your Singing

The main topics in Part II are tone, resonance, vowels, and consonants. Chapter 6 offers you even more information to get you sounding really good when you sing. After you figure out what tone is all about, you find out about the resonance of your tone in Chapter 7. If you aren't sure what resonance is all about, you can read all about the misconceptions of resonance in Chapter 7. This part gets your vowels and consonants moving and grooving, too. If you articulate the vowels and consonants correctly (see Chapters 8 and 9), you make sure that your audience can easily understand you, no matter what style of music you sing. Finally, Chapter 10 is all about practicing and developing a routine to improve your singing voice and apply all the information in the book.

Part III: Advanced Techniques to Improve Your Voice

In this part, you move on to information that helps you apply singing technique. You may have heard people talking about chest voice but may not be quite sure what that means. Head to Part III to find out more than you ever dreamed about the registers of the voice. Chapter 11 takes on middle voice, chest voice, and head voice, and Chapter 12 discusses range. Chapter 13 helps you with your speaking voice and belting. Though you may think that your speaking voice and singing voice are entirely different, you may be surprised by how much your speaking voice can help or hinder your singing. This part also offers some solid suggestions for finding the right voice teacher (see Chapters 14 and 15). In addition, you can find out more about various musical styles — classical, country, jazz, musical theater, opera, pop-rock, and R&B.

Part IV: Preparing to Perform

When you have your technique working well, you may want to test it in public. Before you walk onto the stage, check out this part for great advice on how to prepare before the big debut. Chapter 16 helps you figure out how to choose songs that enhance your technical skills and where to find those lovely tunes. After you find the tune, you want to explore Chapter 17 for help with that new song. Trying to figure out the song alone may seem overwhelming, but Chapter 17 has some helpful hints to make the task manageable.

That new song needs some spice from both the music and the words. Just looking gorgeous on the stage isn't enough; you want to give the audience something to think about as you sing. Chapter 18 explores acting the song while singing: two skills that are important to use together. If you aren't sure you're ready to get out onstage because of butterflies in your stomach, check out Chapter 19 on performance anxiety. Being nervous is okay, but you can explore ways to help you with the anxiety so your sweaty palms don't bother you as you sing beautifully. If you think your butterflies are a sign that you're excited and ready to audition, Chapter 20 gives you some sound advice on taking your song to an audition. Many people dream of auditioning for a show but have no idea how to prepare. The answers to your questions and preparation advice await you in Chapter 20.

Part V: The Part of Tens

If you listen to the top ten songs in your favorite category of music, do you know which singers have good technique? Because the industry tends to favor an ability to make big bucks over talent, find out which singers really have good technique to back up their fame. You may see some surprises on the list. Handling yourself onstage takes some practice if you've never been in the spotlight. In this part, you can find ten tips to help you perform like a pro. You may also have some questions about singing that you just didn't know whom to ask, so I also made a list of the ten most frequently asked questions that my students bring to their lessons and a list of ten tips to keep your voice healthy. You may find the answer to a question that's been nagging you.

Part VI: Appendixes

Appendix A has a list of songs to explore when you're ready, including classical, musical theater, pop-rock, and country songs. No matter what style you like, you can practice your new skills as you work through the book. I chose these songs because of the benefits they provide for your technique. You may not find the top hits of today on the list, but you can find songs that are great for working on singing technique, regardless of style. Appendix B has a chart to coordinate the info on the CD. Use the chart in Appendix B to locate the skills you want to practice today. By working slowly through the exercises on the CD, you give your body time to figure out how to correctly sing the exercises and apply that information to the songs in Appendix A.

Icons Used in This Book

This icon tells you that a track on the CD corresponds to the information in the chapter.

This information is so helpful that you should store it in your memory bank.

This icon highlights detailed explanations that you may find really interesting or may just want to skip right over.

The Tip icon emphasizes good advice from someone who has already made the mistake and wants to save you the trouble.

To avoid making a blunder or injuring your voice, pay attention to what these paragraphs have to say.

Where to Go from Here

If you have no singing experience, you may want to start with Chapter 1 and work your way through the chapters in order. However, this book is designed to allow you to jump in anywhere you want and start swimming through information that's completely understandable. If you have some singing experience, choose whatever chapter appeals to you. You may have to refer to other chapters occasionally if you missed a definition, but otherwise, you're free to roam the chapters at your own pace and in any order. As you work through the exercises in this book, you want to have the basic technical skills of breathing (see Chapter 4) and tone (see Chapters 5 and 6) readily available. If you find yourself struggling, you may want to go straight to Chapter 3 to make sure that you have proper singing posture.

Part I
Exploring Singing Basics

The 5th Wave   By Rich Tennant

TARZAN
VOICE
COACH

"You've got a very nice voice for clubs and small venues, but nothing that would ever inspire an elephant to charge."

In this part . . .

*I*n this part, you get an introduction to singing. You find out about different voice types and figure out which category fits your voice. Then you check out interesting info about the three biggies: posture, breath, and tone. You want great posture to get your body lined up and ready to sing your best, and you need some air moving in and out of your body to keep the glorious sounds coming out. Working on tone allows you to improve on the sounds you're already making or to tweak your tone a little if your engine knocks rather than hums.

Take your time as you read through these chapters. You may even want to come back to the exercises on a regular basis to maintain a smoothly running vocal engine.

Chapter 1

Preparing to Sing

So you're curious about singing. Whatever musical background and experience you have or don't have, this book has something to offer you. The book contains great exercises and even a CD that allows you to hear the exercise and sing along. If you're a beginner, welcome aboard. You can find out all kinds of cool info about singing in this book. This chapter provides an overview of all the great stuff you can encounter in the book.

Singing is one of the coolest means of expression out there. Singing well is about knowing how to work the parts that create the sound for singing. The chapters that you encounter in the book outline what you need to know in just the right sequence. You don't have to read them in the order written to get what you need. Some of the later chapters may be a little difficult if you don't have any singing experience. The only way to know is to jump right in and start reading on whatever topic interests you.

What You Want to Know Right from the Beginning

Before you choose the date for your first big concert or recital, you want to find out about singing. The first part of this book provides you with the big picture.

Determining your voice type

Singers usually are eager to determine their voice type because they want a category to belong to. You may have heard of the categories of singers:

- **Soprano:** Higher female voice

- **Mezzo:** Lower female voice

- **Tenor:** Higher male voice

- **Bass:** Lower male voice

If you aren't sure which one applies to your voice, explore Chapter 2. You can find explanations of what makes a soprano differ from a mezzo, or a tenor differ from a bass. You don't have to figure out your voice type today, but you can explore the chapter so you know what to listen for as you sing.

Locating the notes on the staff

Voice types are probably easier to figure out if you know where to find the notes on a musical staff. (See Figure 1-1 in this chapter.) The names of the notes are A, B, C, D, E, F, and G. Those notes repeat across the piano.

- The treble clef spaces correspond to the notes F, A, C, and E. Beginning on the bottom of the staff and going up, the notes spell *face*. You can use sentences to remember the other notes. Again, starting on the bottom line and moving up, the notes on the lines of the staff are E, G, B, D, and F, letters that begin the words of the sentence *Every good boy does fine*.

- For the bass clef, the spaces are A, C, E, and G, the letters that begin the sentences *All cows eat grass* or *All cars eat gas*. The lines in the bass clef are G, B, D, F, and A, which correspond to *Good boys do fine always*. If you prefer animals, then use *Great big dogs fight animals*.

If I say that a singer's range is Middle C to High C, I have to use ledger lines to notate those two notes because they're not within the five-line staff. Ledger lines are extra lines added above or below the staff for notes that are higher or lower than the notes on the staff. When you find Middle C in Figure 1-1, you can see the extra line added below the staff. The easiest way to find Middle C on the piano is to look at the brand name printed on the lid covering the keys. If you find that brand name, the C right in the middle of that name, or just to the left, is usually Middle C.

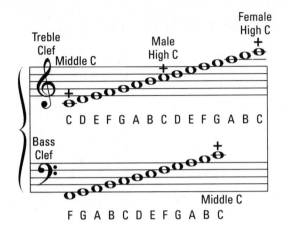

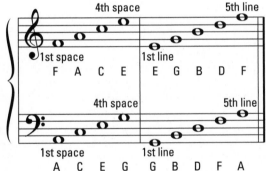

Middle C is called *Middle C* because it's in the middle of the keyboard that contains 88 keys. Middle C is also called C4, because it's the fourth C on the keyboard. If Middle C is C4, then the next C above is C5, and so on. C is the note
just to the left of the pair of black keys. The distance between the two Cs is
called an *octave*. If you start counting at the first *C* and count eight white notes
up, you find another C. That means the E just above Middle C (C4) is E4. Easy
enough, but not every person you encounter knows this system, so I stick to
what works: Middle C.

You also encounter the words *flat* and *sharp* in this book. *Flats* lower a pitch
a half step and a *sharp* raises the pitch a half step. F-sharp is the black key
on the piano between F and G. The same black key between F and G can be
called G-flat.

Considering posture, breath, and tone

First, you want to get yourself aligned — that is, line up all your body parts to get ready to sing — and then explore your breathing. Breathing while singing is different from breathing normally, because you have to take in more air and use more air over a longer period of time. When you get the air flowing, you can explore the tone of your voice.

- **Correcting posture for a better sound:** Posture is important in singing well. If all the parts for singing are lined up correctly, you stand a really good chance of getting wonderful sounds to come flying out of your body. Knowing how to stand isn't rocket science, but it may take a little adjustment on your part. If you aren't used to standing tall all the time, you may feel a bit awkward at first. Chapter 3 explores posture for singing.

- **Knowing the keys to proper breathing:** The big key to great singing is knowing how to use your breath to make the sounds. You may not know how to get much breath in your body and then make it last throughout a long phrase. If you check out Chapter 4, you can find all kinds of exercises and explanations on how to work on your breath so you can sing those long phrases in your favorite song.

- **Finding your tone:** Vocal tone is important because you want the best sounds to come out of your mouth. By exploring exercises on tone, you can make changes to your sound. People often tell me that they want to change the way they sound. To change your sound, you need to know how you create sound. The two chapters on tone, Chapters 5 and 6, give you quite a bit of information about how to start a note and then what to do to make the note sound a specific way.

Developing Your Singing Voice

When you have the basic information swimming around in your head, you can start to work on your singing voice. Chapters 6 through 9 offer you more specific information about how to create a sound that's unique to you. Sometimes singers try to imitate their favorite famous singer. A better idea is to sound like yourself. Your voice can be just as fabulous as that famous singer's. You just have to practice to develop it.

Following are some points to work on:

- **Filling the auditorium with resonance:** Resonance is the echoing of tone. In Chapter 7, you find out how to use resonance to project your voice. Singing loudly makes a lot of sound, but using resonance allows you to project the sound over the orchestra to the back of the concert hall. Find out how your voice can resonate so Uncle Sam can hear you from the back row.

✔ **Fine-tuning vowels and consonants:** A long time ago in grade school, you had to work with vowels and consonants. Well, you can refresh yourself in Chapters 8 and 9. By making your vowels and consonants specific, you can make yourself easily understood when you're singing. You've probably heard someone sing but couldn't understand a word they said. It's even worse when the song is in English or a language that you speak. By knowing how to articulate vowels and consonants, you can create specific sounds that your audience can follow.

✔ **Warming up your voice:** Practice makes perfect! After you discover all this great information about singing, you need to develop a plan for practicing it on a regular basis. If practicing seems like a foreign concept to you, check out Chapter 10. The whole chapter is devoted to helping you figure out what to do when you warm up and how to apply the exercises that you read about in the book to your daily practice routine. Because you can explore so much, make a list of what you want to accomplish today, and then add more to that list each time that you practice.

Working the Different Parts of Your Voice

Your goal is to make your singing voice sound like one smooth line from top to bottom. Your voice may have a few bumps and wiggles as you work your way up and down. That's perfectly normal, but help is right at hand. Chapters 11 and 12 work with specific areas of the voice called *registers* — chest voice, head voice, middle voice, and falsetto. In these chapters, you can discover what each part of the voice feels like and what to do with it. When you're ready, try these tips:

✔ **Strengthening your middle, chest, and head voice to get a complete vocal workout:** The first step in the workout for the voice is to find the different registers of the voice and then notice what each feels like. After you find them, you want to try to smooth the transition between registers. You may find that your chest voice and head voice feel miles apart. The exercises in Chapters 11 and 12 are designed to help you smooth out the bumps. You may not think the exercises are easy in the beginning, which is good. I don't want you to be bored. Even if you've never explored any vocal sounds, you can figure out these exercises and get your voice in good working order — it just takes some time and patience.

Chapter 12 helps you refine your register transitions and extend your range. Some songs require flexibility, and the exercises in the chapter help you develop agility and even try out your agility in some pop riffs.

✔ **Adding belting technique to your list of skills:** Your speaking voice needs a workout to get you started on belting. Belting is the sound that you want to make for musical theater or pop-rock songs. The exercises start from the beginning, so you don't have to know anything about belting to take on the information in Chapter 13.

Applying Your Technique

After you explore your technique through the exercises that I provide, you need to take the next step. Chapters 14 through 18 are about applying your technique. At some point, you want to apply that healthy technique to songs. You also want to maintain your healthy technique and a healthy voice at all times. When your technique is really cooking, you can explore Chapters 19 and 20, about moving your technique into a performance situation. Performances can be big or small. Whatever the size of the audience, you want to look like a pro and feel good about what you're doing onstage.

To start applying your technique when singing songs for yourself or others, consider the following:

✔ **Training for singing:** Finding a voice teacher can be tricky. When you find the right teacher, the experience can be rewarding. If you aren't sure how to go about finding a teacher, explore the tips and suggestions in Chapter 15. Finding the teacher may be the most difficult part. After you answer the questions in Chapter 15, you'll have a better idea of what you want from voice lessons. Whether or not you hire a voice teacher, you can check out Chapter 14 for information about training to sing different styles of music. Knowing what's required of your voice allows you to dive right into the right chapters.

✔ **Choosing appropriate singing material:** Finding new songs to sing can be overwhelming. You have so many choices, but how do you know what works for you? The clues are in Chapter 16. The lists there offer suggestions on what to look for and what to avoid when choosing songs. Whether you want a song to sing for your own pleasure or a song for a specific function, you want a song that accentuates your strengths.

For more suggestions of songs, you can explore Appendix A for a list of suggested songs for enhancing your singing technique. The songs cover different styles of music, from classical to country. After you choose the song you want to sing, check out Chapter 17 for some tips on how to master the song in a short amount of time.

✔ **Feeling comfortable with the music and text:** In Chapter 18, you can explore acting to combine with your singing. Sounding good when you sing is great, but you want to sound good and understand the story behind the music. You don't have to know anything about acting to explore this chapter; it's all right there for you.

✔ **Overcoming performance anxiety:** If your daydreams of singing are clouded with anxiety about singing in front of an audience, Chapter 19 is just for you. By confronting your fear and taking charge, you can make progress and let go of the anxiety. You only add pressure to your performance if you assume that you're supposed to be totally calm. Many famous performers get nervous before a performance. After exploring Chapter 19, you'll know that it's fine to be nervous, but you can still sing while nervous.

✔ **Nailing your audition:** So many singers dream of auditioning for a Broadway show or entering a singing competition that I wrote a whole chapter about auditioning your song. Chapter 20 has information for you on what to expect at the audition, who may be there, what you may have to sing or do, and how to prepare for the audition. Because an audition for a musical is different from an audition for an opera, you want to know what's kosher and what's not.

Having Fun

Singing is about more than just alignment and technique — although, of course those considerations are important. If you concentrate only on the technical aspect of singing, you may end up singing from your head rather than your heart. Remember to let loose every once in awhile and have fun with it!

Some performers are really amazing onstage — obviously having fun — and they also have great technique. Check out Chapter 21 to see whether any of your favorite singers made my list of performers with great technique. And if you want your performance to be spectacular, Chapter 24 has some great tips on performing like a pro. Before your big performance, check out Chapter 22 for answers to the most commonly asked questions about singing, and see Chapter 23 for information on keeping your voice healthy. Maintaining a healthy voice is important. Your cords are really small, and you want to take good care of them. You can also read about medications and other factors that influence your singing voice. A healthy voice and solid technique will keep you singing for years to come.

Chapter 2

Determining Your Voice Type

*F*inding your voice type is a challenge because several ingredients combine to create a voice type. You don't have to know your voice type if you're singing for your own enjoyment, but you may be curious to find out. If you aspire to sing professionally or do some professional auditions, you definitely want to know your voice type. You'll be asked at the audition, so you want to know that answer before someone asks. Chapter 20 has more info about auditions. Determining your *voice type* — soprano or mezzo-soprano for women, tenor or bass for men — enables you to choose songs that are most appropriate for you. After you figure out what category you fit into, check out Appendix A for a list of songs suitable for your voice type. Read on to explore how each voice type sounds and how to determine where your voice fits.

Sifting through the Ingredients to Determine Your Voice Type

Think of a voice type as a series of ingredients mixed together to create a unique-tasting dessert. For singing, the ingredients combine to create a unique-sounding voice. The four common voice types are *soprano, mezzo-soprano* (often called *mezzo*), *tenor,* and *bass* (the next section, "Identifying the Fab Four," tells you all about these four voice types). These five ingredients determine a voice type:

✔ **Age:** Many singers are assigned a voice type as young singers, but voices change with age. In Chapter 11, you can read about the growth of the male singing muscles up to age 20. All voices continue to grow and develop with age. Think about the last time you made a phone call and heard the sound of a stranger's voice. Even if you didn't know the person on the other end, you could guess his age by listening to his speaking voice. Because speaking voices and singing voices change with age, wait until your body is finished growing to determine your voice type.

✔ **Range:** Range is all the notes a singer can hit — including the highest note, the lowest note, and all the notes between. Beginning singers usually have a shorter range than more advanced singers, because the high notes or low notes get stronger with practice. As you practice the exercises with this book and accompanying CD, your range will expand whether you're a beginner or an advanced singer. Knowing your range helps you figure out your voice type, because a bass can sing lower than a tenor, and a soprano can sing higher than a mezzo. The factors that most affect how you determine your voice type are range, in which part of your range you're most comfortable singing, and register transitions.

✔ **Register:** A series of adjacent notes that sound similar are produced in a similar fashion and have a similar tonal quality. The notes sound similar because the same muscles produce them and they often vibrate in a similar location in a singer's body. The transitions between the registers can help you determine your voice type. Keep reading this chapter to find out where each voice type feels transitions to help you decide whether your voice does something similar. The transitions in your voice may change as your voice develops. (Chapter 11 has more on registers.)

The range of the voice where a singer is most comfortable is called *tessitura.* If you hear the word *tessitura* used in a discussion about a song, in that case, it refers to the area where most of the notes lie in the song. The tessitura of a Stevie Wonder song is quite high, because he's comfortable singing a lot of high notes. The tessitura for "God Bless America" and most folk songs is lower. Knowing where your voice is most comfortable, as well as where it's uncomfortable, is a determining factor when it comes to voice type.

✔ **Tone of voice:** Each voice has a specific tonal quality or color. Color is also called *timbre.* Words that describe tone include *strident, dark, bright, metallic, ringing,* and *shrill.* When determining a voice type, the voice tone helps you further determine your category. The tone of voice for a tenor is often much brighter than the tone of voice for a bass.

✔ **Voice strength:** Knowing your voice strength also helps you determine your voice type. Sopranos and tenors have a stronger head voice than mezzos and basses. Likewise, mezzos and basses have a stronger, meatier middle voice than sopranos and tenors. (Chapter 11 gives you details on head voice and middle voice.)

Vocal subdivisions

In classical music or the opera world, voice types can be further divided into categories based on the size and agility of the voice. The first four terms are in order like the soda sizes at the fast-food joint. Light is the small, lightweight cup, and dramatic is the cup so large that it won't fit in the cup holder in your car.

✔ **Light:** A bright, youthful, agile voice.

✔ **Lyric:** A medium-sized voice with a warm color that's comfortable singing long, even phrases. Lyric is appropriate for a romantic character.

✔ **Full:** A louder, stronger voice that doesn't necessarily sing fast lines as easily as a light voice.

✔ **Dramatic:** A voice that's even louder than a full voice and sings a heavier repertoire, such as Wagner. Dramatic voices can peel the paint off the wall from 50 paces. These voices are big and heavier than full lyric voices; they aren't known for subtlety — they're all about power and strength.

✔ **Coloratura:** A flexible voice that moves easily through fast lines in the music.

A singer can be a mix of the terms in the preceding list. For example, a light lyric coloratura refers to a medium-sized light voice that moves easily. Seeing the words combined to describe a voice type isn't so confusing if you understand the definition of each descriptive word. However, only in the classical world is it important for you to know how your voice fits within this list. Don't worry about the specific kind of category you're in until you get some training. Check out the upcoming section, "Identifying the Fab Four," for more information about voice types and their subdivisions.

Don't classify yourself too quickly based on the preceding factors. For the general purposes of singing, focus on building great technique and see how your voice responds. Your voice tells you what voice type it really is; you just have to know how to look and listen.

Identifying the Fab Four

The four voice types are *soprano, mezzo, tenor,* and *bass.* Even though these names sound like characters in a mob movie, I promise you that they're nothing to be afraid of. In the upcoming sections, you discover specific traits about each voice type: the range, register transitions, voice tone, and any subdivisions of that voice type, as well as the names of a few famous singers to help you put a sound with the voice type.

Note that when I talk about register transitions, they don't occur on just one note. That's because not all sopranos (or mezzos, tenors, or basses) are the same.

If you're confused after reading about all the voice types, remember that naming your voice type today isn't absolutely necessary. After you read the descriptions of the voice types in this chapter, you may be ready to vote soprano over mezzo or bass over tenor for now. Try that range for a while and see whether it fits well.

Listen to recordings of singers and read about what they've sung during their careers. If you know of singers who have voices similar to yours, look at the roles they sang. Think about the following factors when you're listening to the singers in Table 2-1:

- ✔ **What's the timbre of your voice?** Is the tone more steely than chocolaty? Steely isn't a negative adjective; it's merely fact. Very often the steely voice is the character audiences love, but they don't want to rush up and put their arms around her and rescue her.

- ✔ **Is your voice light and flutelike?** If so, listen to the lighter voices in Table 2-1. Is your voice loud and heavy even when you're lightly singing? Heavy means the sound that you're making is loud even when you're singing comfortably; listen to the singers in the dramatic list.

- ✔ **What's your singing range and tessitura?** The difference between a mezzo and a soprano often is tessitura. The mezzo can sing the high notes but doesn't want to live up there, and the soprano wants to sing one high note after another. If you're new to singing, you may not be able to tell the difference between a soprano and a mezzo or a baritone and a tenor. No worries. Keep listening to the sounds, and you'll eventually be able to tell the difference between the voice types.

- ✔ **Are you able to move your voice easily?** Do you enjoy the fast passages in the song and think of them as fun? If the fast notes are easy for you, you can add coloratura to your vocal description. The coloraturas in Table 2-1 demonstrate some spectacular fast moves with their voices.

- ✔ **What do you consider the general or overall strengths of your voice —strong middle voice or head voice, perhaps?** Your vocal strengths change as you practice. Notice the differences in the voices in Table 2-1. Compare and contrast the sounds you hear between voice types to hear their strengths.

If you're new to singing, determining your voice type by yourself may take a few months. Your voice changes with practice. So have fun listening and sorting through all the different types.

Table 2-1	Singers from the Opera World
Voice Type	*Examples*
Lighter soprano	Kathleen Battle, Harolyn Blackwell, Barbara Bonney
Lyric soprano	Angela Gheorghiu, Sumi Jo, Dame Kiri Te Kanawa
More dramatic soprano	Hildegard Behrens, Birgit Nilsson, Deborah Voigt
Coloratura soprano	Natalie Dessay, Beverly Sills, Dame Joan Sutherland
Lighter mezzo	Cecilia Bartoli, Susan Graham, Frederica von Stade
Lyric mezzo	Susanne Mentzer, Anne-Sophie von Otter, Wendy White
Dramatic mezzo	Olga Borodina, Waltraud Meier, Dolora Zajick
Coloratura mezzo	Cecilia Bartoli, Marilyn Horne
Contralto	Marian Anderson, Kathleen Ferrier, Maureen Forrester
Lighter tenor	Rockwell Blake, Peter Pears, Fritz Wunderlich
Lyric tenor	Placido Domingo, Luciano Pavarotti, George Shirley
Dramatic tenor	James King, Lauritz Melchior, Jon Vickers
Coloratura tenor	Juan Diego Florez, Jerry Hadley
Baritone	Dimitry Hvorostovsky, Herman Prey, Gino Quilico
Bass	Kurt Moll, Paul Plishka, Samuel Ramey

Highest range of the dames: Soprano

The *soprano* has the highest range of the female voice types. The following aspects are characteristic of her voice type:

- ✔ **Range:** Often Middle C to High C, although some sopranos can vocalize way beyond High C and much lower than Middle C (see Figure 2-1).

  A soprano is expected to have a High C, and many sopranos can sing up to the G or A above High C. Choral directors or musical directors listen for the singer's comfort zone when determining whether the singer is a soprano. Although a mezzo can reach some of these higher notes, a soprano is capable of singing high notes more frequently than a mezzo.

- ✔ **Register transitions:** The transitions usually occur as the soprano shifts out of chest voice around the E-flat just above Middle C and into her head voice around F-sharp (fifth line on top of the staff) in the octave above Middle C.

- ✔ **Strength:** A soprano's strength is a strong head voice.

- ✔ **Voice tone:** The soprano voice is usually bright and ringing.

- ✔ **Weakness:** Sopranos have a hard time projecting in middle voice.

- ✔ **Soprano subdivisions in the classical world** include light lyric, full lyric, light lyric coloratura, full lyric coloratura, light dramatic coloratura, full dramatic coloratura, light dramatic (or spinto), and full dramatic.

- ✔ **Soprano belter:** A soprano belter has an easier time managing her chest voice for belting and usually belts higher than a mezzo. Check out these names to hear some soprano belters: Betty Buckley, Celine Dion, Whitney Houston, Christina Aguilera, Aretha Franklin, Carrie Underwood, Kelly Clarkson, and Jennifer Hudson.

- ✔ **Common performance roles:** The soprano is usually the lead in the show, such as Ariel in *The Little Mermaid,* Marian the Librarian in *The Music Man,* Tosca in *Tosca,* Mabel in *The Pirates of Penzance,* and Mimi in *La Bohème.*

- ✔ **Naming names:** Famous sopranos you may know include Julie Andrews, Sarah Brightman, Kristin Chenoweth, Renée Fleming, Beyoncé Knowles, Audra McDonald, Olivia Newton John, and Dolly Parton.

Figure 2-1: Soprano range.

Middle C (C4) to High C (C6)

How low can she go: Mezzo

The difference between a *mezzo* (*mezzo* is the abbreviated term for *mezzo-soprano*) and a soprano is often tessitura. (*Tessitura* refers to where most of the notes lie in a song — the notes that a voice feels most comfortable singing.) Many mezzos can sing as high as a soprano, but they can't stay as high as a soprano. For example, some roles in operatic literature require the mezzo to sing as high as the soprano lead, but the mezzo usually doesn't have to sing as many high notes as a soprano does — thank goodness — because the mezzo comfort zone is usually different than the soprano; mezzos prefer to live in their middle voices. On the other hand, a soprano hates to live in her middle voice, preferring to sing high notes and soar above the orchestra.

To further confuse you, many sopranos sing mezzo repertoire. How dare they! That's not fair, but it's a fact. As in other aspects of life, after the soprano becomes famous, she sings repertoire that she enjoys and that may be music written for somebody else, such as mezzos. So just because a soprano sings a song doesn't mean that it's a soprano song. You have to look at the details, such as the range of the song, and decide whether that range fits your voice. You can find more information about selecting appropriate songs for your voice in Chapter 16 and a list of songs for each voice type in Appendix A.

- ✔ **Range:** The mezzo range is usually G below Middle C to a High B or High C. Many mezzos vocalize as high as a soprano but can't handle the repetition of the upper notes (see Figure 2-2).

- ✔ **Register:** The register transitions for the mezzo usually occur at E or F (first space) just above Middle C, and the E or F (fifth line) one octave above that.

- ✔ **Strength:** Mezzos have a strong middle voice.

- ✔ **Voice tone:** The mezzo voice is usually darker or deeper than her soprano counterpart.

- ✔ **Weakness:** A mezzo's head voice is often her weakness.

- ✔ **Subdivisions:** One subdivision of mezzo is *contralto*. Singers often mistakenly say that they are altos. *Alto* is the part listed in choral music, but the voice type is either mezzo or contralto. Less common than mezzos, *contraltos* can usually sing from F below Middle C to about an F (fifth line) below High C. A contralto has a darker, richer color and is more at home in the lower part of her voice. Sometimes singers darken their voices intentionally to make themselves sound like contraltos. The contralto may take her chest voice–dominated sound up to a G (second line) above Middle C and shift into head voice around the D (fourth line), an octave above Middle C. Examples of contraltos include Marian Anderson and Maureen Forrester.

- ✔ **Mezzo subdivisions in the classical world** include light lyric coloratura, full lyric coloratura, light lyric, full lyric, and dramatic. The dramatic mezzo is similar to the dramatic soprano. To be fair to the sopranos, I confess that dramatic mezzos sometimes sing roles written for the dramatic soprano. You go, girls!

- ✔ **Mezzo belter:** A mezzo belter doesn't belt as high as the soprano belter. She has a heavier chest voice and is more comfortable singing material that's lower. Listen to these singers to hear the sounds of mezzo belters: Bea Arthur, Pearl Bailey, Kaye Ballard, Carol Burnett, Carol Channing, Angela Lansbury, Lorna Luft, and Leslie Uggams.

- ✔ **Common performance roles:** The mezzo is often the mother, the witch, or the sleazy girl in town. Her roles include such fun ones as Miss Hannigan in *Annie,* Mrs. Potts in *Beauty and The Beast,* Carmen in the opera *Carmen,* Amneris in *Aïda,* and Aunt Eller in *Oklahoma!*

- ✔ **Naming names:** Famous mezzos you may know include Karen Carpenter, Patsy Cline, Marilyn Horne, k. d. lang, and Lorrie Morgan.

Figure 2-2:
Mezzo
range.

G below Middle C to B (B5)

Highest range of the dudes: Tenor

Thanks to the Three Tenors, the Irish Tenors, and even Three Mo' Tenors, you probably have a good idea of what a *tenor* sounds like.

- ✔ **Range:** The tenor range, shown in Figure 2-3, is about two octaves, with many singing a little lower than C (second space in bass clef) and a little higher than the male High C (third space treble clef).

- ✔ **Register:** The tenor voice doesn't make a huge transition from his lower voice to his middle voice. His transition into his middle voice occurs around D just above Middle C or the E-flat just above Middle C and then a transition into head voice around G or A-flat above Middle C.

- ✔ **Strength:** The tenor's strength is his head voice.

- ✔ **Voice tone:** The tenor voice is usually bright and ringing.

- ✔ **Weakness:** His weakness is often his chest voice.

- ✔ **Subdivisions:** In musical theater, a subdivision of the tenor, called the *baritenor*, reigns. This voice type is someone with the power to project in the middle voice and the higher, ringing money notes of the tenor. The other voice type that you frequently hear in the opera world is the *countertenor* — a male singer who sounds like a female. This voice type sings in the same range as the mezzo (sometimes soprano) and sounds similar. When you've heard the countertenor singing enough, you can distinguish him from a mezzo. Until then, just enjoy the unique quality that these gentlemen bring to the singing world.

- ✔ **Tenor subdivisions in the classical world** include light lyric, full lyric, dramatic, and heroic. The heroic tenor is also called a dramatic tenor — the guy who has a large voice with great stamina. Don't challenge him to a singing contest at the local pub.

- ✔ **Common performance roles:** The tenor is almost always the lead who wins the girl at the end of the show. Examples include Rodolfo in *La Bohème*, Don José in *Carmen*, Tony in *West Side Story*, Billy in *42nd Street*, and Rolf in *The Sound of Music*.

✔ **Naming names:** Famous tenors you may know include Placido Domingo, José Carreras, and Luciano Pavarotti, whom you may recognize as the Three Tenors. You also may know Enrico Caruso, John Denver, Elton John, Gary LeVox (lead singer of Rascal Flatts), Maxwell, Justin Timberlake, and Stevie Wonder.

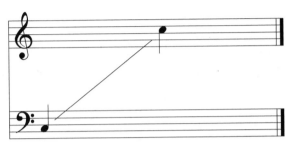

Figure 2-3:
Tenor
range. C one octave below Middle C to C one octave above Middle C

He's so low: Bass

Bass is the lowest of the voice types. The bass is the guy who sings all the cool low notes in the barbershop quartet.

✔ **Range:** His range is usually F (below the bass clef staff) to E (first line treble clef) but can be as wide as E-flat to F (see Figure 2-4).

✔ **Register transitions:** The bass changes from chest voice into middle voice around A or A-flat just below Middle C and changes into head voice around D or D-flat just above Middle C.

✔ **Strength:** His chest voice is his strength.

✔ **Voice tone:** His voice is the deepest, darkest, and heaviest of the male voices.

✔ **Weakness:** His head voice is his weakness.

✔ **Subdivisions:** Filling in the middle between tenor and bass is the *baritone*. Baritones are very common. Young bass singers often start out as a baritone and then the voice changes. The baritone can usually sing from an A (first space bass clef) to F (first space treble clef) below the male High C. The bass-baritone has some height of the baritone and some depth of the bass; his range is usually A-flat (first space bass clef) to F (first space treble clef) and sometimes as high as G below the male High C. The baritone's register transitions usually occur at the B or B-flat just below Middle C and the E or E-flat above Middle C.

- ✔ **Bass subdivisions** include the comic bass (funny guy in the show), as well as lyric and dramatic bass. His subdivision buddy, the baritone, also comes in different shapes and sizes: light lyric baritone, full lyric baritone, and bass baritone.

- ✔ **Common performance roles:** The bass or baritone is often the villain, father, or older man. Examples include Ramfis in *Aïda,* the Mikado in *The Mikado,* and Jud Fry in *Oklahoma!* Some exceptions to this villain image are King Arthur in *Camelot,* Porgy in *Porgy and Bess,* and the Toreador in *Carmen.*

- ✔ **Naming names:** Famous basses you may know include José Van Dam, Tennessee Ernie Ford, James Morris, Samuel Ramey, and Barry White. Famous baritones include Trace Adkins, Billy Currington, Jamey Johnson, Brian Stokes Mitchell, John Raitt, George Strait, and Tom Wopat.

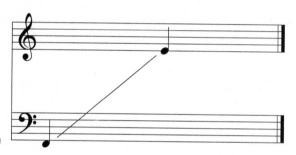

Figure 2-4:
Bass range. F about an octave and a half below Middle C to E above Middle C

Chapter 3

Aligning Your Body for Great Singing

To sing efficiently, you need to line up all your body parts and get them ready to do their job with as little tension as possible. If you're slumped over, you have more trouble taking the breath you need to sing, because posture and tension directly affect the muscles. Tension in your body also prevents you from taking a deep breath and makes singing more difficult. In this chapter, you discover how to create correct, tension-free posture so you can project confidence and sing your best.

In this chapter, I nag you about posture so you become physically aware of your body. In some of the exercises later in the book, you must find your alignment, open your body for breath, drop your jaw, find the correct shape for the vowel, move the breath to begin the tone, and look like you're having a great time. That's plenty to think about. Take some time now to really understand how your body moves and to recognize tension so you won't be so frustrated later when I ask you to do ten things at once!

Evaluating Your Posture

In front of a full-length mirror, look at your posture. Notice the way you hold your body, especially your head, chest, hips, knees, arms, and hands. More than likely, after you looked in the mirror, you changed your posture. Did you change your posture because you thought your body may *work* better or because you thought you may *look* better? For singing, you evaluate your posture for both reasons. Aligning your body properly puts all the muscles that help you sing in the right position. Proper alignment gets you singing better and also makes you appear confident and professional.

Look at Figure 3-1 and check out the alignment of the skeleton. Take some time to study the skeleton and notice the connection of bones. Throughout the chapter, I point out the particular area of the skeleton you're aligning.

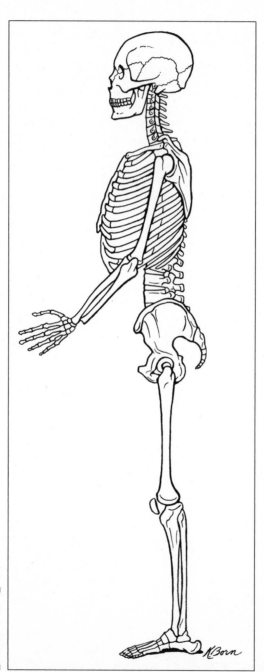

Figure 3-1:
Ideal alignment of the skeleton.

As you continue to evaluate your own posture, notice the posture of others. Observe their movements to better understand what you need to do to change your own alignment.

Creating Correct Posture

Creating correct posture means finding out what correct posture looks like and feels like so that you can quickly make whatever changes you need. By changing your posture, you control what kind of impression you make on others — whether you're on the stage singing or at the audition vying for the show's lead. Good posture keeps energy flowing instead of trapping it in one body part, and it also aligns your body for correct breathing. See Chapter 4 for more information about breathing for singing. Read on for ways to align your body for great singing.

Nervous ticks, such as constant finger wiggling, frequent shifting of weight from one foot to the other, and roaming eyes, are examples of energy that isn't freely flowing throughout the body. If you catch yourself twisting your hands or wiggling your fingers frequently while singing, watch yourself in the mirror to become aware of the movement. Then allow yourself to move around as you sing, to use that excess energy. After you move around, stand still but maintain that same freedom in your body, as if you may move at any moment. Freely flowing energy keeps you looking confident and singing well. Using your acting skills also gives your body something specific to do, so the random wiggles and twitches often subside. See Chapter 18 for more on acting and singing.

Feeling grounded on your feet

The root of good posture is the position of your feet and the balance of weight on your feet. Seems like the feet are a long way from the singing process, but equal distribution of weight on the feet allows all the muscles to stay released so you can make gorgeous sounds. Try this sequence to find the balance of weight on your feet.

1. **While you're standing, roll your foot to find the *tripod*.**

   Roll your foot on the floor to make a circle that moves from your heel through the outside of your foot, across your toes, and down the inside of your foot. As you roll the foot, you feel the heel bone in the back of your foot, a bone or protrusion under your little toe, and another protrusion or bone under your big toe. Roll among these three points several times so that you really feel the points. Some people call these three points the tripod.

If you aren't sure whether you felt the tripod when you rolled your foot, sit down and feel along the bottom of your foot to find the three points. Take your time and feel each point. Look at the skeleton in Figure 3-1. Take special notice of the bones that make up the foot.

2. **When you're confident that you feel the three points on the foot, balance your weight on those three points.**

    The phrase that the three-legged table is always level applies here. You want your weight evenly balanced on the three points. If you intentionally lean back and put your weight on your heels, you feel the front of your body tighten to hold you up. Likewise, if you lean forward and put your weight on the front of your feet, you feel the back of your body tighten. Watch yourself in the mirror or observe the tension in your body. Try to find the center, or the position where you're neither forward nor back; you're evenly balanced on your feet and aligned.

3. **When you find the three points and your balance on one foot, find them on the other foot.**

Practice standing with your weight balanced on the three points to make sure that you're not rolling your weight to the outside of your feet. Some people unconsciously stand with the inside of their feet raised and the outside of their feet pressed into the ground. This stance creates tension in your body. You can feel the tension on the outside of your legs when you press the outside of your feet into the floor. Watch yourself in the mirror to check that your feet are balanced on the three points.

Putting your feet in position

After you find the balance of weight on the feet, place your feet beneath your hips. If you place your hands on your hips, you can feel the muscles of your hips on the sides of your body and you can also feel your hipbone in the front. Directly under the hipbone is your foot (find the hipbone in Figure 3-1).

A lot of people tend to put their feet at shoulder width, which may or may not work for you. Women tend to have narrow shoulders and wider hips, whereas men tend to have wide shoulders and narrow hips. Regardless of the width of your shoulders, you want to align your feet under your hips.

I recommend that you place the feet side by side under your hips so that you feel the equal balance of weight on your feet. When that stance feels familiar to you, change the position of your feet and maintain the balance of weight in your body. You want equal distribution of weight and effort in the body. You can also stand with your toes pointed out, to feel the tension created in the legs. Likewise, you can stand with your toes pointed in and notice that effect on the muscles in your legs. You want to explore the feeling of toes pointed straight and the feeling of parallel feet.

Your toes may seem like cute little extensions of your feet, but they also play a role in your balance. Stand with your weight balanced on the three points. Now lift your toes and notice the sensations of the three points. Most people find that lifting the toes helps them feel the three points. You can put your toes down and feel the same sensation of balance on the three points. Push your toes into the floor and notice the sensation in your feet and your legs. Pushing them down creates tension. Practice without your shoes on so that you can observe your feet and toes while you practice. During your practice sessions, wiggle your toes occasionally to make sure that they aren't tight and that they're ready to help you stay balanced. Notice the bones in the toes on the skeleton in Figure 3-1.

Pretend that you have a tube inside your body that runs all the way from your head down to your feet. Open this tube all the way into your feet each time you inhale. Opening this imaginary tube makes you grounded and ready to sing the next phrase of your song. Each time you inhale, you want to open and release all the way into your feet. It may feel as if your feet open or widen as you take the breath.

Flexing your ankles

You want your ankles open and flexible when you're standing. Sitting in a chair or standing on one leg, move your foot around to feel the flexibility in your ankle. If your ankle feels tight, take your time and move it gently back and forth or in circles to stretch the muscles and release some tension. Move around the other foot or ankle so both are equally released. After you stretch both ankles, notice how they feel. They probably feel open and flexible, as if they can support the weight of your body. Look at Figure 3-1 to see how the foot and ankle are connected. The ankle isn't directly over the heel; it's in front of the heel. If you pretend to sink into your ankles, you feel as if your body is heavier, putting pressure on your ankles and feet. If you visualize a spring (shock absorber) in the ankles, you can feel an opening sensation in the feet and ankles, as if the weight of the body is equally distributed. Go back and forth a few times. Sink into your ankles and then put in the imaginary spring. You want to notice the spring not only when you're standing, but also when you're walking.

Engaging your legs

For singing, you want to engage the entire body in making sound. The legs are your support system, and you want them to hold you up without tightening. Try the following suggestion to discover how to engage your legs.

To feel the legs engage as you sing, use a plié as you take the breath. *Plié* means "to bend," and you want to bend your knees as you inhale. This bending helps you feel an opening sensation through your body and down into your legs. As you sing, you can gradually stand back up from the bend. With each new breath, plié again to create the opening sensation in your legs and gradually stand back up. After you practice this way for a few weeks, you'll be able to sing your song and bend or plié as you inhale. If you visualize that you're bending, you feel your legs open as you inhale and engage as you sing. Review the skeleton in Figure 3-1; notice the bones in the legs and also the shape of the knees.

For singing, you don't want to lock your knees, or push your knees back. Locking your knees also locks your lower back, and you want your lower back to open for inhalation.

Instead, you want to keep your knees released. Released knees aren't locked — but they're also not bent. To find the difference between released knees and bent knees, stand and lock your knees. Without bending the knees, release the muscles around them. Lock the knees again, and when you release the muscles, bend your knees. Move back and forth from the locked position to the bent position. You want to feel the released position, which is between locked and bent. Bent knees make you a little shorter. Released knees keep you the same height, without tight muscles around your knees.

To prevent tension in your knees, you can visualize a spring in your knees or pretend that you have oil in your knees, like the Tin Man in the *Wizard of Oz,* so that they move smoothly. Try using the visual of the spring to feel the difference between weight evenly distributed through the legs and feet and sinking your weight into your legs and knees and creating tension.

Releasing your hips

Go back to Figure 3-1 and look at the hips or pelvis. You may think of the hips as what you try to squeeze into your tight jeans. I want you to visualize the pelvis and not those extra 10 pounds you gained last winter. If you're familiar with the skeleton, you know that I'm talking about moving the pelvis when I say "rock your hips."

To find just the right position for your hips, rock back and forward — push your buttocks back and then push them forward. When you rock the hips back, you can feel the tension created in your lower back. That tension isn't good for singing. Rocking the hips forward helps you feel when they're too far forward — you feel like your hips are in front of your torso. Instead, you want your hips right underneath your torso, with your tailbone tucked under you.

When you're confident that you can feel when your hips are centered under you, you can move your hips from left to right. Many people stand with their hips sticking out to the left or right. That posture may be fine for casual conversation, but it's not helpful for singing. When your hips are off to one side, your back is out of alignment, causing tension. Watching yourself in the mirror, move your hips from left to right or front to back until you feel the centered position underneath your torso. This centered position, neither front, back, right, nor left, is the correct position for singing.

Because most women sink into their hips, you want to understand what it feels like to lift out of your hips. Lifting out of your hips means that you feel an opening between your hips and your torso. You can intentionally sink into your hips to feel the added pressure on your body. You may feel heavier and slumped when you sink into your hips. To lift out of your hips, feel the spring or shock absorber between your hips and torso, and imagine your torso rising out of your legs.

The position of your feet affects your hips. Earlier in this chapter, you may have read that you want to position your feet under your hipbones and keep your toes parallel. This position affects not only the muscles in your legs, but also the muscles in your hips and the positioning of the sit bones. The *sit bones,* or sitz bones, are the bony points of your pelvis that you may feel sticking out inside your buttocks. By positioning the hips and toes in just the right position, you allow the sit bones and hips to stay released and the muscles to stay open. You then have great posture and easy breathing for singing.

Lengthening your spine

The spine is the marvelous curvy set of bones stacked on top of each other inside your body. See the skeleton in Figure 3-1 to discover the natural curve of the spine. Tension in the spine causes tension for breathing. To lengthen and release the spine, you want to open and lengthen your body from the inside out. Visualize your spine as long and flexible, and feel the distance between your tailbone and your skull. For great posture, you want your tailbone under you and headed to the floor while your skull lifts to the sky. You don't want to feel a pulling sensation in your body; you want an opening and lengthening sensation. You can visualize space between each bone or vertebrae of your spine. Your spine connects with your rib cage, and you want your spine to lengthen and open with your rib cage.

Balancing your head and shoulders

At the top of the spine is your neck. The neck is supposed to be curved — check out the curve of the neck in the skeleton in Figure 3-1. If you remember the opening and lengthening of the spine from the previous section, you can continue that idea of lengthening through the neck up into the head so that the head balances on top of the spine. Think of the bobble-head dolls that sit on the dash of the car: The body of the dolls doesn't move, but the head bobs around. You want your head balanced that easily on top of your spine.

To feel the weight of your head, allow your head to feel heavy, as if it sits right on your shoulders. This weight and pressure doesn't feel good after a while, so you want to feel an opening up and lifting of the head that comes from inside the body. Trying to push up the head only causes tension in your neck. Your head weighs about the same as a bowling ball — it's pretty heavy, so it needs some help to stay up.

You can visualize your head balanced on top of your spine. The opposite of this sensation or visual is the head sinking or pressing down on top of the spine.

To keep your head balanced on your body, you want your shoulders to be evenly balanced. Your shoulders sit on top of your rib cage, and their position and balance are important. Roll your shoulders forward to feel how it stretches and curves your back and collapses your chest. Then roll your shoulders back to feel how it thrusts your chest forward. The correct position for your shoulders is neither forward nor back, and pressing neither up nor down; it's an even balance.

When you move your shoulders, you can also feel your shoulder blades moving. If you tighten your shoulder blades, you feel tension in your rib cage. For good alignment, you want your shoulder blades open and released across your back; you want the shoulder blades to release downward as you inhale. To balance the shoulders, you also want to feel the connection between your arms and your chest. Look at the skeleton in Figure 3-1. Notice the connection between the arms and shoulders, and see how the shoulders sit on top of the rib cage.

Releasing Tension

Releasing tension in your body allows for a more open sound and easier breathing. You may notice that I don't ask you to relax. If you relax, you may fall limply on the couch to watch your favorite sitcom. For singing, you want your body aligned but released and free of tension. *Releasing* means keeping your body in a state of readiness: ready to move, breathe, and crawl out of your comfort zone and sing for the world. Think of body movement as fluid motion even when you're still.

Letting go of tension in your upper body

To release any tension in your arms and hands, you also want to check in with the areas surrounding the arms and hands.

- ✔ **Chest:** Check the position of your chest to make sure that it's open and lifted, not pushed up.

- ✔ **Shoulders:** With your chest in the right position, notice the position of your shoulders. You want your shoulders centered, neither too far forward nor too far back.

- ✔ **Arms:** Tighten your arms and notice what that feels like. When your arms are tight, you feel tight across your back and perhaps across your chest. Release the tension in your arms and notice that they feel as if they opened.

- ✔ **Elbows:** You may have discovered that when your elbows are tight, your back and shoulder blades are really tight. All your muscles are connected and need a balanced relationship to support the body. Your elbows can also feel like they have a spring in them, similar to the visual you may have explored with your ankles and knees earlier in the chapter. Your elbows and your body should have distance between them; you don't want your elbows to press against your body or push out from your body.

- ✔ **Hands:** The same tension release can apply to your hands. If you tighten your hands and wrists, you can feel the tension move all the way up your arms and across your back and chest. When you release the tension in your hands, you may feel as if they aren't as heavy as they were when you tensed the muscles in your hands.

Opening space in the head

Believe it or not, tension in the head and face is pretty common in singers. You can see tension in the face when the eyebrows lift or the brow furrows. The facial muscles may also hold tension, even though you may not see the face wrinkle. Read on for information about how to release both obvious and invisible tension.

Look in the mirror at your face. Tighten your face so that you can see the muscles squeezing together. Now release that tension and notice what it feels like. When the tension releases, your face may feel wider or more open. Tense and release several more times so you can really feel the difference. Notice any tension in your forehead from the muscles wanting to either lift or furrow the brow.

One area that commonly generates tension is the forehead. If you notice your forehead wrinkling as you sing, stick a piece of clear tape vertically on your forehead between your eyebrows. You can feel the tape move when you tighten your forehead. It's normal for your eyebrows to move as you sing or speak, but keeping your forehead free of tension is the goal.

Next, notice any tension in your eyes. Tension in your eyes feels like squinting or a tightness behind your eyes. When the eyes are open and free of tension, it feels similar to the opening you feel behind your eyes when you see something that surprises you. Pretend that a friend you haven't seen in a long time walks through the door. Notice the opening of your eyes and a feeling of space behind your eyes. The opening or release of tension behind the eyes also helps the forehead to relax.

Releasing the tension in your head and opening the space involves allowing the muscles to stay pliable on your head. If you squint or concentrate really hard for a long time, your head may start to hurt from a tension headache. To prevent that tension, massage your scalp. See whether you can get the skin on your head (your scalp) to move around. It might not move much if it's tight, but you may get it to move a little by massaging and stretching it. You can also visualize your head expanding from the inside out.

Look in the mirror again and notice the space around your mouth. When you're annoyed or frustrated, the muscles around your mouth may tighten. To release the tension around your mouth and face, look bored. If you pretend to be really bored and dull, you'll feel tension around your mouth release.

Walking with ease

Maintaining your posture while you walk makes a big difference in your appearance and your ability to sing while walking or moving. You may actually have to sing while walking around the stage. Church choirs sing as they process, and backup singers groove to the music as they dance. What if you have to cross the stage? You want to look glorious for the entire time that you're onstage and not just when you land in place next to the piano.

To maintain your posture while walking, keep your eyes up and look ahead as you walk. You can still see where you're going even if you're not looking at the ground. You also want to be able to land in correct alignment. When you have to walk onto the stage for a performance, you want to land in alignment so you don't have to adjust your position.

Practice finding your alignment when you're standing still. Then walk a few steps and land in place. Did you land in the same alignment? Look down at your feet to see whether they're parallel and the same distance as your hipbones. If not, try again: Walk around and then land in alignment. Eventually, you'll confidently land in alignment and know that your body is ready for some fabulous singing.

You also want to practice walking with an awareness of the weight and pressure on your legs. You want to feel the sensation that your weight is evenly distributed on your legs and feet and have a sense of buoyancy. Feeling your weight sink into your legs makes you feel much heavier. Pushing into the floor or pavement causes you to feel pressure and tension in your legs. Of course, you want to connect your feet to the floor, but you want to feel an opening sensation, as if your feet touching the floor causes your legs and muscles to open — not contract and tense. Try walking and pushing into the floor, and then walking and visualizing your body with springs that open when your feet connect with the floor.

Projecting confidence through posture

Projecting confidence onstage is important because you want to feel good about your performance and you want the audience to be comfortable watching you perform. Audiences are usually apprehensive about performers who project fear. Luckily, that's not a crime, or I would've been shot by a firing squad as a young singer. Projecting confidence involves finding your correct posture and maintaining it throughout a performance. If you maintain that posture and a calm expression even if you forget the words to your song, many people probably won't even notice. I've seen it many times: The performer is onstage making up the words, but he looks as terrific as if he'd intended to sing those words. By maintaining poise and posture, the performer projects to the audience that everything is fine and assures them that they needn't worry, as if to say, "I'll get back to the original words in a moment." The performer also walks away feeling good because he stuck to a basic singing rule: Good posture enhances good singing.

To explore how correct posture exudes confidence, pretend that you're a king or queen. Strut like you own the place. Notice your posture. Now pretend that you're really sick and that your whole body aches. Doesn't a ruler move differently than someone who is ill? It's possible for a king or queen to be ill, but not in this scenario. A king walks tall, carries himself with great dignity and grace, and glides around the room. A sickly person can barely stand, much less project confidence. In this scenario, which one are you? Are you the king with a dignified posture, or are you stooped and closed off from the world? You're probably somewhere in the middle. Strive to be the king or queen when you sing.

Chapter 4

Breathing for Singing

. . . .

In This Chapter

▶ Getting down to the brass tacks of breath control

▶ Inhaling and expanding your body

▶ Exhaling and extending your breath

▶ Discovering how your body moves while breathing

. . . .

*H*ow you manage your breath when you sing can drastically change the sound of your singing voice. If you try to hold your breath and sing, it doesn't work. You also can't sing a loud phrase without using some air — that is, without exhaling. Most people think of exhaling as involving air, not sound. When you sing, exhaling encompasses both at the same time. Although breathing is natural — you don't have to think about it — when you sing, you need to train your body to breathe in a certain way so that you breathe efficiently throughout an entire song. You don't want to run out of breath in the middle of a word. The exercises in this chapter help you master breath control so you can sing through all those long phrases in your favorite songs with ease.

Try not to push yourself too quickly when you're working on breath. Work slowly and allow the movements described in this chapter to become habit.

Breathing Basics

When you breathe normally, you automatically make a shallow inhalation and an even exhalation, followed by a pause before it all starts again — you don't even need to think about it. On the other hand, when you sing, you need to not only inhale quickly and exhale slowly as you sing the phrases of a song, but also maintain proper posture. (See Chapter 3 for more information on posture.) Breathing in this manner gives you the breath control you need to sing efficiently. However, because controlled breathing doesn't come naturally, you need to train your body to breathe for singing. Keep reading for the breathing basics.

The easiest way to find out how to breathe for singing is simply to feel it. Being able to visualize and feel the proper way to breathe makes the process more natural for you, too.

Inhalation refers to air moving into your body — breathing in. *Exhalation* is blowing out the air. You exhale when you speak or sing.

Inhaling to sing

Singing songs requires getting a full breath quickly — a quick inhalation — because the orchestra can't wait five minutes for you to find the air. Knowing how your body feels when you inhale helps you quickly get air in your body so you can sing the next phrase. Use the following exercise to explore your own inhalation and get a feel for how your body needs to move when you inhale and exhale.

Pretend that you see someone you're really happy to see. The surprise breath that you take feels like the air just rushed into your body. You can also pretend that someone told you something shocking.

You probably just took a really quick breath. Quickly filling your lungs with air is the way you have to breathe when singing. As you read this chapter, you discover how to open your body so the breath intake is silent.

When you're working on breath control, you may find yourself yawning. The body gets confused with the different amount of air coming in, and you yawn. My students yawn plenty during lessons and are embarrassed at first. I have to tell them that it's okay to yawn when working on breath.

Exhaling to sing

Singing requires you to control your exhalation. You want to have a sustained and smooth exhalation so you can sing those demanding high notes and long, slow phrases.

To explore exhalation, try this exercise: Take a breath and say "Shhhh," as if you're trying to quiet some noisy children. Take another breath, and this time sustain the "Shhhh" as long as you can. While saying the "Shhhh," notice what moves in your body as you exhale. You may feel that your abdomen or ribs are moving. At the end of the "Shhhh" (exhalation), you should feel the need to immediately inhale again.

Breathing like a bellows

Attached to your ribs, your lungs are made of pliable tissue — not muscle. When you inhale, the muscles between the ribs (*intercostals*) move the ribs up and out as the lungs expand downward. When the intercostal muscles relax back inward, the lungs move back to their normal resting position. Another muscle that moves when you breathe is your *diaphragm,* a dome-shaped muscle located underneath your lungs and attached to the ribs and the spine. Your diaphragm is actually attached to the rib cage in the front of your body and the ribs and spine in the back, and it doesn't descend below your ribs. When you inhale, the diaphragm flexes downward and moves back upward as you exhale. If the diaphragm flexes downward as you inhale, the organs below your diaphragm (such as the liver and your stomach) have to move out of the way. The organs move down and out, which is why your abdomen moves out as you inhale. As you exhale, the organs gradually move back to their normal resting positions.

Breathing can be confusing for a singer who's just starting out, because you have to pay attention to so many things at one time. Different people who know something about singing also may tell you about yet another breathing method to use for singing. One friend may say that his teacher wants him to leave his muscles out — sides, ribs, back — and distended as he sings or exhales; another friend may tell you that the abdominal muscles must move in when you exhale. Who do you believe? Both of them.

More than one method of breathing is useful, so you need to explore what works for you and understand why. You'll likely encounter someone who claims to know all the answers about breathing, and I want you to be familiar with your own breathing to understand your options.

Being an "innie" or an "outie" doesn't refer to just your belly button — it also refers to how you breathe. Both methods are valid; you just need to understand how breath works in your body. Here's more info about each:

- ✔ **The innie method** focuses on moving the ribs and abdomen in gradually during exhalation. If you're exploring breathing for the first time, start with these exercises.

- ✔ **The outie method** requires the singer to focus on keeping the ribs or abdomen out during exhalation.

For many singers, the outie method is helpful because beginners have a hard time preventing the ribs and abdomen from moving back in too quickly during exhalation; visualizing the abdomen staying out helps them slowly move back in. After their abdomen moves back in, some singers squeeze their throat to continue singing. You can explore the outie method to see whether imagining your body staying wide during exhalation helps you slow the movement of your ribs and abdominal muscles and extend your breath.

Posturing yourself for breathing

Breathing efficiently when you sing is a combination of great posture (see Chapter 3) and skillful inhaling and exhaling. (See the sections "Practicing Inhalation" and "Practicing Exhalation," later in this chapter.) Remember the importance of good posture: It allows you to get a deep, full breath. If you slouch or you're too rigid, your diaphragm locks and prevents you from getting a correct breath for singing. (See the "Breathing like a bellows" sidebar in this chapter.) If your breathing and your posture work together as a team, you can improve your singing.

To sing your best, you want to develop good posture while you breathe. When your body is aligned correctly, taking and using an efficient breath is easier.

Your own two hands can help you maintain great posture while breathing. As you work through the breathing exercises in this chapter, place one hand on your chest and the other hand on your abs and your sides. As you inhale, use your hand to feel whether your chest stays steady; you want it to stay in the same position for both the inhalation and the exhalation. (If your chest rises during inhalation, you create tension in your chest and neck.) You'll feel your other hand moving out with your abs and sides as you inhale, and back in toward your body as you exhale.

Practicing Inhalation

When you sing, you want to be confident that you can take in air and then use it efficiently to sing your song. Knowing how to open your body for inhalation allows you to get the breath in your body skillfully and with little effort. Inhaling is simple: Open your body, and the air comes rushing in. Read on for exercises and information to develop skillful inhalation technique.

Inhaling through the nose and the mouth at the same time is ideal for singing. Taking in air through just the nose isn't the best idea, because you won't be able to do that if you have a cold. If your nose is stuffed up, you'll be distracted when singing and your breath will sound very noisy, because you're trying to suck air through congested nostrils. Instead, allow air to come in through your nose and your mouth when you breathe. Getting accustomed to air coming in through both your nose and your mouth takes some time, but it's a worthwhile technique.

Breathing jargon

If you've had some singing lessons, you may be confused by all the phrases and terms singers use to describe breathing. Your voice teacher or choir director may have said, "Support that note" or "Sing on breath!" If those commands make sense to you, congratulations! I always thought they were confusing, because the word *support* can mean so many things.

- ✔ **Support** probably became a popular term for breathing for singing because of the Italian word *appoggio,* which means "to support" or "to lean your body into the breath." *Support* means using your body to control the breath and sound so your throat stays free and open.

- ✔ **Appoggio** also implies that singers flex their body or ribs open as they sing and leave the body open during exhalation. (This is similar to the outie method mentioned in the "Exhaling to sing" section in this chapter.)

This may sound confusing, but it will make more sense as your understanding of your own breathing habits improves with practice.

- ✔ **Singing on breath** is what you're supposed to do all the time. If someone says, "Sing on the breath," he's probably telling you to connect the breath to the tone or start the sound by connecting air. You can grunt and make a sound, but that's not applying air or singing on the breath. You can also blow too much air and make a breathy sound, which isn't what it means to sing on the breath. The process in between those two is what you're looking for.

In the future, ask the person to be more specific if you're confused by the phrase he uses. But it's okay if you don't know every singing cliché. How can you know them all yet? The singing world uses just too many.

Opening your body

Taking in air quickly and quietly is one of the goals for singing. To get the air in quickly, you want to open your body — your back, ribs, sides, and abs. You can open all these areas at the same time, but explore each area separately before trying to activate them all together.

Moving back for inhalation

If you think of your back or spine connected to your ribs, it makes sense that opening your back helps your breathing. You want to quickly open your back so air falls into your lungs. Remember that the lungs are connected to the ribs, so moving the ribs and the back moves the lungs.

Try this suggestion to quickly open your back for an easy inhalation:

1. **Assume a huddle position, as if you're on the football team ready to hike the ball to the quarterback.**

In the huddle position, you stand and lean forward, with your hands on your bent knees and your back straight. You don't have to bend over as far as the football players — only far enough to allow your back to relax.

2. **With your hands on your knees, take a breath and imagine that you can put the air into your back — as if your lungs are all along your back and you want to fill them with air.**

   You may notice that the muscles in your back feel like they're lifting and opening for the air to come in the body.

3. **Take a few more breaths and notice the sensations of your back opening.**

4. **When you think you feel your back releasing and opening as you inhale, try opening your back more quickly.**

   Open the same muscles along your back without worrying about inhalation. When you open the muscles, the air comes into your body and you don't have to worry about inhalation — the inhalation happens because you're opening the muscles.

You can also squat down and place your hands on your back to feel the movement of the muscles. If you have a practice buddy, ask her to put her hands on your back as you try expanding your back. Or you can ask her to try the same exercise so you can feel how her back moves. Feeling the movement of someone else's body may help you know what's happening to yours.

If the huddle position isn't comfortable, try lying on your back with your knees bent to feel the opening of your back. Lie on the floor and feel the opening of your back along the floor as you inhale. Notice the movement of the upper part of your back and the lower part of your back, all the way down to your hips.

Flexing the ribs

The rib cage has 12 pairs of ribs. (Yes, men and women have the same number of ribs.) You can view the skeleton in Chapter 3 to see that the last two ribs aren't attached in the front of the rib cage; these ribs are called floating ribs. The first seven pairs of ribs are connected to the sternum, and the last three ribs are connected to rib #7, to make the curved shape in the front of the rib cage.

You don't have to remember the number of ribs, but you want to remember that the top of your rib cage has more movement from front to back in your body and that the lower ribs open more laterally, or out to the side of your body. Knowing how your ribs move, you can visualize the side-to-side opening near the bottom of your ribs to get the most air into your body quickly. And if you're a dancer, you want to know how to quickly open the upper ribs and your back when you're dancing across the stage.

You may be asked to sing and dance at the same time. Because dancers have to keep their body moving while singing, they can't always let their abdominal muscles release. But dancers can allow the ribs to open when breathing. If a dancer allows his ribs to open upon inhalation and slowly lets them close upon exhalation, he doesn't have to worry so much about letting the abdominal muscles be loose. When you understand the way the body was designed to breathe, take it a step farther and practice working with your ribs for dancing while singing.

Move your arms in the following exercise so that you can feel the opening of your chest and ribs:

1. **Raise your arms over your head.**

2. **Take a breath and feel your ribs open.**

   Keep your chest stable. You don't need to raise your chest; merely let it open. Repeat several times to feel the movement of your ribs.

3. **Put your arms down and place your hands on your ribs.**

   Put your palms against your lower ribs with your thumb facing forward and fingers pointing to your back. To feel the movement higher in your rib cage, turn your hand the same way with the thumb facing forward, or cross your arms so that your right hand is on your left ribs and your left hand is on your right ribs.

4. **With your hands on your ribs, open the ribs slowly to feel the stretch of the intercostals — the muscles between the ribs.**

   Repeat several times.

5. **Send air to your ribs or flex open your ribs as you inhale.**

6. **As you sing, allow your ribs to gradually move back in.**

If raising your arms over your head isn't comfortable, you can lie on your side. Putting your arms above your head is ideal, but you can get the same sense of movement in the ribs with your arm bent at the elbow or extended in front of you. Other positions you can try are standing with your arms extended straight out on each side. Position the arms just slightly behind your body so your chest is open. In this position, you may especially feel the opening of the upper ribs. When your arms tire, you can put your hands on your hips and continue exploring the opening of the ribs. It's fine to practice with your hands on your hips to remind you to open your sides and ribs. When the opening is familiar, you can put your arms down by your side and find the same opening.

It's okay if you're really confused right now or feel short of breath. Feeling short of breath when you begin working through these exercises is normal. Be patient, and you'll begin breathing efficiently. Creating a new habit in your body takes a while, and breathing for singing is definitely new. Your inhalation was perfect when you were a baby. If you watch infants breathe, you can see that they know exactly what to do. As people age and life becomes more complicated, however, stress affects the body. People start to carry unnecessary tension in various parts of the body, which can prevent correct breathing. The body gets stressed out. But not in this book — stress busters are on the way!

Stretching the sides

Another area of the body that you can open for inhalation is your sides. For now, think of your ribs and your sides as separate. The sides are the love handle area — the area right below your rib cage and above your hips — the oblique muscles. This area may automatically open when you open the ribs, but you want to be sure.

Place your hands on your hips and then move them up a couple of inches so that you feel the indentation just above the top of the hipbone.

Pretend that your lungs are on your sides and inhale, to help open that area. You may also be able to open this area by placing your hands on your sides, exhaling, and then opening your hands. You may need to provide a little resistance with your hands so you can figure out how to open those muscles.

Your sides are a great place to notice exertion in the body. When you cough, you may feel your abs move in and your sides expand. The movement for singing is similar but happens more slowly. The sides also engage when you sing loudly. For now, be aware of how your sides move; later, you can move your sides when you need an exertion of energy to sing loudly.

Singing with a clear tone doesn't use as much air as singing with a breathy tone. See Chapter 6 for more information on singing with clear tone. You can sing with a breathy tone on purpose, but it requires a lot more air and it's more difficult for a microphone to amplify a fuzzy tone.

Releasing the abs

Many singing teachers feel strongly about the movement of the abdominal muscles (abs) and singing. You may have been told to control your abs to control your exhalation. That idea is a good one, but you also want to control the other muscles in your torso, because the abs aren't the only muscles that control exhalation.

To feel the release of the abs with inhalation, get down on your hands and knees. You can get something soft to put under your knees if this isn't the most comfortable position for you. Exhale and notice the movement of your abs. You probably feel them moving in, and that's great. Notice how they move when you inhale. If you feel them dropping down with gravity, you're on the right track. If you don't feel them drop, you may be trying too hard to move your chest to breathe. Allow your chest to remain steady and try again.

Taking in too much air is called *overbreathing,* which can cause adverse tension in the body. When you get used to breathing for singing, you can judge how much air you need to take in for each phrase.

The following exercise enables you the opportunity to let breath fall into your body, releasing the abs.

1. **Exhale.**

   As you exhale, your abs move in.

2. **Hold your breath and silently count to ten.**

   Don't inhale while you're counting to ten.

3. **After counting to ten, inhale.**

   Most likely, you need the breath so badly that it just falls right into your body, and your abs release and drop.

4. **Notice the movement of your body as the air comes rushing in.**

   Your throat opens and your abs release so the air can drop in.

After expelling all your air on a long musical phrase, let that air that you need just drop into your lungs by opening your body.

Breathing, slow and steady

The goal for inhalation is to open the body quickly so the air drops in quietly. If your muscles don't know how to open quickly, you can slow down with this exercise and find how to open the muscles.

When you were a kid, your mom probably told you not to suck air through your straw, right? It makes that horrible slurping noise after all the liquid is drained from your glass. Now you need a dry straw that doesn't have any leftover milkshake stuck inside. Breathing through a straw helps the air that you breathe drop into your body, making it easy to feel your body expand as you breathe. You also can't gasp or suck in air too quickly with a straw.

1. **Find a straw and cut it down to 3 inches.**

2. **Insert one end of the straw into your mouth.**

3. **Breathe through the straw, making sure that you don't raise your chest or shoulders, and notice how your body opens as the air drops into your lungs.**

4. **Inhale for three slow counts and exhale for three slow counts.**

   Repeat this step five times. Remember to keep your alignment. Chapter 3 has tips for great alignment.

5. Inhale for four slow counts and exhale for four slow counts.

As you inhale, notice what's moving in your body. You want your ribs to open, your sides and back to expand, and your abs to release and drop. If the motion is still unsteady, keep practicing until you really feel the movement in your body. It may take a couple of weeks to feel the movement enough that it becomes familiar.

Catching a quick breath

Your song may have a long phrase and then a very short rest to catch a breath. The struggle is to get in enough air in a short time. To understand how to catch a quick breath in your song, you want to know how to quickly open your muscles. If you opened the muscles slowly in the preceding exercise, you may be ready to open them quickly. Try this exercise to explore a catch breath.

Get yourself slightly winded by running in place, dancing around, or doing any other movement that gets you moving. When you start to breathe faster and get winded, stand and sing part of your song. Your body really wants to inhale. When you finally take a breath, notice how the breath drops quickly into your body. Most people describe the sensation of the body opening quickly to get air in. It's different from pulling in air or gasping. With a gasp, your throat is tight and you're pulling or sucking in air. Opening the body (including your throat) helps you make a quick and quiet inhalation.

Although inhaling may be natural for everyone, you need to practice the correct way to inhale while maintaining correct posture, in order to breathe your best while singing. Correct inhalation means keeping yourself properly aligned, with your body free of tension, your throat open, and your shoulders steady to allow the most air to fall into your body. Try the following to feel the difference between incorrect and correct inhalation:

- ✔ If you gasp, you can feel a tight sensation in your throat as you try to squeeze air in while your vocal cords are closed. However, if you pretend that you're hiding and don't want anyone to hear you breathing, you leave your throat open and can take in plenty of air.

- ✔ If you inhale and intentionally raise your shoulders or chest, you can feel that, as your shoulders rise, your neck gets tense. However, if you keep your shoulders and chest steady and inhale, you get more air into your body.

It's tempting to push down the tongue as you inhale. You may feel like pushing down the tongue helps you get the air in faster, but it doesn't. To help release any tension in your tongue as you inhale, release the tongue forward. Your tongue then moves forward, or toward your teeth, as you inhale instead of pushing back or pressing down. Compare the two. Push down your tongue as you inhale, and then try releasing your tongue forward as you inhale. You may find that the release forward helps you get the air in quickly and has your tongue released to start the first note.

Inhaling properly should now be fairly easy for you. Singing "Happy Birthday" tests your ability to inhale correctly and then sing a song. Before you start the song, feel the breath moving into your body. When you're in the groove, go for it.

1. **Sing all the way through the song "Happy Birthday."**

2. **Take a deep breath and sing the first phrase again.**

3. **Pause.**

   Before you sing the second phrase, remember all that you recently discovered about inhalation. Take your time and find the correct way to take in that breath. You don't have to rush.

4. **Calmly take the breath back in.**

5. **Take the time to find the correct motion of the breath and then sing the next phrase.**

6. **Repeat this series of steps until you finish the song.**

   Remember to get the breath right instead of rushing to the next phrase or gasping for air.

Each time you try this exercise, it gets easier. Try it the next time you sing a new song to coordinate your breathing properly.

 You're not alone if you feel like you can't remember how to breathe. Your body gets confused putting all this information into practice, so just work on the inhalation until it's easy for you; then move on to another exercise. Go back and reread the explanation about how the breath works in the body, and then try some of the exercises again. You may find that they're easier now that you can picture the movement of the air as well as feel it.

Practicing Exhalation

When you sing and exhale, remember not to collapse your body too quickly. Keep the same aligned position that you had for your inhalation: Keep your chest steady, and have your abdomen and ribs gradually move inward as you release the breath. When you aren't singing or speaking, and as you go about your everyday business, you normally exhale much more quickly than you should when you sing. When you sing, however, you have to inhale quickly and extend the flow of air over a longer period of time. It takes practice to be able to sing a long phrase without stopping in the middle to breathe. Practice a steady, controlled exhalation while maintaining good posture.

Blowing in the wind

This exercise helps you develop the control needed when you sing a long phrase of music. The object of the exercise is to make a candle flame flicker by exhaling and not blasting hot wax onto your hand! Make sure that you exhale with a steady, slow stream of air — just enough to bend the flame. If you don't have a candle handy, you can blow air across the top of a hot cup of cocoa or tea, or just use your imagination. You can work this exercise with your imagination, or you can actually light a candle.

Please be careful with the candle if you use a real one. Hold or set down the candle in a holder that's at least 8 inches from your mouth so you don't burn your eyebrows.

Follow these steps:

1. **Light a candle and hold it 8 inches from your face.**

2. **Take a deep breath, keeping your shoulders and your chest nice and steady.**

3. **As you exhale, blow gently on the flame to make it bend but not flicker wildly.**

4. **Continue the steady stream of air to keep the flame bent, counting silently to see how long you can bend the flame.**

Be careful that your body doesn't collapse quickly as you exhale during this exercise. Instead, feel a steady movement in your body during the exhalation. If you can bend the flame for the count of five the first time, try to make it to six the next time. Bend the flame for six counts several times in a row before you try for seven. Each time, make sure that you notice what's happening in your body.

Trilling for exhalation

A *lip trill* is an itchy exercise, but it's great for feeling the movement of the exhalation. The vibrations of your lips may make your nose itch after a few minutes. No problem — scratch your nose and keep going. What's a *lip trill*? Ever see a horse blowing air through his lips? The horse's lips flap in the breeze. This may seem silly, but it's a great test of your exhaling endurance. Take a breath, and send the breath between your lips and let them vibrate. If your lips don't vibrate like Mr. Ed's, it's probably because they're too tight. Loosen your lips and just let them hang free as you blow air between them this time. If your lips are tight, place a finger at the corners of your mouth and gently push the corners toward your nose as you do the lip trill.

1. **Practice trilling your lips.**

2. **When you have the lip trill moving easily, start counting silently.**

3. **Sustain the lip trill for four counts; inhale slowly for four counts and repeat the cycle.**

   Make sure that you take a good breath before you begin. As you count to four, notice what moves in your body as you exhale. Try not to collapse your chest as you exhale; let your lower body do the work.

4. **Sustain the lip trill for four counts again, but this time, inhale for two counts and repeat the cycle.**

5. **Sustain the lip trill for longer periods of time as your endurance improves.**

   Lip trill for six counts and inhale for two counts. When you can easily do the lip trill several times in a row, increase the number by two counts (lip trill for eight counts, inhale for two counts, and so on). The object of the exercise isn't to count to 50, but to work the endurance of the breath and make sure that the body is working properly as you exhale.

6. **As your skill increases, vary the lip trill count.**

   Notice how your body changes on a two-count trill compared to an eight-count trill. It adjusts by moving more slowly on the eight counts. This variation happens in songs — you have short phrases followed by long phrases, and you have to adjust your breath control for the phrase.

When the lip trill is a piece of cake for you, add a tune: Lip trill a song. You can easily lip trill "Happy Birthday." Let each note connect to the other without a pause and without pushing your tongue against your teeth for each note. In other words, make it *legato* (smooth and connected).

To practice more lip trills, check out Figure 4-1.

1. **Sing through the lip trill pattern in Figure 4-1.**

2. **Play the track again, and this time, try a tongue trill.**

   Many people find that they can make good sounds with a tongue trill. The tongue trill works like the lip trill. Leave your tongue loose in your mouth and blow air between your tongue and the roof of your mouth. Make sure that your tongue is released or this won't work. As the air moves over the tongue, the tip of the tongue raises and vibrates against the roof of your mouth.

3. **Play the track for a third time, alternating between doing the tongue trill and singing on the given notes.**

   You can easily go right from the tongue trill to a vowel. For example, sing the first two notes on the tongue trill and the last two notes on *ah.* Make a smooth transition from the tongue trill to the *ah.* See whether your airflow remains the same.

TRACK 2

Figure 4-1:
Lip and
tongue trills.

1. Lip trill   Br _____

2. Tongue trill   Tr _____

3. Tongue trill to "*ah*"   Tr _____ *ah*_____

Recognizing resistance and suspending the breath

Earlier in this chapter, I tell you about breathing basics. Singers often think that they can control their diaphragm movement and achieve great breath control. What most people don't know is that the diaphragm is passive during exhalation. Your diaphragm moves down as you inhale and as your lungs expand to fill with air, but the diaphragm isn't active when you exhale. You control exhalation by controlling all the muscles that affect the movement of the lungs — the muscles between the ribs (intercostals), the muscles on your sides (obliques) and your back, and your abs. Knowing how to control the movement of these muscles controls your exhalation and allows you to sing long phrases.

Because your body is used to opening for the inhalation and then a quick exhalation, you have to resist the normal movement of your body when you're singing. This resistance is a good thing. Think of resistance as a slow movement of the body back in for exhalation, or a friendly resistance to keep the body from collapsing.

One way to explore exhalation and resistance is to suspend the breath. If the normal movement of your body is to take a breath and gradually exhale, or allow the body to move back to its resting position, I want you to explore taking a breath and then waiting before you exhale. It feels like your body is suspended in motion: You're ready to exhale, but the muscles just aren't moving yet. This feeling of suspension is what I mean by resistance. Your body wants to close, but you aren't allowing it to collapse just yet. Resistance doesn't involve tension; it's more like hesitation. Notice the feeling of your body staying open as you take the breath and then wait. You can practice suspending for three or four counts and then gradually exhale. The goal isn't to figure out how to suspend for long periods of time, but to understand the sensation of the body resisting the normal urge to close after an inhalation.

Try this sequence to develop your ability to suspend the muscles of exhalation:

1. **Breathe in for three counts.**

2. **Suspend for three counts.**

   As you suspend, pay attention to the sensations in your body. Your body wants to close, but you make the choice to suspend and stay open.

3. **Exhale for three counts.**

4. **Gradually move the exhalation number higher.**

   Breathe for three counts, suspend for three counts, and exhale for four counts. Notice how your body adjusts to the slower exhalation.

You can exhale in one count or in ten counts, and the body adjusts the movement of the muscles. For today, I recommend that you try the sequence with three counts for each step. Tomorrow you can move the exhalation up to four counts, and the next day move the exhalation to five counts. Explore this exercise slowly to develop control over the muscles. Moving too quickly doesn't allow you to explore the sensations of adjustment in your body as the exhalation gets longer. The next section in the chapter has more exercises that explore longer exhalation.

Testing Your Breath Control

If you've been working on the exercises in this chapter, you've probably explored your inhalation and exhalation enough to know what's moving and grooving as you breathe and sing.

Athletes know that they have to train consistently to teach the muscles in their body to respond exactly the way they want. Gaining coordination of the muscles that control breathing takes time and consistent practice. Some people call it developing muscle memory. Over time, the muscles remember how to move and you don't have to think about it. You want this to happen for breathing and singing: You want to practice the breathing exercises enough that you can rely on them to work efficiently so you can focus on the story you're telling.

Athletes also know that working out and doing physical conditioning is crucial to develop the ability to transport oxygen quickly throughout the body. When you're singing, you're moving a lot of air and your body needs to be in good shape so you can handle the endurance required to sing for an entire performance. You don't have to be thin, but you have to be in good shape. Your workout at the gym also helps your breathing for singing.

Pushing yourself just a little beyond your comfort zone helps you develop stamina and endurance. Your muscles may feel warm or tired after you work on the breathing exercises, which is perfectly normal. Extreme fatigue is a sign that something isn't right in your practice session, but it's normal to feel tired and need to rest for a time before you can practice more.

To give yourself an opportunity to work on more advanced breathing exercises, keep reading and working through the exercises. They aren't too advanced for you, especially if you've been exploring other exercises and are comfortable with what moves as you breathe.

If you're new to singing, moving too quickly to the advanced exercises without practicing the basics doesn't give you an opportunity to make the movement a habit. It took some time for me to make correct breathing a habit, but now I don't have to worry about changing gears when it's time to sing. I breathe in the same manner when I sing as when I speak, because the movement has become so natural for me.

Releasing abs and then ribs

Because your lungs are housed within your rib cage, allowing the ribs to open as you inhale and letting them stay open as you exhale is beneficial. This is also known as *outie* breathing, or *appoggio* (that's Italian for "support" or "lean"). Don't *force* your ribs to stay open, but *allow* them to stay open. Even if the words *force* and *allow* seem similar, they're different. Forcing the ribs to stay open results in pressure being put on your body and a tight sound.

When you've been working with breath for some time and you can easily manage quick, efficient inhalation and have some control over longer exhalation, try the exercise that follows.

1. **Practice flexing open your ribs.**

   Stand in front of the mirror and try to open your rib cage. You want to open your ribs on the side of your body, not raise your chest. Watch the movement in your body to make sure that you're not lifting your chest. It may take a few tries before you can figure out how to open the ribs. When you know how to move them, allow the ribs to open as you inhale. The area that you're trying to move is at the bottom of the rib cage.

2. **Inhale and open your ribs.**

   Practice inhaling and allow your ribs to open. If you aim the air at the lowest rib, you can open the ribs without forcing your chest to rise.

3. **Work for a time just allowing your ribs to open when you inhale and to close as you exhale.**

    As this becomes easier, allow the ribs to stay open longer on the exhalation.

4. **Inhale and allow your ribs to open.**

    Leave the ribs open as you exhale. Take the next breath and allow your abdominal muscles to expand.

5. **Now that your ribs are open and your abdominal muscles are expanded, exhale.**

    As you exhale, allow the abs to move in as the ribs stay out.

6. **As you reach the end of your breath, allow the ribs to gradually close or collapse back to their normal position.**

The long-term goal of this exercise is to provide you with the option of opening the ribs as you inhale and letting them close by choice, depending on the length of the phrase you're singing. I keep my ribs open if I have to sing a long phrase. This motion may take a month or more to master. Keep trying.

Singing slowly

Earlier in this chapter, I suggest simple tunes, such as "Happy Birthday," so that you can easily concentrate on many details at one time. However, it may be time for you to try a tougher song. Think of a song that gives you trouble when it comes to managing the long phrases. It can be a hymn or familiar tune in which you just can't quite conquer the phrases. Some familiar tunes with long phrases are "Danny Boy"; "Come Unto Him" from *The Messiah;* and "Over the Rainbow." Sing through the song to refresh your memory of the words and the tune. When you're ready, sing through the song at a slow pace. You want to sing more slowly so you extend your exhalation. By singing more slowly, you have to figure out how to extend your breath over a longer period of time. Singing faster songs with short phrases doesn't require a long exhalation, and it doesn't require that you control your exhalation over long phrases.

Practice the exercise that follows to move on to the next level of breath control so that you can manage your breath easily during longer phrases.

1. **Sing the song slowly.**

    If you've chosen a long song, sing through part of it. If you've chosen a shorter song, sing it all the way through.

2. **Sing through each phrase with a consistent exhalation for a smooth, connected line.**

   Make sure that you inhale slowly before the beginning of each phrase.

3. **Sing through the song again slowly, but inhale quickly, while taking in the same amount of air that you did when you were inhaling slowly.**

Be careful not to gasp when you're singing through this exercise; open your throat and allow the air to come in. Gasping prevents you from getting the air in quick enough.

In exhaling, your ribs and abs must be moving in. Then try letting the abs move while the ribs stay open.

Gaining weight or losing weight quickly can totally confuse your body. If your body is used to moving a certain amount of weight around, it affects your breathing. You have to slowly get used to your body being a different size after the weight change, especially if you've gained weight. Take your time when you lose weight to allow your body to slowly adjust.

Chapter 5

Toning Up the Voice

· ·

In This Chapter
▶ Changing the tone of your voice
▶ Discovering your larynx and vocal cords
▶ Exercising to improve your tone
· ·

In this chapter, you discover what to release to help you create that gorgeous tone — and even find a little *vibrato* (the variation of a sustained pitch) along the way. I also include some helpful exercises for those of you who are *tone deaf* (not able to accurately distinguish between differences in pitch). Relax. By the time you finish this chapter, you'll be better at not only controlling your singing voice, but also locating some fun body parts to brag about at your next family gathering. "Hey, wanna feel my larynx?"

Defining Tone

If you turned on the radio, would you recognize your favorite singer? Elvis, Toby Keith, Ethel Merman, Maxwell, Luciano Pavarotti, or Lady Gaga? You probably would. How? If you answered, "By their voices," you're partly right. More specifically, you recognized your favorite singer by the *tone* of voice. *Tone* is what's known as the *color* or *timbre* of your singing voice. Every voice has a specific color, which can be described as warm, dark, or strident. Two singers singing the same song in the same key may sound different — the reason is tone.

Creating unique tone

A lot of people just open their mouth to sing and produce wonderful-sounding tone. Others have to work to create beautiful tone. The tone of your voice is unique to you, but if it's tight and pressed, you may need to work on the exercises in this book to help you create great tone. You also want to make sure that the tone of your voice matches the style of music you're singing. If you've ever heard opera singers try to sing pop music, you know that they sound funny — their tone is too full and rich when it needs to be more casual. Check out Chapter 2 for more information on the sounds different voice types make in different styles of music, and read Chapter 7 for more information about creating a resonant singing voice and understanding the differences in resonance among various styles of music.

Identifying factors that affect tone

The shape and size of your body and your body coordination partly determine your tone. In addition, your tone changes with your moods or emotions. Check out the following list for factors that affect tone:

- ✔ **Body coordination:** Coordinating the muscles in the body is important for creating lovely tone for singing. That coordination includes breath coordination, alignment, and articulation. You can read about breath coordination in Chapter 4 and alignment in Chapter 3. Chapter 8 outlines articulation of vowels, and Chapter 9 covers articulation of consonants. Check out the other chapters in the book so your entire body is ready to help you make great sounds.

- ✔ **Emotions:** Your emotions directly affect the tone of voice. You know when someone is happy or sad by the tone of voice. When you're acting, you want to tap into your emotions so that the tone of your voice reflects the story you're telling. Of course, it's also possible to go overboard and let the emotions overtake you. If you go too far emotionally, you end up crying and won't be able to sing your song. Or maybe you'll be so angry that you tense up and can't sing well. Using your emotions is good, but allowing emotions to overtake you isn't good. Work on the exercises in the book to develop your technique. When your technical skill is solid, you'll be able to maintain your technique even during the more emotional sections of your song.

- ✔ **Shape and size of your head and throat:** If your mouth and throat are small, you have smaller vocal cords and probably a higher voice type. Singers with large mouths and heads tend to have bigger voices and can make bigger sounds.

- ✔ **Size of your body:** Singers with a big, round chest tend to have a large lung capacity for nailing those high notes. You don't need to have a big body to sing well, though — good singers come in all shapes and sizes.

- ✔ **Space:** The amount of space you open for tone to resonate is a key element in the tone of your voice. If the space is tight, the tone is tight. If the space is open, the tone has room to resonate. You can read more later in the chapter about opening the space in the mouth and throat.

- ✔ **Tension:** Even body parts far from your singing voice need to be free of tension to keep the tone of the voice free.

Considering tone, pitches, and notes

Whether you sing just for fun or you dream of performing professionally, you can count on frequently encountering three terms: *pitch, note,* and *tone.* These three terms are often incorrectly used interchangeably, but understanding their true relationship to one another may make your journey through the world of singing less confusing.

- **Pitch** is the high or low frequency of a sound. When you sing, you create pitch because your vocal cords vibrate at a certain speed. As an example, a foghorn emits a low frequency or pitch, whereas the sound your smoke detector emits when you press the test button is a high frequency or pitch. In singing, when your vocal cords vibrate at a faster speed, you sing a higher pitch than when they vibrate more slowly. The A just above Middle C vibrates at 440 cycles per second — your vocal cords open and close 440 times per second.

- **Notes** are musical symbols that indicate the location of a pitch.

- **Tone** is the *color* or *timbre* of pitch. Tone can be described by many different words, including *warm, dark, brilliant, ringing, rich, lush, shrill,* and *strident.* An example of a singer with a warm tone is Karen Carpenter; someone with a strident tone is Eddie Murphy playing the role of the Donkey in the Shrek movies.

Based on these definitions, it makes more sense to say that someone is *pitch deaf* rather than *tone deaf.* You may also hear singers say that they're afraid to sing high *notes* when they should say that they're afraid to sing high *pitches.* Although knowing the exact definition of these terms is good, I doubt that anyone will correct you if you mix up the words *tone* and *pitch.*

Flexing Your Singing Muscles

Within your head and neck, groups of muscles help create tone. At the same time, the brain sends a message to the muscles that create your singing voice: The air in your lungs begins moving out and the vocal cords move into position to create the pitch. The color of the pitch is the tone. Does it seem complicated? Well, it isn't — this is exactly what happens every time you speak.

To change the tone, you change the space in your mouth and throat, your posture, and the amount of breath moving as you sing. The exercises in Chapter 6 help you create the right tone and adjust the space in your mouth and throat so that you can change your tone and make your voice sound great.

Discovering your own bands

Many different parts of your body influence how you sing, but understanding how they all work together to produce the best sound is the key to great singing. Chapters 3 and 4 are devoted to the big anatomical influences, such as breathing and posture, but knowing where those tiny little bands of tissue called *vocal cords* — your muscles for singing — are located and how they make tone is just as important. When developing good vocal technique, you need to understand how your breath, posture, and tension affect the way your vocal cords work.

Your vocal cords are inside your *larynx* (pronounced *lar*-inks, not *lar*-nicks), which is the source of your singing voice. Your vocal cords are two small bands of tissue stretching across your larynx that vibrate to create pitch.

Your vocal cords coordinate with your breath to release a pitch by opening and closing (vibrating) as air (your breath) passes through. Each vibration is called a *cycle of vibration* or *glottal cycle*. If you're singing the same note that an orchestra plays to tune the instruments, your vocal cords are vibrating at 440 cycles per second — yes, that fast. To make those fast vibrations, you need to keep your breath flowing; otherwise, you run out of air and won't be able to sustain the tone. (See Chapter 4 to discover techniques for improving your breathing.)

Making the first sound

You already can make singing sounds — you just may not realize it. Working through the sounds in the following steps can start you on the road to singing. Making these sounds helps you discover how to make tension-free sounds that explore your entire singing range.

Make the following sounds:

1. **Try sighing — a nice, long sigh.**

   A sigh is that sound you make as you feel the warmth of the whirlpool or the relaxation of your body as someone massages your shoulders. As you sigh, make the sound as long as possible. Start higher and gradually slide lower.

2. **Imitate a siren.**

   Slide up and down or around in circles a few times, exploring high and low pitches. Those pitches in the siren are the same pitches you sing in the exercises later in the book.

3. **Whoop with joy.**

    Another way to explore the first sounds is to use your imagination. Pretend that someone just told you that you won the lottery. Rather than screaming, try whooping with joy.

Dropping the jaw

When you sing, you have to drop your jaw much farther than you do in everyday conversation and you have to open your mouth and throat much wider. If you don't drop your jaw and open your mouth, the sound gets trapped inside your mouth and can't make it past the first row of the audience.

Your neck and jaw need to be free of tension and ready to move. If they aren't, check out the exercise in the "Checking for neck or jaw tension" section, later in this chapter, to release tension from your neck and jaw.

To properly open the throat and mouth for singing, you need to feel around a bit first. Place your finger on your chin and trace your jaw line back to your ear. At the back of the jaw, you can feel a curve under your ear. This is the area that I want you to focus on when you drop your jaw. Instead of trying to drop your chin, I want you to drop it from the area right underneath your ear. The back space gives the tone room to resonate.

Practice dropping the jaw to discover how to open the space in the back of the mouth — called the back space — and space in the throat; dropping just the chin doesn't open the back space. To practice dropping the jaw, follow these steps:

1. **Massage all the muscles around your face to make sure that they're free of tension and ready to open.**

2. **Try yawning and dropping your jaw at the same time.**

    Remember, you want to drop the jaw, not just move the chin down. Your chin does move, but you want to open the space in the back by your ear (back space), not just the front (front space).

3. **Yawn inside your mouth and throat without opening your lips.**

    To do this, pretend that you're at a boring dinner party and you don't want the hostess to see you yawning. You feel an opening sensation inside your mouth and throat when you're starting to yawn. At the beginning of the yawn, you can feel the muscles stretching and opening. By the end of the yawn, the muscles are tight from the huge stretch. You want to remember the beginning of yawn, when the muscles are opening, not the tense phase at the end of the yawn.

Finding front space

To understand the difference between back space and front space, first find the front space. Open the front space, or only the front of your mouth, by following these steps:

1. **Open your lips really wide, as if the corners of your mouth are moving out toward your ears.**

When you open your lips, notice what that opening feels like inside your mouth.

2. **Open your front teeth really wide.**

Notice the sensations in your mouth.

Putting your larynx into position

Throughout this book, you explore different sounds that you can make with your singing voice. Knowing where the larynx rests in your throat makes it easier for you to tell whether your larynx is too high or too low. If it's too high, I tell you how to drop it.

Finding your larynx

Because the position of the larynx affects the tone, you want to know where your larynx is. The larynx can move up or down. A low larynx helps create a full, open sound. Raising the larynx too high creates a tighter and more strident sound.

Place your fingers on the middle of your throat underneath your chin. Now swallow. As you swallow, you can feel something move up and then down. That's your larynx.

The bump in the middle of the larynx is called the *Adam's apple.* Because men usually have a larger, more pointed larynx than women, guys can feel their Adam's apple more easily.

Keep your fingers on your throat and yawn. Feel that? The larynx went way down. When you sing, you want the larynx to be in the middle of your neck, (a neutral position) or lower. A low larynx helps create a nice, full, open sound for classical music. The larynx in a neutral position is closer to what happens when you belt. (See Chapter 13 for more info on belting.) Raising the larynx too high creates a tight or squeezed sound. Some teachers talk about a raised larynx for belting. If you drop the larynx low for classical singing, the position of the larynx is higher for belting. I prefer to call it a *neutral position* because thinking of a raised larynx may encourage you to push up or press to raise your larynx.

You want to release the larynx on the inhalation so that it opens. Not releasing the larynx upon inhalation can cause fatigue, because the muscles in the larynx are always in action when you're singing. Those muscles need a rest between phrases. See Chapter 4 on breathing for information on dropping the larynx when you inhale.

With your finger on the middle of your throat, hum a few bars of your favorite song. The buzzing sensation that you feel is your vocal cords vibrating and creating tone. Awesome! You may feel that buzzing sensation in your lips or around your nose. You can even feel the vibrations on the crown of your head. Because you can't see your voice, feeling the vibrations of sound is important. Your singing voice makes vibrations that you can feel in your body and hear resounding in the room. Trusting the feeling of good technique is important, because each room that you sing in has different acoustics. To monitor your tone, learn to feel the vibrations instead of relying on reverb.

Dropping your larynx

Nonsingers usually have a high-resting larynx. That's because most of the muscles in the neck are designed to keep the larynx high — which isn't what you want for singing. You have to figure out how to keep the larynx in a lower or more neutral position in your throat for singing.

To drop your larynx, you can use the beginning of the yawn, as you did in the earlier section, "Dropping the jaw." Avoid intentionally pushing down the back of your tongue, as most people do when first trying to drop the larynx: If you push your tongue down, you also feel the larynx push down and you feel a tightening of the muscles under your chin. This tight sensation isn't what you want for singing. It may take you a while to feel the difference between pushing down and dropping. The correct sensation is to feel your tongue moving forward and stretching the space between the parts of the larynx so that the bottom part of the larynx drops. You can also try the following suggestions to drop the larynx without pushing the tongue:

- ✔ **Smell something yummy.** Inhale slowly as you smell something positively wonderful. When you smell something yummy — or even pretend to — your throat opens and your larynx drops. Try smelling something yummy a few times and just notice what you feel. After a few tries, smell something yummy again and put your hand on your throat to notice whether your larynx dropped.

- ✔ **Open the space behind your tongue.** If you release your tongue forward, inhale, and pretend that the space behind the tongue opens — or the space between your tongue and the back wall of your throat — you may feel your larynx drop. Releasing or opening the back wall of the throat while releasing the tongue forward helps you drop your larynx.

Now, how do you keep the larynx dropped when you make sound? Good question — and it takes some practice for you to maintain the lower position of your larynx. Remember, the larynx is designed to ride high in your throat, but you want it to lower for singing classical music or at least stay in a neutral position for singing more contemporary music. Try the following suggestions to drop your larynx and leave it there while you make sound:

- ✔ **Drop and breathe.** When you feel the dropping sensation of the larynx, just breathe in and out (inhale and exhale) and leave the larynx in the low position. It may take a few days of experimenting before you can keep it steady while you breathe. When you can keep it steady while breathing, try the next suggestion.

- ✔ **Drop and make sound.** Say "ah" on a low note. Notice whether the larynx stays in the same place when you say "ah." Make the same sound several more times so you can really feel what's happening. If the larynx bounced up when you said "ah," try again. Release the larynx down and say the "ah" again. It seems simple, but it may take a couple of days of experimenting before you can make sound without the larynx jumping up. Remember to make a sound low in your range; trying to make a sound too high in your range is hard for a novice. It took me several days to learn to keep my larynx steady when I made sound. When you're confident that your larynx can stay steady with the "ah" sound, try the next suggestion.

- ✔ **Drop and slide around on pitch.** Drop the larynx, say "ah," and slide around a little bit in pitch, almost like you're saying "ah-hah." This sound is the one you make when you finally understand what someone told you. Keep exploring the "ah-hah" or sliding around on pitch before moving on to the next suggestion.

- ✔ **Drop and sing.** When you can keep the larynx steady while breathing or making simple sounds, try singing. Sing a simple two-note pattern or three-note pattern similar to what you see in Figure 3-1. Use this pattern, but sing it low in your range. When you're confident that the larynx stays steady, you can gradually sing higher.

Keep the larynx steady as you sing by visualizing the space in your throat opening farther as you ascend in pitch and by keeping your breath moving steadily. The larynx may tilt as you ascend, but shouldn't rise.

Matching Pitch

You may be familiar with the phrase "He can't carry a tune in a bucket" or "She's tone deaf." If either phrase sounds familiar, I have some good news. You can develop a sense of pitch, so you *can* carry a tune in a bucket.

Perfect pitch

Perfect pitch involves naming a note and singing it without hearing the pitch first. For example, singers with perfect pitch can sing Middle C correctly without hearing it first. They can also pick up a piece of music that they've never heard and sing all the correct notes without hearing the first note. You can't develop perfect pitch — you're either born with it or you're not — and even if you have it, you don't automatically sing every note in tune. Relative pitch, however, can be developed. *Relative pitch* involves guessing at the note and usually getting close to the exact pitch. Most singers develop relative pitch from singing their scales or even singing a certain song over and over. They often begin on the correct note just by knowing the way it feels. Perfect pitch may sound cool, but it's not necessary for good singing.

Being able to hear a pitch in your head or from an external source, such as the radio or a piano, and then sing it is called *matching pitch.* The first step to matching pitch is figuring out how to hear the pitch in your head so you can match it. The second step is matching it with your voice. Matching pitch is a skill. Perhaps it's not your strongest skill today, but you can improve with some practice. Using my suggestions in this section, you can improve your ability to match pitch and join in at the next campfire sing-along.

Matching pitch may be tricky for you in the beginning. If you've never been able to do it, matching pitch won't happen instantly, but you can improve with some practice. Be patient and keep trying!

Sliding up and down on pitch

Sliding up and down on pitch gives you the chance to hear a pitch from an external source, such as a piano, and then sing that pitch or slide around until you match it. Sliding away from the right note allows you to hear the vibrations of your voice clashing with the wrong note and then match the right note.

With practice, you can match any pitch, but start in the middle part of your range and work your way up.

1. **Play a note on any instrument.**

2. **After you play the note, feel it in your body — visualize yourself singing the note before you actually sing it.**

3. **Play the note again and sing it.**

   If you didn't match the pitch, slide up and down until you match it.

You can keep playing the note on the piano until you match it. How do you know when you've matched it? You'll hear that the vibrations of your voice and the vibrations of the note sound similar. The sounds will blend together.

4. **Play a different note.**

5. **Visualize it and hear the note in your head before you sing it.**

6. **Now sing the note.**

If you miss again, slide up and down until you match the pitch.

If you sang the correct note after some practice, good for you. Play the note again. This time, intentionally slide above the note or higher than the note, and then slide back down and match it again. The next time, try sliding below the pitch and then back up to match it. This exercise trains your ear to hear the matching vibrations of your voice and the instrument.

You can also ask someone to sing a note and hold it out. Listen to the person sing the note for a moment, and then try to match the pitch. Make sure that the note isn't too high; matching pitches that are close to your speaking range is easier than matching pitches that are outside your speaking range. As your partner sings, try sliding around until you match his pitch. If you still aren't sure, ask him to tell you when you get it right. This buddy system is beneficial for you because your buddy can be the pitch monitor. As you explore pitch, find a buddy of the same gender: It's usually easier to match the pitch with someone who's the same gender.

TRACK 3

On Track 3, listen to the note played on the piano and then listen to the singer sliding above and below the pitch. This exercise helps you understand what I mean about the vibrations of your voice matching the correct pitch. You can hear the clashing of the sounds when the singer is too high or too low, and you can hear the similar vibrations when she matches the pitch.

Developing muscle memory

For some folks, a link is missing between hearing the pitch and singing it. Developing what's called muscle memory can bridge the gap, however. *Muscle memory* refers to your body remembering how to do a task — like riding a bike or typing. In singing, your voice remembers how it felt to sing a certain note or exercise so that you can recall that feeling the next time you sing the note. Practice the following exercise so you can develop muscle memory for matching pitch.

1. **Find a quiet place and take a few moments to listen to your favorite tune in your head.**

2. **Take a moment and try to feel the pitch in your body.**

   What does that mean? If I asked you to imagine yourself speaking, you'd feel or imagine the sensation in your body. You hear the sound of your speaking voice in your head when you're rehearsing that funny joke for the dinner party or practicing your acceptance speech for the big awards banquet. Now I want you to feel the sensation of singing the tune that you hear in your head.

3. **Visualize yourself singing the notes in the first few lines to process the message that your brain sends to your vocal cords.**

4. **Sing a few lines of the tune.**

   Were you close? If you got part of the song but not the high notes, try singing the song again in a lower key that's more suited to your voice.

   If you sang most of the notes on target but missed a few, go more slowly. Take more time between hearing the pitch in your head and singing it. You can even sing a nursery rhyme that isn't as complicated as your favorite tune.

Recording yourself and singing along

Another way of discovering how to match pitch is to record yourself singing along with another recording. This exercise gives you a chance to compare the notes you sing with the notes that the singer on the recording sings. Listening to yourself singing on a recording is different from listening to yourself singing live. You can be more objective and hear the difference between what you sang and what was on the original recording.

1. **Choose your favorite song and select a recording device.**

   Recording with a digital recorder offers a better quality than a tape recorder.

2. **Start playing the song at the same time you begin recording.**

3. **Hold the recorder near your mouth and sing along with the song.**

   Sing at least half the song.

4. **Stop the song and the recording.**

5. **Be brave and play the recording.**

   Were you close to matching the pitches? Did you hit most of the notes? Missing only the high notes is fine for now. You can read more about singing higher notes in Chapters 11 and 12.

If you missed most of the notes, go back and review the previous two exercises (from the sections "Sliding up and down on pitch" and "Developing muscle memory").

Not liking what you hear on the recording is normal. Don't give up yet! You'll get used to hearing your voice recorded. Comparing your sound to the artist's recording isn't fair, because the artist probably spent thousands of dollars for a sound engineer to make her sound incredible.

Releasing Tension for Better Tone

Anytime you sing, be aware of how your body moves to create tone. When you sing, you want your body to be free of tension so that you create a round, full sound. For example, if you're singing and your body is tense and your throat is tight, the tone will be tight, thin, or strident. You don't want that.

The following exercises in this section help you discover how to release tension from your neck, jaw, and tongue to create that beautiful tone. But before you try those exercises, get your entire body into alignment by reviewing the exercises in Chapter 3.

Checking for neck or jaw tension

Having a loose jaw and flexible tongue is important. The tighter your jaw, the tighter the sound — and the tighter your tongue, the more difficult it is to make your song understood.

Become aware of the back of your neck and jaw as you sing so that you can monitor whether you have a flexible jaw and tongue. Follow these steps:

1. **As you step into alignment, notice what you feel in the back of your neck.**

2. **Massage the back of your neck to release any tension.**

   As the tension melts away, notice how easy it is to move your head without tension in the back of your neck. Feel your head floating above your shoulders as if your neck is long.

3. **When your neck feels tension-free, notice what your jaw is doing.**

   Without even realizing it, most people clamp down on their jaw. Everyday stress can lead to clenched teeth and clamped jaws.

4. **To relieve a cramped feeling in your jaw, let your jaw hang loose as if you were asleep.**

   I know that you've seen someone snoring away with his jaw hanging wide open for any old bug to fly right in. Allow yourself to explore this feeling of release and openness in your jaw.

5. **When you feel the fluid motion, try singing a few lines of a song.**

   Combine correct posture and breathing and open space in the throat and mouth with fluid motion of the jaw and neck. Whew! That's plenty to think about, but you can do it.

Bouncing the tongue and jaw

To create great sound, your tongue needs to be just as released as the rest of your body while you sing. The tongue is a huge muscle, and if it's tense or bunched up in the back, it blocks or squeezes the tone, making it sound tight. Your tongue should just lie like a rug — relatively flat — in your mouth except when you're making consonant and vowel sounds that require you to arch your tongue. (You can find exercises for singing vowels in Chapter 8 and consonant exercises in Chapter 9.)

Isolating the movement of the tongue and jaw is important because you don't have to press your tongue down to move your jaw or move your jaw when your tongue moves. The tongue and jaw are members of the same team, but they don't have to play at the same time. You can do the following to make sure that your tongue is released and working on its own:

1. **Without moving your jaw, say "Yuk."**

   Saying the *y* allows you to move the back of your tongue.

2. **Again, without moving your jaw, say "Ya-ya-ya-ya-ya."**

   Did you notice how your tongue was bouncing?

3. **Bounce your tongue again and then let it rest in your mouth.**

   Notice what the tongue feels like when it's resting in your mouth. It's not tense or pushing up or down. It's just lying in your mouth.

4. **Bounce your jaw and say "Ya-ya."**

   Say "Ya-ya" several times, and let your jaw bounce or move up and down as you say it. Notice how it rests in place after you say the syllables. You want your jaw, like your tongue, to hang loose, ready to move at any moment — but not tense.

Use the musical pattern in Figure 5-1 to practice the following exercise (don't forget to step into your alignment and breathe):

1. **Sing "Yah" on each note to feel the movement of your tongue.**

   For now, don't move your jaw. Just use your tongue to sing the "Yah."

2. **After you explore that sensation, sing the pattern again, but sing an "ah" with your tongue resting in your mouth.**

   Notice how released your tongue can be when you sing the *ah* vowel.

3. **Sing the pattern again. This time, bounce your jaw and sing "Yah-yah."**

   Allow the jaw to move as you sing. You'll still be able to sing.

4. **Sing the pattern again, using the *ah* vowel, and let your jaw be still.**

   Notice that the jaw is hanging loosely and is open.

TRACK 4

Figure 5-1:
Bouncing
the tongue
and jaw.

1. yah-yah- yah-yah-yah-yah- yah-yah- yah
2. ah _____

In the musical example in Figure 5-1, notice how the syllables are divided underneath the note. The *yah-yah* is written underneath every note, but the *ah* has a line moving off to the right. That line indicates that you sing "ah" and hold it out for the length of the pattern. You don't have to re-sing the *ah* vowel for each note. Get out some music to see how the syllables are divided for some familiar words. Understanding this process helps you master a new song because you can guess which note and which syllable belong together.

Part II
Improving Your Singing

"Here's a little technique I use to help people reach the high notes."

In this part . . .

The meat and potatoes of technique are in this part. Tone is an important topic, so you get more information in this part to keep you moving in the right tonal direction. Because resonance seems to be a misunderstood phenomenon, you can debunk all the myths that you hear and find out the real story. Inquiring minds want to know, and it's all in this book waiting for you to gobble it up.

The big workout in this part centers on vowels and consonants. Your audience won't understand you if your vowels and consonants aren't distinct. The exercises in this part get your vowels and consonants whipped into shape. After you read through some of the chapters on technique, you may want to develop a practice routine to polish your technique.

Chapter 6

Acquiring Beautiful Tone

To create your own beautiful, engaging tones, you need to make space for the tone to resonate, and you need to apply the breathing skills that you can pick up in Chapter 4. Space and breath are great partners in tone production. If you invite space to the singing party and don't invite breath, the space closes down. So think of those two factors as a team, and keep them working together. This chapter gives you all the tools you need to create your space and breath team while creating and sustaining beautiful tone and vibrato. See Chapter 5 for information about tone in different styles of singing.

Creating Tone

When you sing, you want to create tones that are clear and ringing. But making a clear tone takes practice and know-how. You need to know how to control your muscles and the movement of air.

You don't want to produce breathy or tight tones:

- ✔ **Breathy:** A breathy tone is fuzzy and unfocused. To get an idea of what a breathy tone sounds like, pretend that you're whispering a juicy secret to a friend. The fuzzy tone that you use when whispering isn't clear or ringing. When you sing with a breathy tone, you lose plenty of air. It takes much more air to sing a breathy tone than it does to sing a clear one.

- ✔ **Tight:** When your muscles are so tight that they squeeze the sound out, you get a tight tone. If you've ever run out of breath but kept singing by pressing or squeezing, you've produced a tight tone. Imagine using that sound to sing an entire song. Whew, how tiring!

Instead, you want to move air (exhale) to create a free, large, colorful, open tone. Using too much physical pressure in the throat (which feels like squeezing) creates a tight, constricted sound; not connecting enough air creates a fuzzy or airy tone. You need to find the happy medium — a tone that's connected to air and sounds clear. By coordinating the flow of air from the breathing skills you developed in Chapter 4 and by keeping the space in your throat open, you can control the quality of your tone.

Starting the tone

Onset of tone refers to starting a tone for singing. You can start a tone in two ways: with physical force or with air. You have to use some physical exertion to sing, but the exertion comes from energy moving to coordinate the muscles for breathing. Too much physical force results when the muscles in the throat press together with very little air flowing. By starting the tone with a consistent breath flow and an open throat, you create a tone that has a better quality. Starting the tone with air applies the same idea as producing the lip trill (see Chapter 4) or tongue trill. When you start the lip trill, the air passes between your lips, suction pulls them together, and they flap in the breeze. Your vocal cords do the same when you start the tone by coordinating a consistent flow of air.

The easiest way to start the tone, *humming,* involves singing or making a tone with your lips closed. Think of humming as a prolonged *M.* Try it. If you aren't sure whether your tone was clear, say, "Uh-huh," with your mouth closed — the sound you make when you're reading the newspaper and someone asks you a question. Say "Uh-huh" again to hear and feel the clarity, and then use that same feeling to hum part of a song. The clarity of tone from your "Uh-huh" is different from the whisper you use to explore breathy tone. You can feel the difference in vibrations between a breathy tone and a clear tone. The clear tone creates stronger vibrations in your throat, mouth, and nasal passages. You may feel vibrations in all three locations, or the vibrations may vary depending on how high or low you're singing or speaking. Remember this feeling so that you can start the tone clearly each time you sing it.

When you start a tone, don't rely on the sound. The sound may be different in each room, so you want to rely instead on the feeling, which should be more consistent from room to room and day to day in your singing. See Chapter 7 on resonance for information about projecting sound and how it may vary in different rooms.

Creating back space

In the days before computers, people often used the phrase *back space* to refer to moving the carriage of a typewriter back one space. In singing, *back space* refers to the space in the back of your mouth and in your throat. Just opening your teeth or the front of your mouth (front space) shows off your gorgeous pearly whites, but it doesn't do enough for your tone. Yes, you do have to open your teeth to create enough back space, but the big opening has to be in the back of your mouth and your throat. For space and breath to work together, you need to open the space quickly and then move the breath. (See Chapter 4 for more information about breathing.)

To create the open space necessary for great tone, pretend that you have an egg in the back of your mouth. You can use other images, such as a golf ball, if you don't like eggs. Compare the feeling of the space when it's closed and when you have the egg sitting on the back of your tongue. Practice opening that space quickly. Allow your tongue to release down, not press down.

Try singing part of your favorite song. Find the openness from the imaginary egg in the back of your mouth, and begin singing with the throat and the back of your mouth open. Remember to find the same clarity that you had when you were humming. You can compare the tone change by first singing with the throat and back of the mouth closed and then singing with the space open. If you aren't sure about the difference in the sound, record yourself and listen.

The first few times you open the space in the back of your mouth, the resonance may sound hooty, as if the sound is in the back of your mouth. Allow the tone to be hooty while you learn to coordinate the space. Eventually, you will be able to open the space and send the sound forward.

Coordinating air with tone

When you have the space open, you want to coordinate breath with tone to sing. You want the movement of the air to happen at the same time the tone starts.

Try these three ways of coordinating breath and tone:

- **Whistle:** Whistling requires that you move some air between your lips as you make tone. This coordination of breath is similar to singing. Whistle a tune or whistle at an attractive person. Notice how your body moves. You can't whistle without using air, and the air movement and start of the tone happen simultaneously.

- **Laugh:** Laughter is mostly about connecting air with the start of the tone. Take a few minutes to explore that feeling of boisterous laughter. Let the sound vary in pitch and change to higher and lower pitches as you extend the laughter. Notice the movement in your body as you laugh. More than likely, your body moves exactly as I describe in Chapter 4. That means your lower *abs* (that's short for *abdominal muscles*) move in and your sides move out as you exhale to make the sound.

> ✔ **Play:** Pretend that you're on the playground, having a blast on the swing or the merry-go-round. Kids often exclaim "Weeeeeeeee!" when they're delighted by moving fast. The "Weeeeeeeee" may start on a high pitch and gradually slide down, or you might extend the sound without changing pitch. Notice that this exclamation is clear and that you're moving breath as you sustain the sound.

After you explore these three suggestions, try singing part of a song to notice the flow of your air as you start the beginning tone of each phrase. You want the air to be moving consistently the entire time you sing, and you want the open space to remain open as you sing.

Sighing your way to clarity

Certain styles of music don't require clarity in the tone, but you want to be singing a breathy tone by choice instead of having no idea how to sing clearly when you really want to. Sighing helps you focus on finding this clarity of tone. It allows you to make sounds without worrying about singing precise pitches, which you needn't bother with for this exercise.

Start a sigh at a comfortable pitch, and maintain the sound of a sigh as you slide down pitches. The sigh can also be called a siren. Sigh or siren as if the sound moves up and down a three-story building. If your sigh is clear, continue your exploration and move to higher pitches. If your tone isn't clear, try to make a more-energetic sigh. Adding more energy to the sigh means connecting your body to the sigh. Engage your entire body in sighing by moving as you sigh. Move your body in such a way (leaning, bending, stretching) that you feel as if your entire body is surging and sighing. Using this exertion of energy when you sing also helps you find clarity in your tone. Your breath is flowing to complete a specific physical movement, which helps with the onset of tone. Filling a room with a clear tone is easier than filling it with a fuzzy tone. Without a microphone, you need a clear tone to be heard when you sing.

Younger singers often have a breathy tone, caused by lack of coordination. To create a clear tone, you need to use correct technique without adding pressure. Doing so involves getting the breath ready and then adding the energy that I just described. If you have a breathy tone, work on your breathing skills (see Chapter 4) to better understand that movement in your body. When you've polished your breathing skills, focus on tone production. Your tone may also continue to change as you mature, which is normal. Just remember what good technique feels like and keep working to make it a habit in your body.

If you aren't sure whether your tone is clear, record your practice session and imitate Marilyn Monroe's unfocused tone when she sang "Happy Birthday, Mr. President"; then imitate Pavarotti to find clear tones. The point is to find out what your tone sounds like and know when a clear tone is appropriate. You can use a breathy tone if you want that style and sound. Norah Jones has a breathy tone, but she's an example of someone singing pop and jazz music, using that tone on purpose.

Releasing Tone

Releasing a tone doesn't sound nearly as important as singing the tone. You sing a tone and then release it or stop singing. Singing requires that breath move out of your body (exhale), and releasing the tone simply requires that you inhale. Sounds easy doesn't it? Practice the following two exercises a few times to get the feeling in your body. In the heat of the performance, you want your body to remember how to let go of the tone so you can quickly take in that next breath.

Inhaling to release tone

An easy way to practice releasing tone is to inhale. Sing an *ah* vowel and, when you're ready to stop the tone, simply inhale. The first few times you try this, it may feel funny. You may think that you haven't done it right, because it was too easy. Practice singing the *ah* and releasing several times in a row: *ah,* inhale, *ah,* inhale, *ah,* inhale. Although this exercise may have you momentarily sounding more like a sex kitten than a professional singer, it allows you to feel that singing is exhaling, releasing a tone is inhaling, and the breath is always in motion, whether going in or out. Remember that when you inhale, you want to release the muscles in your throat. If you keep the muscles tight, you gasp, because the air is trying to pass through a tight space.

Letting your throat go

After you explore inhaling to release the tone, try letting your throat go and releasing all the muscles in your throat. You may still have enough air to keep singing, but you have to release the tone if you're at the end of the song or the end of a phrase. Just think of releasing in your throat by letting go of all the muscles to stop the tone. You may end up inhaling, but you don't have to worry about that action, because your body took care of it. As a young singer, I was afraid to sing higher pitches because I didn't know how to stop them without choking on the consonant. Think of the release as a liftoff from the tone or a liftoff from the consonant, and don't worry about stopping the tone.

Sustaining Tone

Sustaining tone is a singing must. Have you ever run out of air before the end of the phrase in your song and then had to sneak in a breath? Sneaking in a breath is legal when you sing, but I want you to sneak a breath because you choose to, not because you have to. Among the times you ran out of air, you may even have had to take a breath in the middle of a word. Yikes! It's not a federal crime, but you came to the right place for some tips on applying your breathing skills to sustain tones.

Connecting the dots with legato

Those gorgeous tones that professionals sing so effortlessly happen because they know how to connect the pitches of a song. Singers sometimes sing a melody one pitch at a time, not thinking of a continuous line or phrase. To make the phrases *legato* (smooth and connected), think of the pitches as having no empty space in between. The sound needs to flow from one pitch to the other, and the feeling in the throat must be a continuous sound even while you change pitches. Singing a long line of tone is possible because of breath control. If you haven't read Chapter 4 on breath control, do so now so that you can apply those skills as you attempt to sing legato lines.

While singing the pattern in Figure 6-1, focus on making the sound legato and concentrate on the connection between pitches. Find your alignment, practice the breath a few times, open the back space, and begin. Allow your body to open as you inhale and steadily move back in as you sing.

TRACK 5

Figure 6-1:
Creating a
legato line.

1. oh _____

2. *ah* _____

Trilling the lips or tongue

The lip trill is an exercise that I explain in Chapter 4. This time, you're going to really let those lips trill on a longer, slower musical pattern. The purpose of the lip trill is to monitor the flow of air — you can't continue the lip trill without the air flowing. By making the pattern longer, you get an opportunity to sustain the tone longer. If that lip trill is just too much for you, feel free to use a tongue trill. The principle is the same: trilling the tongue but maintaining a consistent flow of air. For this pattern, you want to monitor how your body moves as you trill — gradually moving. Review the exercises in Chapter 4 for tips on how to manage exhalation.

Focus on creating a legato line as you sing the pattern in Figure 6-2. Find your alignment, prepare your breath, and begin.

TRACK 6

Figure 6-2:
Trilling a
long legato
line.

1. Lip trill: br _____

2. Tongue trill: tr _____

Working your breath control

The pattern in Figure 6-3 gives you the chance to sing and put all your eggs in the basket. Instead of playing the exercise faster, I slow it down to make it harder, so you really have to work the breath. Think through all the skills that you can apply (using great posture, opening the space in your throat and mouth, and getting breath in your body) so you're ready to put it all together when you sing this pattern.

The pattern in Figure 6-3 is played slowly to allow you to lengthen your breath and sing long legato lines. You have time between each repetition to get your breath. Remember to find your alignment, open the back space, allow the breath to drop in your body each time, and keep your chest steady throughout the pattern. You can review the exercises on breath control at the end of Chapter 4 if you have trouble with this pattern.

TRACK 7

Figure 6-3:
Managing
long
phrases.

1. oh _____

2. ah _____

Finding Your Vibrato

Vibrato, the variation of a sustained tone or pitch, is one of the differences between singers and styles of music — how much vibrato they use and whether they use it all the time. A normal vibrato rate is five to eight pulses or fluctuations in the tone per second.

Vibrato can be fast or slow, depending on the singer. A really slow vibrato is sometimes called a *wobble,* which is often created by a lack of breath coordination. Vibrato that's too fast is called a *tremolo* and usually results from too much tension somewhere in the throat or neck area. Keep reading to find out what exercises can help you find your vibrato and to discover the difference between *straight tone* (no variation in pitch) and vibrato.

When you sing, one option is to use straight tone, with no vibrato or variation in the tone. You can use straight tone when you sing various styles of music, but you want the straight tone to be a choice, because it's a different sound. Knowing how to move from straight tone to a tone with vibrato is important in adding variety to your singing tone. Young male singers (before they hit puberty) don't have vibrato, but almost everyone else has it or can acquire it.

One way to understand vibrato is to listen to other singers, especially classical singers. Almost every classical singer has vibrato. Listen to the pitches as the singer holds them out, to hear the variation of the tone. After you spend some time listening to others, record yourself singing a song that has sustained pitches. Listen to the recording of you singing. Notice the variations of your tone as you hold out the pitches. You may find that the vibrato was there all along, and you just didn't know it or didn't know what it was called.

Moving from straight tone to vibrato

When you sing, you can choose to create tone that has variation in pitch (vibrato) or not (straight tone). Absolutely nothing is wrong with straight tone singing, as long as that's your choice. Your choir director may have asked you to sing straight tones when performing some styles of music (see the nearby sidebar, "Vibrato in different styles," for more info). Many people sing with straight tones because they have too much tension in their neck or throat. You don't have to squeeze in your throat to create straight tone — actually, just the opposite is true. You need to keep the throat open for a tone with or without vibrato.

Vibrato in different styles

Classical singers use vibrato on sustained tones except in some contemporary or modern music and early classical music. For this material, they use straight tone and vibrato.

Musical theater singers use both vibrato and straight tone. Vibrato is commonly used in earlier musical theater and straight tone is often used in contemporary material. Musical theater singers often start the note with straight tone and then allow the vibrato to come in.

Folk singers tend to use straight tone and some vibrato. The rate or variations in pitch during vibrato are not as drastic in the folk singer compared to the classical singer. If you think of vibrato as an ornament to the sound, then the classical singer uses lots of vibrato to ornament the material and the folk singer uses only some vibrato.

Rock, pop, country, and R&B singers often use straight tone and some vibrato on sustained tones. Because these styles of music have fewer sustained tones than classical music, the singers have fewer opportunities to use vibrato; therefore, it isn't considered a characteristic of the style. That doesn't mean the artists don't use it, but they use it more sparingly than a classical singer. The artist singing the style of music may have to adjust the use of vibrato when singing different styles of material because some artists cross over between styles of music.

TRACK 8

On Track 8, listen to the singer demonstrate the difference between a tone with and without vibrato, as well as how she moves from straight tone to vibrato. Then you try it. Sing a tone that has vibrato, and then sing a tone that has no vibrato. Now try starting the tone without vibrato and sliding into a tone with vibrato. As the vibrato begins, you feel something release and the movement of the vibrato begin. It's not a huge difference; it's subtle. Try this several times in a row to feel the difference. If you still aren't sure which sound you're making, try whining, which is usually made with a straight tone. Listen to the sound when you whine your way through part of a song, and then open up and really sing.

Imitating another singer's vibrato

Singers who have good coordination of breath and open space usually have vibrato. Think of a singer (probably someone you've heard singing opera or classical music) who makes a huge sound when singing. Now imitate that singer.

Find a quiet place where you can make plenty of sound. Hear the singer's voice in your mind and then imitate that singer. If it helps, open your arms wide, hold a towel, or stand on a chair, so you feel enormous. Imitating someone with good technique doesn't hurt your voice. You may discover that you can make some pretty big sounds yourself.

If you imitate a singer with vibrato, you can probably figure out how to imitate that vibrato, too. When you do, continue to explore that sound and notice what your voice sounds like. You can even record yourself, just to prove that you made that much glorious sound.

If you didn't find a different sound, imitate a different singer. This time choose a larger-than-life opera singer. Be flamboyant and pretend that you've been called in to sing because the star is ill. Fake it and sing some of this singer's songs — even make up the words.

The key to singing with vibrato is to make the sound happen naturally — don't force it. Explore different kinds of sounds, and work with space and breath to find vibrato.

You may be tempted to create vibrato by bouncing your abdomen or your larynx — but don't. Bouncing your abs or larynx doesn't consistently produce vibrato; instead of forcing it, let the vibrato happen because you keep air consistently flowing, as you did in the exercises in Chapter 4. Ham it up and enjoy vibrato!

Chapter 7

Exploring Resonance

. . . .

In This Chapter

▶ Separating the truth from fiction

▶ Putting your sound out where folks can hear it

▶ Understanding what resonance is not

▶ Moving your soft palate to achieve the best resonance

. . . .

*H*ow do all those singers project so much sound without microphones? They take advantage of resonance, the vibrations that create tone. Resonance is the glorious magic that allows a singer to fill a large hall with sound without electronic amplification. Creating tone is the first step in the singing process. (See Chapter 5 for more information on creating tone.) The next step is to refine your tone depending on which style of music you want to sing. Read on to find out more about what type of resonance is desirable for different styles of music, such as classical, pop-rock, country, and jazz, among others.

Sound vibrates in canyons, and you need to take advantage of the small canyons in your body called *resonators* — your throat, mouth, and nasal passages. Chapter 6 discusses how to open the space in the throat and mouth to get the most benefit from those resonators. And by lifting the soft palate, you adjust the resonance in the throat and nasal passages. (For more on your soft palate, see the section "Eliminating Nasality," later in this chapter.)

In this chapter, you explore the sounds and feeling of resonance and discover where sound can resonate in your body.

Good Vibrations

Resonance is vibrations that create tone through and within your mouth, throat, and nasal passages. Large, full resonant tones are desirable in some styles of music but inappropriate in other styles. Keep reading to find out what's customary in your favorite style of music.

✔ **Choral music:** If you're a choral singer, you need resonance so you can be heard when you sing a solo. Use less resonance when you're asked to blend with other singers.

✔ **Classical music:** Very full resonant tone is desirable in classical music, especially operas. Classical singers try to generate as much resonance as possible to fill the large concert halls when they sing opera. To generate these large resonant tones, you need to really open the space in your throat and the back of your mouth to create a space for the sound to resonate in. Good breath coordination and precise shapes and sounds of vowels further enhance the resonance. (See Chapter 8 on vowels and Chapter 4 on breathing.) For early classical music, you want resonant tone that's slightly less than what's required for the later operas of Puccini, Verdi, or Strauss.

✔ **Country music:** Country music is currently very similar to pop music. Country singers are great storytellers and they often write songs that are very close to speech. They use resonance as they would in speaking — forward and chatty. Early country singers used a lot of twang — forward nasal resonance similar to their speaking voice.

✔ **Jazz:** Jazz singers almost always use a microphone and sing with instruments. When you use a microphone, you don't have to work so hard to generate resonance to carry your voice to the back of the club. You need to know how to create clear tone (see Chapters 5 and 6 about tone) and create enough resonance that the microphone picks up your voice.

✔ **Musical theater:** For this style of singing, you want to create resonance, but not as much as for classical singing. Musical theater singers often wear microphones onstage in productions, so the sound engineer is largely responsible for getting your voice to carry to the back of the hall. If you generate too much resonance, you sound like a classical singer trying to sing musical theater. Some musical theater roles require a full resonant tone, but classical music requires the most resonance. For musical theater, you want to know how to open the space to generate a lot of resonance when you sing the more legit material (*The Light in the Piazza,* Maury Yeston's *Phantom,* or Rodgers and Hammerstein musicals such as *South Pacific* or *The King and I*), and then adjust the space and resonance when you sing contemporary musical theater material that is more conversational (such as *In The Heights, Memphis,* or *Spring Awakening*).

✔ **Pop-rock and R&B:** These styles of singing require mostly forward nasal resonance. You need to keep from squeezing the space in the throat and mouth, but you also don't need to be as fully open as classical singers do. The space may not be as wide open but it should be free of tension. Pop-rock and R&B singers also use a microphone. If your tone doesn't have resonance, the microphone will have trouble picking up your sound and projecting it over the instruments. You want enough resonance to sing the style of music, but not as much as classical singers need.

Resonance: From crying to crooning

Listening to popular music on the radio provides you with an opportunity to hear different types of resonance. Pop and country singers use much more *twang* — that sound that's similar to a cry or whine. The resonance isn't made with a wide-open throat and a low larynx, but it still can be a pleasant and enjoyable sound. Other singers, like Frank Sinatra, are called crooners. Crooning is like lazy singing — for example, Sinatra always had a microphone in front of him and wasn't worried about projecting to the back of the hall. Classical singers use a lower larynx and have to use plenty of brilliant resonating tones, because they don't have microphones on the stage. See Chapter 5 for help with finding and positioning your larynx. Some opera companies amplify the singers, but it's not common practice.

As you listen to your favorite singers, note the difference in the sound and think about what you have to do with your own voice to imitate those sounds. You probably have to change the space in your mouth and throat, and sometimes even change the position of your larynx. Have fun exploring these sounds as you discover the secrets of resonance. By experimenting with all the different resonators, you can better achieve a balanced resonant tone in your own singing voice. If you want some ideas of who to imitate, try listening to these pairs of singers to hear drastic differences in resonance: Loretta Lynn and Leontyne Price, Gracie Allen and Kathleen Turner, Steve Urkel (Jaleel White) and James Earl Jones, or Marlon Brando and John Wayne.

Recording artists spend a lot of money altering sounds in the studio. In the studio, you can record until you get it perfect or the engineer can paste the fabulous segments together. A live concert requires that you get it right the first time. You want great technique so you know you can rely on your voice under pressure. Attend live concerts so you can hear the difference in sounds — even the best performers aren't perfect.

Exploring your resonators

When you sing, you want to open the space in your throat and mouth to generate sound in all your resonators (mouth, throat, and nasal passages). Opening the space allows the tone to resonate in the space, but tone needs to move forward when you sing for everyone to hear you; otherwise, you're just staging your own private concert inside your head. Moving the sound forward means taking advantage of the resonators and allowing the sound to really ring in each resonating space while you intentionally propel the sound forward and into the room.

Try to propel the sound forward by visualizing the tone moving out of you and into the room. Some singers intentionally visualize that they swallow the tone to understand the opposite of moving the tone forward. When you feel that sensation, you can compare it to what you feel when you visualize the tone moving forward and into the room. Read the section "Ringing it out" to explore the feeling of the sound moving forward. Knowing how to access all that resonance can help you fill an entire concert hall, instead of just your car, with great tone.

Keep reading for more information about resonance in the nasal passages, which you feel as vibration in your face. You can check out the information in Chapter 6 on opening the throat, which helps create resonant tone in your throat and mouth. Read Chapter 8 for more about producing equally resonant vowels and making your words heard from the back of the concert hall.

Ringing it out

Swallowing vowels moves the sound into reverse — it's the opposite of propelling the sound forward to achieve the resonance you want. To create resonant tones that resound around the room, allow the sound and sensations of the resonance to move forward. Follow these steps:

1. **Sustain an *M* consonant.**

   Notice the buzzing sensation in your lips and around your face.

2. **Sustain an *M* consonant again for a few moments, and then sustain an *ee* vowel.**

   It sounds like "MMMMMMeeeeeeeeeee."

3. **Now sing the same "MMMMMMeeeeeeeeeee."**

   Note whether the *ee* buzzes or resonates in the same vicinity as the *M*. Most people say that sustaining the *M* consonant creates a buzz of vibrations around their lips or in the front of their face, so look for that same sensation when you move to the vowel *ee*.

4. **When *M–ee* is easy and you've explored the buzzing sensations for both sounds, try *M–ooh*, *M–oh*, and *M–ah*.**

   M–ah may be harder to feel, but try to sing *ah* and keep the same vibrations you found in *M–ee*.

5. **When that's easy, roll between consonants and vowels, singing words like *many* and *moment*.**

   Maintain the same ring or buzzing sensation of resonance each time as you go from the consonant to the vowel.

Eliminating Nasality

Your *soft palate* is the soft tissue on the roof of your mouth. Knowing where it is and how it moves can help you make resonant tones. A soft palate that lifts helps create the ringing sound that you want. If the soft palate doesn't lift, the sound is nasal. Exercise your soft palate so that it lifts on command and you avoid that nasal sound.

To check for a nasal sound, sing part of your favorite song and hold your nose. If you have a balanced, resonant sound, your sound won't change and you can successfully sing while holding your nose. If the sound does change, you likely have a nasal sound.

Getting the feel for soft palate work

Seeing your soft palate in action helps you visualize it working correctly. But before you watch it work, you need to find out where it is in your mouth.

Run your tongue along the back of your front teeth and then along the roof of your mouth. You can feel a ridge right after your gums, then the hardness of the hard palate, and then the soft tissue at the back. That soft tissue is your soft palate.

To see your soft palate move, follow these steps:

1. **Shine a flashlight in your mouth while looking in the mirror.**
2. **Yawn so that you can see the soft palate lift.**
3. **Say "Hung" or "Ugh" to see the tongue and soft palate touch.**

If you aren't sure what your soft palate feels like when it moves, then I give you my permission to cut some zzzzz's and snore — just don't try this as an excuse for your nightly snoring habit. Snoring helps you feel your soft palate moving.

To feel the soft palate, pretend that you're snoring in your sleep. Snore with your mouth open and take in air through your nose. If this only gets your nose quivering, put your fingers on your nose and close off your nostrils. When you close your nostrils, try snoring again by breathing through your mouth. That quivering you feel is your soft palate moving.

As you practice the exercises in this section, bear in mind how it felt and looked to have your soft palate lift and to have your tongue touch your soft palate. These movements, when coordinated, keep your sound from being too nasal.

Coordinating your soft palate and tongue

When you know where your soft palate is and how it feels when it moves, you need to discover how to coordinate that movement of your soft palate with your tongue. Knowing how to move the soft palate is important for speaking and singing, because you want the soft palate to lift for a resonant tone. If the soft palate doesn't lift, you make a sound that has too much resonance in your nose, or a "nasal sound," as you may have heard someone say. To make a sound that has a resonant tone, explore the following exercises to help you feel the movement of the tongue and soft palate in words. You can then apply that same knowledge to your singing. When it's time to sing a consonant that requires moving the soft palate, move the tongue and soft palate until they touch and then lift the soft palate back up and release the tongue down.

In Chapter 9, you can explore consonants. To prepare for some of the movements you need to make in your mouth, you want to be able to move your tongue to touch your soft palate and then go back down and rest in your mouth. To feel how the back of your tongue raises to meet your soft palate and then moves back down, do the following:

1. **Move the soft palate up and down.**

   Stand in front of the mirror and shine a flashlight at the back of your mouth. Locate your soft palate and try to move it. If you aren't sure how to move it, say "Hung-ah" and watch the soft palate and tongue meet and then separate. Say the "Hung-ah" several more times until you can feel the muscles that move the soft palate. Try to move the soft palate up and then release. If it still won't move, yawn. The soft palate moves up at the beginning of a yawn. The tongue usually releases down at the beginning of a yawn. You don't want the tongue to push down as it does toward the end of a yawn; you want the tongue to release down as the soft palate moves up.

2. **Lift your soft palate and keep it up for four counts.**

   Review the preceding step to figure out how to lift your soft palate. When you can execute that motion, lift the soft palate and practice keeping it up for four counts. Release it and then hold it up again for four counts. Holding up the soft palate is what you want to do when you sing or speak. Keeping the soft palate up keeps the resonance just right, because dropping the soft palate too low makes the sound nasal.

3. **Move the tongue up and down.**

   Say the "Hung-ah" again and watch the back of your tongue move up. See whether you can move the back of the tongue up and down, as you do when you're repeatedly saying a *K* sound. Practice moving the back of the tongue up and down until you're confident that you know how to move it up and then release it.

4. **Separate the tongue and the soft palate.**

   Lift the soft palate and release the tongue. Don't press the tongue down, but release it so there's space in the mouth or distance between the soft palate and the tongue. This opening is what you want to feel when you inhale and when you sing.

Moving air through the nose

Nasal resonance is different from a nasal sound. *Nasal resonance* involves taking advantage of the sound resonating in the nasal passages. If all the sound resonates in your nasal passages, the sound is a nasal sound or too nasal. Air shouldn't be moving out of your nose unless you're humming or for the split second it takes for you to make a nasal consonant *(M, N, NG)*. To help you feel the sounds of nasal resonance and feel the air moving out of your nose, try the following exercise:

1. **Hum a few bars of a song to feel buzzing around your lips.**

   Humming is prolonging an *M* consonant. You should be able to feel the buzzing or resonance of that consonant in your nasal passages.

2. **Try humming while holding your nose.**

   Doesn't work, does it? When you close your mouth and hold your nose, the air has no escape route.

3. **Hum again without holding your nose.**

   Notice the flow of the air coming out of your nose. This escape route is just fine when you're singing, as long as you allow the air to escape only when you're pronouncing nasal consonants, such as *M, N,* or *NG*. When the soft palate lifts again, the air escapes out of your mouth, creating a more balanced resonant tone.

When you open your mouth for a vowel, you want the air to come out of your mouth. If it doesn't, the sound is nasal. Remember that you can have air coming out of your nose as you're singing nasal consonants, but not while you're singing a vowel sound. If air comes out of your nose while you're singing a vowel, you create an undesirable nasal sound, which doesn't take advantage of all the resonators. See Chapter 4 on breathing for help with coordinating your body on sustained tones.

Debunking Common Misconceptions

Now that you understand what resonance is, finding out what it isn't is important, too. Myths and misconceptions about resonance abound, and most have to do with what is — and is not — a resonator.

If you buy into these myths, the tone of your singing voice may not be as good as it can be.

Misconception: Tone resonates in your sinuses

Sometimes a voice teacher says, "Let the tone resonate in your sinuses." It's a nice image, but sound doesn't resonate in the sinuses even though you may feel the vibrations in your face. Sound may resonate in the nasal passages but not in the sinuses. You're feeling *sympathetic vibrations,* also known as *sympathetic resonance.* What the teacher is trying to get you to do is explore the vibrations of sound in your face — or in the mask, as some teachers like to call it.

Your *mask* is the front of your face. Think of the bones and skin on your face as a mask sitting on top of another face. You may feel the sound vibrating like crazy as if you have some metal substance on the front of your face.

No need to correct someone who says, "Let the tone resonate in your sinuses." Just keep exploring sympathetic resonance, and everyone wins.

Misconception: You have to place every tone in the same location

The word *place* is misleading. You can visualize and feel, but you can't literally *place* a tone anywhere. *Place* is a common word voice teachers use, and it's not all bad. What they really want is for you to explore the sensations and get the most resonant tone as possible from your singing voice. They may say to focus the sound to get the most resonance. Think about how you focus a flashlight to get a strong, clear beam of light. Keep focusing your sound, and know that focusing is often called *placing* or *placement.* Remember, these images can help you achieve the sound you're trying to produce.

Also confusing is the fact that you don't feel every tone in the same location. Again, you can focus and try to feel sound in the same place. You probably feel head voice vibrations more in your head or on the top of your head, and you feel chest voice in your chest. Feeling the sounds of chest voice in your head is much harder, so "placing the tones in the exact same location" is tough. Work to find brilliance and focus in all tones, and then remember that feeling, no matter where it is.

Some time ago, I worked with a wonderful director who kept asking me to place the tone outside my lips. When he finally said, "That's right; that's the place," I didn't feel the sound anywhere near my lips. I realized that I had to find the correct sound, notice where I felt it, and remember what it felt like. Remember that every body is different. Where I feel a vibration, you may not. Work to achieve the quality of tone, and remember that the vibration you feel is a result of this.

Misconception: You're supposed to keep your tongue completely flat

The tongue has to move to shape vowel sounds and consonant sounds, so it can't stay down all the time. Releasing tongue tension is different from keeping the tongue down. You can read about releasing tongue tension in Chapter 4. After releasing the tension, you can move the tongue to shape vowel sounds and consonant sounds without pressing up or down. As you can read in Chapter 8, your tongue arches to make certain vowels. Sometimes the arch is in the front of the tongue, and sometimes it's in the back of the tongue. If you're trying to keep your tongue down at all times, you may end up muffling your vowels. Allowing your tongue to do its job when the time comes is easier.

Misconception: You need to open your mouth as wide as possible

Opening the mouth for singing is good. Opening the space in the back of your mouth is excellent. Opening your mouth too far isn't good, however, because the sound spreads. Dropping the chin too far actually closes off the back space. See Chapter 4 for an explanation about opening the jaw. To find the right space, put your second and third fingers together with one finger on top of the other. With your fingers parallel to the floor, place your two fingers in your mouth between your teeth, and see how that space changes the sound when you sing *ah*. Create the space and then remove your fingers. You really can have too much of a good thing if you open your mouth too wide. Open your mouth to let the sound come out, but don't show your tonsils, no matter how beautiful they are.

Misconception: The more forward the sound, the better

It's true that if you swallow your vowels, you create a backward sound, which isn't so great. However, by thinking only of projecting your voice forward as much as possible, you create a piercing sound. You may want to use that sound for a character voice (imagine Fran Drescher singing), but I don't recommend doing it for every song. Variety in resonance is important in a song. As an actor you want to create a variety of sounds to represent the story you are telling — every song has a story to tell. See Chapter 18 about acting and creating a journey.

Misconception: You have to smile to stay on pitch

The other counterpart of the smile-to-stay-on-pitch myth is raising your eyebrows to stay on pitch. Raising your eyebrows creates a lift that many people believe helps you stay on pitch. The problem is that this lift can cause unnecessary tension — plus, it makes you look surprised all the time. The same is true about smiling. A smile is a beautiful thing, but it can cause unnecessary tension in your face while singing. Smiling usually pulls the corners of the mouth toward the ears and tightens the muscles inside the mouth. You can still use this idea if you think of a smile gently lifting up the cheeks and opening behind your eyes.

You may also have explored pushing the lips out to focus a pitch. It changes the sound, but you can't always depend on adorable fish lips for ringing sounds. Find the bright resonant sound by exploring sympathetic vibrations so your lips can round to shape the vowels. Read Chapter 5 for more information about matching pitch and Chapter 8 about vowels. If your pitch is good and your vowels are precise, you don't need to tighten anything to help the pitch.

Chapter 8

Shaping Your Vowels for Clarity

- -

In This Chapter

▶ Knowing your back vowels from your front vowels

▶ Dropping your jaw and using your tongue and lips

▶ Singing and pronouncing distinct vowel sounds

- -

Y our grade school teacher taught you that vowels are *A, E, I, O,* and *U.* However, the name of a vowel may differ from its pronunciation. For example, the name of the letter *A* sounds like *Ay,* although that same letter can have one of several different sounds, depending on the word it's in (as in *always,* *after,* and sof*a*). Those sneaky little vowels disguise themselves with different pronunciations in various words: American English has 15 vowel sounds — not 5. Such news may sound like a mouthful, but you make all 15 vowel sounds every day without even thinking about it.

When you hold out a note, you sustain a vowel sound. Therefore, making clear, precise vowel sounds is important if you want to be understood. And to make those precise vowel sounds, you need to know how to shape the vowels quickly, using a specific tongue shape or arch, forming a certain lip shape, and correctly opening the jaw or mouth. If you fudge your vowels, "I miss pizza," may come out as, "A mus pit suh." So if you don't want Aunt Geraldine in the back row turning up her hearing aid until it squeals, check out the exercises in this chapter. I provide you with the information to shape most vowel sounds using your tongue and lips, to pronounce vowel sounds clearly in a sentence, and then to sing vowel sounds to make yourself clearly understood.

You want to generate a consistent resonance for all vowels. Even when the shape changes, the resonance needs to remain solid. Work the vowel exercises in this chapter to produce precise vowel shapes, and check out Chapter 7 for help on keeping the resonance consistent when you change vowels.

To make vowel sounds, you poise your lips in a certain position and arch your tongue in a specific way. But you need to keep the tip of your tongue against your bottom front teeth for all vowel shapes. Think of this as home base — the tongue stays at home on all vowel sounds. The tip of the tongue moves to make consonants but always returns to home base after you finish the sound of the consonant, to hold out the vowel as you sing a note.

Symbols used for pronunciation

In the front of your dictionary, you can find a chart of symbols that the dictionary uses to help you pronounce the words correctly. Linguists have their own symbols for notating the sounds of vowels and consonants, called the International Phonetic Alphabet (IPA). The system was designed to give a common language to the pronunciation of sounds. Anyone who knows IPA can read a transcription of the words in IPA and sound familiar with the language. Singers usually study IPA in diction classes. Without focusing on the translation, singers pronounce different languages using IPA symbols. In this book, I spell out the vowel sound for you or use symbols found in *Webster's* dictionary, because that's more common to new singers or nonsingers.

Getting Your Backside into Shape — Back Vowels, That Is

Now you get the chance to explore your *back vowels*. You make these vowels by arching or raising the back of your tongue near the roof of your mouth, while keeping the tip of your tongue behind your bottom front teeth and keeping your lips rounded. You may be familiar with these vowel sounds (such as *ooh, oh,* and *ah*) because of how you shape your lips. Even so, you need to make sure that you keep the tip of your tongue against your teeth and keep your lips poised for action. Keep reading to discover how to quickly move from one vowel sound to the next with clarity and precision.

Exploring the shape of back vowels

In Table 8-1, you can read down each column out loud to feel and hear the same vowel sounds in several words. Then you can read across the page to explore the differences. When you understand the sound and shape of each vowel, you can isolate just the sound, without the word, to move quickly from one vowel sound to the next when you sing.

If you read the words across the page from left to right in Table 8-1, you can feel your

- **Jaw** dropping the farthest for the vowel *ah*.

- **Lips** moving from rounded and slightly open for the *ooh* sound to relaxed and open for the *ah* sound. Picture five circles in a row, representing rounded lips. The circle on the left is *ooh;* the lips are close together, with a small, round opening. The second circle is *OOh;* the opening of the lips is slightly larger than with *ooh.* The third circle is *oh;*

the opening is slightly larger than with *OOh*. The fourth circle is *aw*, and the opening is slightly larger than with *Oh*. The fifth circle is *ah;* it is the largest of the circles and represents the full opening of the lips.

✔ **Tongue** arching higher in the back of your tongue on the *ooh* vowel sound and arching only slightly for *ah*. The illustration in Figure 8-1 demonstrates the arch of the tongue for back vowels.

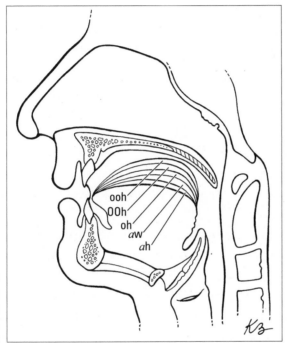

Figure 8-1:
Back
vowels.

The *OOh* and *aw* sounds are tricky, even if your first language is English. Practicing the *ooh* and *OOh* helps you learn to distinguish between the two sounds. *OOh* is similar to the sound of *und* in German. You also want to practice *aw* and *ah* to make a difference between these two sounds.

Table 8-1		Exploring Back Vowels		
ooh	*OOh*	*oh*	*aw*	*ah*
woo	foot	old	awe	father
moon	took	obey	fraud	blah
two	should	hotel	fought	bra
who	put	over	talk	plaza

Most of these words are pronounced differently across the United States, but the sound of the vowel in *blah* should be the exact same sound for the words *bra* and *plaza*. These pronunciations are for standard American dialect — how American English is supposed to be pronounced. Edith Skinner is considered the authority on standard American dialect. You can explore her book *Speak with Distinction* (Applause Books) for more information about standard American dialect. Singers can use their regional dialect when they sing folk music, country, and sometimes pop, but not when they sing classical music or perform musical theater.

Just when you were beginning to make sense of all these vowel sounds, along comes a tricky consonant to muddle things further. *W* is considered a consonant, but it sounds like *ooh* (a back vowel sound) and the lips round as in *ooh*. Because the *W* sound glides into another vowel, you make the sound of the word *we* by moving from *ooh* to *ee*.

Lipping around your back vowels

The sentences in the following list give you the chance to put all those shapes you discover in Table 8-1 into action, speaking through a series of similar vowel sounds. Try to recall the shape of each vowel so you can easily differentiate among the vowel sounds when you sing.

- ✔ **ooh**

  Whom do you boot?

  "Oops, noon hoops," cooed Bruce.

  Whose pooch did Schubert smooch?

  Loose roots spooked Pooh.

- ✔ **OOh**

  The cook mistook your foot for soot.

  She took good sugar cookies.

  The bull stood in the crook of the brook.

  The rookie forsook pulled wool.

- ✔ **oh**

  Omit overt ovations.

  Olivia obeys Joanne.

  The motel located the oasis.

  Rotate the robust mosaic.

✔ **aw**

She s<u>aw</u> the fl<u>aw</u> in the l<u>aw</u>.

He <u>ough</u>t to have b<u>ough</u>t the <u>aw</u>ful s<u>aw</u>.

P<u>au</u>l, ch<u>al</u>k the w<u>al</u>k.

F<u>aw</u>ns gn<u>aw</u>ed the r<u>aw</u> str<u>aw</u>.

✔ **ah**

Put the c<u>a</u>lm b<u>a</u>lm on my p<u>a</u>lm.

F<u>a</u>ther made m<u>a</u>cho t<u>a</u>cos.

The s<u>a</u>ga at the sp<u>a</u> was a faç<u>a</u>de.

Su<u>a</u>ve dr<u>a</u>ma at c<u>a</u>sa L<u>a</u>s Vegas.

Singing the back vowels

Sing the pattern in Figure 8-2 to practice shaping the back vowels. (See Chapter 1 for some help with the musical notation in Figure 8-2.) By making precise shapes with the vowel sounds (as you do when speaking through the words in Table 8-1), you can easily make yourself understood when you sing words. When the series of vowels becomes easy for you, look at Table 8-1 to find words that go with each of the vowel sounds and sing through them.

Figure 8-2:
Alternating
vowels for
precise lip
shapes.

TRACK 9

ooh — OOh — oh — aw ——— ah

Mastering the Front Vowels

Your tongue arches in the front of your mouth to sing *front vowels*. Your tongue does most of the work shaping front vowel sounds, but make sure that both your lips and tongue are released and free of tension. The front vowels don't require as much lip action as the back vowels.

Exploring the shape of front vowels

The front vowels are much less open than the back vowels. I'm not saying that your mouth lacks space, but these vowels aren't as wide open as the back vowels. It may sound odd, but it's true.

The vowels in Table 8-2 are called front vowels because the tongue arches in the front of the mouth to make these sounds. Keeping the tip of your tongue touching your bottom front teeth, say the vowel *ee*. Notice how your tongue arches in the front of your mouth when you make the sound. You also feel the sides of your tongue go up. Another difference between back and front vowels is that, when the tongue arches in the front, the sides of the tongue also raise and touch the upper teeth. As you speak through the vowels, you feel your

- ✔ **Jaw** drop slightly for the *ee* vowel and gradually move down more as you move from *ee* toward *a*.

- ✔ **Lips** slightly open for the *ee* vowel, and open more as your jaw drops when you move to the most open vowel, *a*.

- ✔ **Tongue** arching in the front, the highest on the *ee* vowel and the lowest on the *a* vowel, and the tip of the tongue resting against your bottom front teeth.

Figure 8-3 shows the arch of the tongue for front vowels.

Table 8-2		Exploring Front Vowels		
ee	*ih*	*ay*	*eh*	*a*
me	kiss	ate	bed	asked
eagle	myth	gain	head	passed
flee	wig	day	heaven	master
ski	busy	they	guess	danced

Some words in Table 8-2 have two vowels. I'm referring to the vowel sound that comes first — in the first syllable.

The name of the consonant is pronounced like *why*, but that's not the sound it makes. *Y* is considered a consonant, but it sounds like *ee* (as in the word *you* — ee-ooh). The sound of the *Y* glides right into the next vowel.

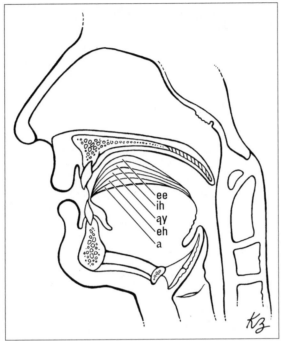

Figure 8-3:
Front
vowels.

Speaking the front vowels

Now it's time for you to put all the front vowels in sentences to practice speaking. Using these vowels gives you an opportunity to return to the correct arched position of your tongue after moving through the consonants. You can even use the sentences with front vowels to sing the musical example found in Figure 8-4 when you're confident singing the individual vowels.

✔ ee

> We meet lean, mean fiends.
>
> He greased Phoebe's knees.
>
> Greedy eels eat cream.
>
> Leave me peas teased, Eve.

✔ ih

> Hip chicks knit big mitts.
>
> Cliff fixed its clipped wick.
>
> Tim's busy with his chips.
>
> Dig Phillip's little sister Lilly.

✔ **ay**

Great Dane saves whale.

They say Abe gained weight.

Kate saves pale ale.

James blames Dave's fame.

✔ **eh**

Deb's pet pecked every peg.

Ed shed wet red.

Edge any hedge, says Ned.

Kelly's mellow fellow fell dead.

✔ **a**

Lance can't glance last.

Ask half after Fran.

Vast masks pass fast.

Prance aghast past grassy path.

The *ay* vowel is actually a diphthong, or two vowel sounds together. I include it in the front vowel list because the arch of the tongue is important for making the correct sound. As you make an *ay* sound, just know that it's a diphthong and that you move through two vowel sounds.

Singing the front vowels

You want to make precise vowel sounds as you sing. Singing a song requires you to move quickly from one vowel sound to the other; you must quickly change the arch of your tongue to accommodate the different vowel sounds. You have to make the shape happen at the speed of the music. If you practice singing the vowels alone, you give yourself the chance to really get them solid before you add consonants in words.

You may not be able to tell the difference between each vowel sound as you're singing the pattern in Figure 8-4. So record yourself singing along with the CD and then listen to the recording. Pretend that you've never seen the pattern and try to distinguish which vowel you're singing. Notice which vowels aren't as precise as others, and you can make those a priority in your next practice session. If they aren't clear, go back and practice making the shape, saying the words with the vowels, and then singing again.

More than just *A, E, I, O,* and *U*

By now, you may be amazed to find that you have to reckon with singing 15 vowel sounds, not 5. Even more amazing are all the names given to vowels and their sounds: back vowels, front vowels, diphthongs, and so on. But to get even more technical, vowels can also be *open* or *closed.*

✔ Open vowels refer to vowel sounds that require you to open your lips wider, such as *ah* or *aw.*

✔ Closed vowels refer to vowel sounds, such as *ee* or *ooh,* because your lips aren't far open when you say those vowels. Think of it as semi-closed to get just the right opening.

All these names for the five little vowels can be confusing or interesting, depending on your point of view. Just tuck away this info so you can understand your director or voice teacher when he talks about vowels or wow your colleagues with your understanding of vowels the next time you're at the water cooler.

Work the vowel sequence in Figure 8-4 to get that tongue arched quickly to get the right vowel sound. If your tongue doesn't move fast enough, you may sing a different vowel. No problem — just keep trying. When you're able to clearly distinguish each vowel sound, insert some words into the pattern for variety and spice in your practice routine.

Figure 8-4:
Arching the tongue while alternating vowels.

TRACK 10

ee — ih — ay — eh —— a

Singing vowels in English

If English isn't your first language, knowing which vowel or syllable to emphasize when you're singing can be a mystery. In fact, people who speak English as a second language often stand out precisely because they emphasize the wrong syllable in certain words. Sometimes a composer puts a weak syllable of the word on a very strong beat in the music. What to do? You can look up the words in a dictionary to determine which syllable to emphasize and then practice speaking through the text. If you speak through the text, you practice the shapes of the vowels and can familiarize yourself with the flow of the syllables. After you speak through the text, sing through the text of your song. Knowing which syllable to emphasize now makes you sound like English is your native language. Practicing with the exercises in this chapter not only helps you create precise vowel sounds, but also helps you sound like a native English speaker if you emphasize the right syllable. Even if your English is fabulous,

you still want to look up words to make sure your pronunciation is correct for singing. Regional accents are great but you want neutral speech (with no accent) when you sing your classical or musical theater songs.

Composers also have to know which syllable is emphasized in a word so they can put it in the right place in the musical phrase. If the word in your song normally has the accent on the second syllable (dir<u>ect</u>, res<u>olve</u>), the composer may put the first syllable on a long note and accent the weak syllable. Instead of singing <u>Die</u>-wreck-t, keep your focus on the second syllable. You're then closer to the right vowel, which is Dih-<u>rect</u>. Similarly, instead of focusing on *Reeee*-zolve, keep the musical line moving to the second syllable so that you sing Rih-<u>zolve</u>. You have to know which syllable gets the emphasis, just in case the composer gets carried away and emphasizes the weak syllable on a strong musical beat.

Chapter 9

Exercising Consonants for Articulation

*N*o doubt you remember from grade school that consonants make up the bulk of the alphabet — they're all the letters except *A, E, I, O,* and *U* — but just knowing which letters are consonants isn't enough to sing 'em. You have to understand how to shape consonants with your tongue and lips so that you can sing them with clarity and precision.

Most people who mumble aren't working and shaping their mouths properly to make distinct consonant sounds. The same is true when singing: You need to understand how to articulate consonants so that what you sing is clear to the audience. After all, the words of a song are the vehicle for telling your story. Knowing how to move your lips and tongue as you sing consonant sounds makes all the difference.

This chapter offers help so that you can clearly enunciate those consonants without sounding forced or tense. I start by telling you about voiced and unvoiced consonants, and then I offer tips on singing soft palate, lip, and combination consonants. Throughout the chapter, I tell you how to shape consonants. (By *shaped,* I mean that your mouth has to *shape* itself in a particular manner to pronounce the consonant.)

When you come to the tables in this chapter, practice reading the words across the page to compare similar consonant sounds. Read down the column to solidify that particular consonant sound. Solidifying a consonant's sound and recognizing its differences from similar sounds helps you to quickly move with precision from one sound to the next while singing.

Your tongue is an independent mover and shaker. You don't have to open or close your jaw to move your tongue. Allowing your tongue to move all by itself helps you keep your jaw and the back space open for your high notes. It also helps you look more polished when you sing a fast song if your jaw isn't bobbing at every syllable.

The name of the consonant isn't the same as the sound. The name of the consonant *D* may sound like *Dee,* but when you sound out the consonant, it sounds like *Dah.*

Saying Voiced and Unvoiced Consonants

Students often ask about the correct pronunciation of words for singing and speaking. Knowing the difference between voiced and unvoiced consonants can help you figure it out.

- *Voiced consonant* sounds are produced by adding vocal sound. An example is the letter *M.* If you say the word *make,* you have to add sound to the letter *M* before you even get the vowel. (Other voiced consonants include *B, D, G, J, L, N, NG, V, W, Z,* and *ZH.*)

- *Unvoiced consonants* are produced by momentarily stopping the flow of air and making no voice sound. The unvoiced consonant has sound, but the sound comes from the flow of air. The consonant *T* is an example. If you say the word *to,* you don't make any sound with your voice until you get to the vowel. (Other unvoiced consonants include *CH, F, K, P, S, SH,* and *WH.*)

As you read this chapter, practice the pairs of consonants in the tables so you know when you have to use your voice to help make the consonant sound.

When you're sounding out the ends of words, follow these general rules. The *ed* at the end of a word is pronounced with a *D* sound if the *ed* is preceded by a voiced sound (vowel or consonant), as in the words *headed, lingered,* and *roamed.* However, if the *ed* is preceded by an unvoiced consonant, it sounds like a *T,* as in such words as *picked, yanked, joked,* and *wrapped.*

You may also notice that some consonants can be either voiced or unvoiced based on what follows them. For example the *th* in *bath* is unvoiced, but the *th* in *bathe* is voiced. *Sh* in the word *shoe* is unvoiced, and *zh* in the word *visual* is voiced. *J* in the word *jump* is voiced, but *ch* in the word *champ* is unvoiced. Because most printed dictionaries don't include a guide on which consonants are voiced and unvoiced, you can search for pronunciation Web sites to hear a particular word pronounced for you.

Making Tip Consonants

You shape *tip consonants* with the tip of your tongue as it touches the *alveolar ridge*. If you slide your tongue along the roof of your mouth, you first feel your teeth, then a small section of gums, and then a ridge — the *alveolar ridge*. The only tip consonant sound not made on the alveolar ridge is *TH*, which is shaped with the tip of the tongue touching the upper front teeth. Keep reading to discover how to shape the tip consonants correctly as well as sing them. Practicing consonant shapes gives you not only the precision you need to sing, but also the confidence that you're putting your best tongue forward while articulating the tip consonants.

Shaping tip consonants

To sing a song, you take a breath, open the space in your throat and mouth, and then shape for the vowel and consonant. That's a lot to do in the first moment of your song, and all these shapes continue as you sing through the words in your song. Until you're confident that you can shape tip consonants without thinking about it, practice them. *D, T,* and *S* are the most commonly mispronounced tip consonants. *D* is often mistakenly pronounced like a *T.* Be sure to listen for the sound of your voice when you make the *D.* Practicing these shapes every day will help you quickly get the hang of tip consonants.

Working out with D, T, L, N, S, and Z

To shape the tip consonant sounds in Table 9-1, the tip of your tongue touches the alveolar ridge. The voiced consonants are *D, L, N,* and *Z.* The *T* and *S* don't require any voice, so they're unvoiced consonants. While shaping these tip consonants, make sure that your

- ✔ **Tongue's** tip is moving from your bottom front teeth to the alveolar ridge behind your front teeth. The tip of your tongue curves for the *D* and *T* and flattens more on the alveolar ridge for the *L* and *N.*

- ✔ **Lips** are released and free of tension. In Tables 9-1 and 9-2, as you move from the consonant to the vowel, your lips may be shaped for the vowel sound as the tongue's tip touches the alveolar ridge.

The consonants in Table 9-1 may be pronounced differently in other languages. For American English, you want the tip of the tongue to touch the alveolar ridge for the tip consonants. For other languages, the consonants may be made with the tip of the tongue touching the teeth. For this exercise, practice curving the tip of the tongue slightly so it touches the alveolar ridge for the *D* and *T,* and flattening on the alveolar ridge for the *L* and *N.*

Table 9-1		Practicing *D, T, L, N, S,* and *Z*			
D	*T*	*L*	*N*	*S*	*Z*
do	to	Lou	new	sip	zip
doe	toe	low	no	sap	zap
dab	tab	lab	nab	sing	zing

If you have a lisp, make your *S* with the tip of the tongue against the roof of your mouth (not your teeth) while the sides of your tongue touch your teeth. If your *S* sounds too similar to a leaky tire, release the grip on the tip of your tongue. Practice saying the word *its.* You say *ih* and then place the tip of the tongue against the alveolar ridge for the *t.* Then the tip of the tongue releases in the center for a tiny stream of air. Release the air slowly to feel and hear the *s.* Hold out the *s* to feel the movement of the airflow.

When singing the words *don't you, can't you,* and *could you,* or any other combination that has a *D* or *T* next to a *Y,* make sure that you say, "Could you?" and "Don't you?" and not, "Could jew" or "Don't chew." You can get a laugh in a song in the wrong place if you chew too much on the wrong consonant combination.

Trying a TH

In Table 9-2, you explore the other consonant sound made with the tip of the tongue — *TH.* Unlike the other tip consonants, the *TH* is made with the tongue tip touching the edge of the upper front teeth instead of the alveolar ridge. The first column uses a voiced *TH* sound, and the second column uses an unvoiced *TH* sound.

Practice saying the words in Table 9-2. While shaping the *TH* in Table 9-2, take note that your

- ✔ **Tongue's** tip is touching your bottom front teeth and then moving to touch your upper front teeth.
- ✔ **Lips** may move to shape the vowel sound following the *TH.*

For American English, the *TH* sound requires air to move over the tongue. If American English isn't your first language, you may confuse the *TH* sound with *D* because the *TH* sound doesn't exist in every language. To make the *TH* specific, put the tip of the tongue against the teeth and blow a little air. The voiced *TH* sound has the sound of the voice plus air moving. That is different from a *D* sound, which temporarily stops the flow of air.

Table 9-2	Practicing *TH*
Voiced TH	*Unvoiced TH*
this	theater
the	thin
brother	tenth

Tipping for R

The sound for the consonant *R* is the hardest to shape. An *R* can be confusing because it sometimes stands alone as an individual sound and sometimes is closely linked with a vowel. It is a voiced consonant. When you sing words that contain a consonant *R*, you may notice that your

- ✔ **Tongue's** tip rises toward the roof of your mouth behind the alveolar ridge for this consonant.
- ✔ **Lips** shape for the vowel sound that follows the *R*.

In other languages, *R* is rolled or flipped. Flipping an *R* means saying the *R* like a *D*, and rolling an *R* means touching the tip of your tongue on your alveolar ridge as you would with a *D*, and then blowing air over it to make your tongue vibrate like the tongue trill in Chapter 6. Flipped or rolled *R*s aren't appropriate for American English. Try the following sentences to practice *R:*

- ✔ Row, row, row the boat.
- ✔ Right the wrong.
- ✔ Race red rover.
- ✔ Run, rabbit, run.

Singing tip consonants

As you practice the pattern in Figure 9-1, speak through the syllables a couple times to get the feeling of the tip of your tongue moving to make the sound of the consonant. Practice the lines until each one is clear. Record yourself as you sing along, and listen back to hear whether your consonants were distinct.

Singing through the tip consonants in this way helps you feel how the right movement of your tongue makes each consonant easy to sing and easily understood. Watch yourself in the mirror to check the movement of your tongue. Listen for the voiced consonants *L, N, D, Z,* and the voiced *TH.*

1.	loh	noh	loh	noh	loh
2.	dooh	tooh	dooh	tooh	dooh
3.	zah	sah	zah	sah	zah
4.	thy	thigh	thy	thigh	thy
5.	row	row	row	row	row

Figure 9-1: Singing tip consonants.

Making Soft Palate Consonants

If you slide your tongue along the roof of your mouth, you first feel your teeth and then feel a small section of gums, a ridge (the alveolar ridge), a hard surface, and, at the very back, a soft surface. That soft surface is your *soft palate,* where you shape the soft palate consonant sounds. To say the soft palate consonant sounds *K* (as in the words *cat* or *king*), *G* (as in the word *go*), and *NG* (as in the word *sing*), you raise the back of your tongue to meet the soft palate. Just after your tongue touches your soft palate, the back of your tongue moves back down and your soft palate raises back up. The movement happens quickly, and the back of the tongue remains flexible and free of tension during this movement. You notice that the *K* sound occurs in words even when you see the letter *C,* as in the word *cat.*

The *Q* is included in this list even though the sound of a *Q* is the same sound as a *K.* The unvoiced *Q* is most often followed by a *W* or *ooh* sound, as you see in the list in Table 9-3. By practicing both the *K* and *Q* you get the hang of the *K* sound followed by most any vowel and the *Q,* which is followed by the *ooh* vowel sound.

Shaping soft palate consonants

To shape soft palate consonants, keep the tip of your tongue against your bottom teeth, lift the back of the tongue to touch the soft palate, and shape your lips for the vowel sounds before and after the consonant. The *K* consonant is unvoiced, and *G* and *NG* are voiced.

While shaping the soft palate consonants in Table 9-3, see to it that

- ✔ **The back of your tongue** rises to meet the roof of your mouth at your soft palate, while the tip of your tongue continues touching your bottom front teeth.

- ✔ **Your lips** stay free of tension and ready to make the vowel sound that follows the consonant.

If you have trouble with the sounds of *K* and *NG* because English isn't your primary language, practice saying *sing* and *sink* to feel and hear the difference between the *NG* and the *K*. The *NG* is voiced and the *K* is unvoiced.

Table 9-3	Practicing *G, NG, K,* and *Q*		
G	**NG**	**K**	**Q**
get	sing	keep	quiet
gild	hung	cup	quote
gore	bang	key	quarrel
guppy	clang	caper	queen

If you struggle to sing a soft palate consonant, try this. For the first few practice sessions, make the consonant sound with the middle of your tongue arching to touch the back edge of the hard palate. By moving the consonant out of the very back of your throat, the sound won't get trapped in the back of your mouth. As you become more comfortable with keeping the back space open while making soft palate consonants, you'll be able to touch the back of the tongue in the right spot on the soft palate.

Singing soft palate consonants

Singing the soft palate consonants, such as in Figure 9-2, gives you an opportunity to make the sounds of these consonants and practice keeping the back space open at the same time.

TRACK 12

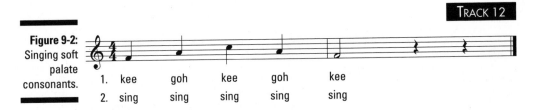

Figure 9-2: Singing soft palate consonants.

1. kee   goh   kee   goh   kee
2. sing   sing   sing   sing   sing

Working Lip Consonants

In this section, you can explore making consonants with your lips. Use both lips for the consonants *P, B, M,* and *W,* or touch your bottom lip to your top teeth for *F* and *V.* To make these sounds, keep your teeth apart and close your lips. It's similar to having an egg in your mouth and closing your lips.

Shaping lip consonants

Lip consonants are different from tip consonants (see the earlier section, "Making Tip Consonants," for details on these consonants) because the lips move instead of the tip of the tongue. The similarity is that you can move the tip of your tongue and your lips without moving your jaw. Figuring out how to keep the space inside your mouth open as you close your lips helps you continue making those round tones as you articulate a consonant sound. The voiced consonants are *B*, *M*, and *W*; *P* and *WH* are unvoiced.

Saying P, B, M, W, and WH

While shaping the consonants in Table 9-4, you can feel your

- ✔ **Tongue** staying steady for all these consonants.
- ✔ **Lips** close as you make each consonant sound. (But note that your teeth remain open.)

W is different from *V*. You make the *W* sound with both lips, and you make the *V* sound with the bottom lip touching your upper teeth. *W* can also be confusing because it sounds like *ooh*. You glide from the *ooh* sound into the next vowel. Remember that the name of the consonant may be different from the sound. Make *WH* unvoiced when you read the words in Table 9-4.

Table 9-4		Practicing *P, B, M, W,* and *WH*		
P	**B**	**M**	**Voiced W**	**Unvoiced WH**
pop	Bob	money	wear	when
puppy	bubba	music	weather	whether
pope	bib	mother	witch	what
pencil	bulb	mimic	winter	whisper

If you go overboard pronouncing the ending in some consonants, such as *B,* you may hear a shadow vowel of an *uh. Bob-uh* isn't what you want your audience to hear if Bob is the name of the man you're singing about!

Rehearsing with F and V

While shaping the consonants in Table 9-5, your

✔ **Tongue** stays touching your bottom front teeth.

✔ **Bottom lip** moves up to touch your upper front teeth, but your teeth stay open. You won't need to use your voice when your lips touch for the *F* because it's an unvoiced consonant. The *V* is voiced. Practice with a mirror to check that your bottom lip is touching your top teeth for the *V* and the *F*.

Table 9-5	Practicing *F* and *V*
F	**V**
father	vapor
feather	vintage
Phillip	vacant

As you may have noticed, different consonants can make the same sound. In Table 9-3 you see different words that make the sound of a *K* (keep, cup). The letters *F* and *PH* make the sound of *F*. The *P* consonant alone makes a different sound than *PH* together. You can read about the sound of *P* using both lips in Table 9-4 and *PH* using only the bottom lip touching the upper teeth in Table 9-5.

Singing lip consonants

Singing the lip consonants (see Figure 9-3) gives you a chance to make the sounds of the consonants and practice moving easily from a vowel to the consonant. Watch yourself in the mirror to make sure that you're keeping your jaw steady, your teeth open, and your lips moving. Record yourself singing so you can listen back and distinguish between voiced and unvoiced consonants.

TRACK 13

Figure 9-3:
Singing lip
consonants.

1. pooh - boo   pooh - boo   pooh - boo   pooh - boo   pooh
2. woh - moh   woh - moh   woh - moh   woh - moh   woh
3. *fah - vah*   *fah - vah*   *fah - vah*   *fah - vah*   *fah*

Working Combination Consonants

Sometimes two consonants are combined to make a specific sound. Knowing how to articulate the sound makes it much easier to sing. The combinations of sounds listed in Table 9-6 are the few sounds that are made by closing the space in the front of your mouth when you're singing. They require special attention in practicing to be able to make the sound without totally closing down the space in the back of your mouth and changing the tone.

Shaping combination consonants

For the consonant pairs in Table 9-6, your

- ✔ **Tongue's** tip moves toward the alveolar ridge and the sides of your tongue touch the upper side teeth and gums at the side at the same time. You feel air blowing between the tip of your tongue and the gums. The tip of the tongue touches the alveolar ridge momentarily at the beginning of the *CH* and *J* sounds. (See the earlier section, "Making Tip Consonants," for more info on the alveolar ridge.)
- ✔ **Lips** should protrude slightly forward. The protrusion is slight and the movement happens quickly. When your lips move for the *ZH* and *J,* you use your voice. The *SH* and *CH* are unvoiced.

The position of the tongue is important. The *SH* requires you to blow air between your teeth and tongue, whereas you make the *CH* by momentarily stopping the flow of air, by putting the tongue's tip on the alveolar ridge and then blowing air. Listen to the singers on the CD on Track 14 demonstrate for you. Be sure to note the difference between *CH* and *Y.* You make *Y* by moving the back of the tongue, and you make *CH* with the tip of the tongue.

Table 9-6	Practicing *SH, ZH, J,* and *CH*		
SH	**ZH**	**J**	**CH**
show	visual	jump	chump
plush	pleasure	June	choose
shop	measure	age	chance

Cutting off a note

One tricky part of singing is knowing how to cut off a note that has a consonant at the end of a word. Some people think you have to squeeze to cut off the last note of a phrase. Squeezing creates a tight grunt to cut off the last note of your beautiful song. You have several options, depending on the last sound in the word. For example, if the last word you sing ends with a vowel, you can simply inhale to stop singing the last note or cut off the last note. Try it: Sing out the words "I love you!" Sustain the last word for a few moments. When you're ready to cut off the note, just inhale. It feels funny at first, but it makes releasing the note a lot easier. If that last word ends with a consonant, you want to sing through the last consonant and inhale right away. Sing out the words "Come back." As you prepare to release the end of the word *back*, move your tongue to create the *K* sound and inhale at the same time. It feels as if you sing through the *K* sound and then lift off. Some singers focus on singing through the last consonant and forget to prepare the breath for the next word or phrase. If the *K* sound is the last sound of the song, you can focus on only the consonant. If you have to sing another phrase, you want to sing the consonant and inhale right away so you're prepared for the next phrase.

The consonant *G* can be pronounced two ways, as in the words *go* and *George*. I use the consonant *G* in this chapter to describe the pronunciation of the consonant *G* in the word *go*. I use the consonant *J* to describe the pronunciation for the consonant *G* in *George*.

ST and *SH* are often mistakenly interchanged. An example is the word *street* — it shouldn't be *shtreet*. Practice *sh-t* and *s-t* so you can get it just right in your song and when you give your new friends your street address.

Singing combination consonants

Sing through the sentences in Figure 9-4, following the words under each note. Sing through each one until you feel the fluid movement from consonant to vowel. Doing so enhances your ability to keep your back space open as you momentarily close the space in front.

Sing through the consonants in Figure 9-4 with a *legato* (smooth and connected) line, and try not to anticipate the next consonant. Allow yourself time to extend the vowel before jumping to the next syllable and consonant. Anticipating the next consonant means closing down the space in your mouth too early, and that affects the shape and sound of the vowel you're currently singing. Notice that you have to use your voice to sing through the *ZH,* but the *SH* is unvoiced. You'll feel the difference, because the *SH* is just flowing air, whereas the *ZH* requires you to make sound with your voice and move air.

TRACK 14

Figure 9-4: Combining your consonants.

1. zhah_____ shah_____ zhah shah zhah

2. Joe _____ Choh_____ Joe Choh Joe

Chapter 10

Crafting a Practice Routine

- -

In This Chapter

▶ Creating your own practice routine

▶ Knowing when, where, and how to practice

▶ Choosing exercises that fit your needs

▶ Keeping track of your progress

- -

Maybe you daydream of singing on a big stage, being the star of the show, taking a bow after thundering applause, and thanking your agent as you accept the award for the world's most fabulous singer. Well, I just have one little question: How do you get to Carnegie Hall? Practice, practice, practice.

Singing is no different from any other art; you have to work at it on a regular basis to improve. Knowing how to practice properly is key to making consistent progress toward that big dream of being the star attraction. A proper practice session consists of physically warming up; doing vocal exercises to improve tone, range, articulation, and breath; and then applying that work to songs. If you aren't sure how to practice your singing, this chapter is just for you: I outline some of what I routinely suggest for my students and also apply to my own practice sessions. Call me odd, but I love to practice. After reading this chapter and realizing the benefits of practice, hopefully you will, too.

Knuckling Down to a Practice Plan

Organizing your practice session greatly increases your chances of accomplishing something. If you have only 30 minutes to practice, you don't want to waste the first 20 minutes figuring out what you need to do. Make a plan.

Planning your practice time also keeps you from getting overwhelmed. I suggest many great exercises throughout the book for you to use to improve your technique. If you think about all the details of singing, you'll get discouraged. Pinpointing your goals for each practice session enables you to focus on two or three skills in each session. If you really work those areas, you can add new exercises quickly. You don't have to plan your time so much that you have no room for exploration, of course. Read on to discover other elements to include in your practice session.

Every practice session should include the following elements:

- ✔ **A warm-up period:** In this part of your session, you warm up both your body (yes, your body) and your voice. Head to the section "Warming Up," later in this chapter, for details on what to include in your warm-up and how long to spend warming up.

- ✔ **The practice period:** After you warm up, perform various exercises that you discover in the book and hear on the CD. Chapters 11 through 13 cover specific areas of the voice.

- ✔ **An update on how you're progressing:** To know whether you've made the progress you want, keep a practice journal (described near the end of this chapter) and listen to your recordings from previous practice sessions. See the "Recording yourself" section, later in this chapter.

Getting Answers to Your Practicing Questions

Don't worry if you aren't sure what to do when you practice. Students frequently ask questions about practicing, so I answer them here before you start practicing. Knowing where to practice, when to practice, and what to use when you practice puts you on the right track for technique work.

Where should I practice?

The number-one question concerns location. Your practice space can be anywhere you can be alone and can concentrate. You simply need space to move around comfortably during the warm-up and when you set the scene for your song. Regardless of wherever else you do your practicing, devote some of your time to standing up and practicing several times a week.

"Hey! Will ya pipe down?"

Echoing sound is great for the singer but not so great for the neighbors. Apply these tips to cut down the noise:

✔ Put rugs on the floor to absorb sound (carpeting is great).

✔ Close the door or hang a thick blanket over the doorway to absorb sound.

✔ Talk with your neighbors or roommates and ask them about their schedule. They may hate to hear you sing at 8 a.m. but may not mind around noon.

✔ Move the back of the piano away from the wall or tack a cloth on the back to dampen the sound.

✔ Use the soft pedal (the pedal on the left that dampens the sound) if you accompany yourself.

If you want to avoid the issue altogether, consider renting a practice room from a music store, recording studio, or church.

What's the best time to practice?

Anytime that works for you is best. Schedule a specific time and duration for practicing each day. If you allot time on your calendar to practice, you're more likely to practice. Many singers practice more efficiently at night because of their body clocks. You can also practice on your lunch hour or right before or after work. To maximize your concentration, turn off the TV, cellphone, and computer during your daily practice time.

Have your practice space set and ready each day. If you have to search the entire place to find all your practice tools, you're wasting valuable singing time. Stay organized so you can enjoy your time being creative!

How long should I practice?

The length of the practice session depends on your level of expertise. Someone who is new to singing can benefit from practicing 15 to 20 minutes a day. Gradually increase your practice time to 30 to 60 minutes per day. Your voice is like any other muscle group in your body: It becomes fatigued and needs rest. As long as your voice is back to normal after a few hours of rest, your practicing is on the right track. Improvement happens with frequent practice.

What do I need besides my voice?

Of course you need your voice to practice your singing. However, you need some other tools as well:

- **Keyboard:** Just about any new or used electronic keyboard works. A piano is fine, too, as long as it's in tune. You don't have to know how to play the piano to sing, but if you want to get a better understanding of what keyboards and musical notation are all about, pick up a copy of *Piano For Dummies,* 2nd Edition, by Blake Neely (Wiley).

- **Recording device:** A recording device is super useful because all you have to do is record the music once and then play it back during your practice time.

  Recording your practice sessions is a great way to monitor your progress, too. Record yourself singing through the exercises, and then rewind to hear whether you were right on pitch or whether a vowel really was precise. If you want a sound that's a bit more sophisticated, use a digital recorder (such as an iPod or recording application on your phone designed for recording music or singing) — the sound quality is much better than with tape recorders. The sound of your voice played back on a quality digital recorder is closer to what you actually sound like.

- **Pitch pipe:** The leader of the choir or barbershop quartet whips this gizmo out of his pocket and blows into it to sound the starting pitch. If you don't have a keyboard or a recording with your exercises handy, you can get a pitch pipe and play your starting pitch. You can also play a pitch occasionally to see whether you're still on target.

- **Metronome:** This gadget monitors speed and maintains rhythm — not like a radar gun, but more like a ticking sound that encourages you to stay at the same speed or tempo when you practice. Most songs have a tempo marking at the beginning. You can set your metronome to this speed to experience the tempo that the composer intended. See Chapter 17 for more information about tempo.

  If you can't locate a metronome, look at the clock. The second hand on the clock is ticking 60 beats per minute. You can practice your song or vocal exercise while keeping a steady pace with the ticking of the clock.

- **Mirror:** Mirrors are so helpful for practicing. By watching yourself in the mirror, you become much more aware of how you move your body as you sing. You can find more tips on watching your practice sessions in the mirror in Chapter 3 (alignment) and Chapter 9 (consonants).

- **Music and pencil:** As you listen back over the recording, take notes in your practice journal or on your music. Seeing the notes from your last practice session helps you remember your goals.

Warming Up

A good vocal warm-up gets your body limber and your voice ready to practice singing. Make your body warm-up (stretching and limbering up your body) last about five minutes — long enough to get your body flexible and warm. Then spend the next ten minutes on vocal exercises that get your singing muscles warm (humming, lip trills, sirens). You need to discover what works for you; some people take longer to warm up than others. If I haven't been practicing for a few weeks, I sometimes need 10 minutes to get my body awake and 15 minutes just to get my voice warmed up to practice. During times when I'm singing quite a bit, I may need only a few minutes to get myself ready to practice because my voice warms up quickly. I know I'm warmed up and ready to practice when my voice and body feel warm enough that I can move around and engage my entire body when I sing.

Stretching to warm up your body

No matter how easy the day is, start your practice session by stretching out. You want to get your entire body ready to sing, not just your singing muscles. For the breath to really move in your body, you need to be connected to your lower body. I recommend the following stretching routine, which begins with your head and moves to your toes. For each segment, remember to continue breathing as you move.

1. **Shake out any tension in your entire body.**

   Wiggle around until you feel the stiffness in your joints melting away. Use the exercises in Chapter 3 to help your posture and to release tension.

2. **Release your head forward.**

   Gently drop your head toward your chest at a slow pace and inhale. As you exhale, allow your head to drop a little farther. Repeat this several times, allowing the head to drop farther each time to stretch the neck muscles. Inhale and lift your head back to its balanced position.

3. **Move your head.**

   Turn your head to the left and to the right. Roll your head around, starting from the left side and rolling your chin near your chest to the right side. Don't roll your head back unless you've worked with this kind of movement before. The vertebrae in your neck may not respond well to pressure from your head rolling backward.

4. **Gently stretch your neck.**

   Gently drop your left ear toward your left shoulder and pause. Inhale and, as you exhale, drop your head a little farther toward your shoulder. Repeat several times, and then repeat the sequence over your right shoulder.

5. **Move all the muscles in your face.**

   Tighten them and then release, to feel the flow of energy in your face.

6. **Move your tongue in and out.**

   Stick it out as far as possible and then move it back in. You can also lick your lips — move your tongue in a circle around the outside of your mouth to stretch the muscles in your tongue.

7. **Work your shoulders.**

   Lift your shoulders and then push them down. Move your shoulders forward and then back. Make circles with shoulders in one direction, and then reverse. Keep your chest steady and open.

8. **Swing one arm (and then the other) in circles.**

   As you swing, wiggle your fingers and wrist to get the blood flowing all the way down your arm. Be careful; watch out for furniture. Repeat with the other arm.

9. **Stretch your side.**

   Lift your left arm over your head and lean to the right. As you lean, feel the muscles between your ribs opening on your left side. Reverse: Lift your right arm and stretch your other side.

10. **Swing those hips around to loosen that tension.**

    Many women hold tension in their hips. You don't have to be tough now. Let 'em loose. Let the hips rock back to front, as well as around in circles.

11. **Warm up your legs.**

    Stand on your toes and then lower your feet back to the floor. Stand on one leg and shake out the other. Reverse to get the other leg in motion. Move up on your tiptoes, and then drop back to the floor and bend your knees.

12. **Finally, take a nice deep breath and feel the energy flowing in your body.**

Getting your blood pumping while warming up helps you focus on your task at hand. If you're having trouble connecting your breath to your song, try being more physical in your warm-up or practice session. One way to connect your body is to shoot basketball granny shots. Bend your knees, drop your arms between your legs, and throw the invisible ball up with two hands.

This motion gets you connected to your lower body and really helps you connect energy to sing higher notes. If you shoot a regular free throw, you lift your body up to sing the note. I want you to "think down" — releasing down into your legs instead of pushing up — to sing the notes. See Chapter 3 for more information about releasing down into the body and engaging your legs. You can use any number of different physical movements.

Keep in mind that you want fluid motion. Any movements that cause you to jerk your body are going to jerk the singing voice also. Doin' the twist is better than doing jumping jacks.

Warming up your voice

If you were scheduled to run a race this afternoon, would you just show up and start running? I doubt it. You'd work for weeks or months to prepare your body for the big event, and just before the race, you'd warm up your body. That may sound odd for singing, but remember, your singing voice is made up of muscles just like any other part of your body. These muscles need a specific type of warm-up. Baseball players spend time stretching before the big game, and you need to stretch your singing voice before practicing.

What's the difference between practicing and warming up? A warm-up gets your body ready for practicing. The difference between the end of the warm-up and the start of the practice may be only slight. Think of the warm-up as the beginning of your practice session. Everything that you do in the warm-up leads you to the work you do in your practice session.

Vocal warm-ups include making sounds to get your singing voice awake and ready to work out. Some good choices of warm-ups include the following:

- ✔ Humming a familiar tune or one that you make up (see Chapter 6)
- ✔ Sighing or doing vocal slides (see Chapters 5 and 6)
- ✔ Doing lip trills (see Chapter 4) or tongue trills (see Chapter 6)

The basic ingredients of a good warm-up work the body, blood, and breath: You get your body moving, your blood pumping, and your breath ready to move out and sing.

Experimenting with different postures allows you to feel your entire body, as well as the movement of the breath. Don't always stand erect to sing — sometimes sit, squat, lie down, slump over, or create other positions that allow you to explore what's moving in your body as you breathe. Try singing in these various positions, and then compare the feelings in your body to the feelings when you're standing upright and singing. Watch out for any tension that may creep into your body while you're experimenting. If you're momentarily confused when you finally do stand up, review the alignment exercises in Chapter 3.

Don't let anyone's comments discourage you from singing. Everyone is capable of singing well with practice. Have a family meeting to explain that you won't tolerate tacky comments about your singing. Inform family members that what they think of as joking is really unacceptable. Be tough! Take no prisoners! Train your friends and family to respect your practice time.

Exercising Your Voice

This is huge! This is big! Inquiring minds want to know, what do you actually practice and how do you practice it? I thought you'd never ask. You can find many exercises throughout this book to help you develop your technique. By breaking down the practice session, you develop a routine that touches on all areas of your voice.

Picking exercises that work for you

The exercises for posture in Chapter 3 offer fun ways to create great posture. After reading Chapter 3, choose the exercises that appeal the most to you and write them in your practice journal. A *practice journal* is a notebook or journal (on paper or on your computer) that you use to take notes on your practice sessions. On each page, list the date and what exercise you need to work on. This is your to-do list for your practice session. After your practice session, write down what you discovered — what worked and what was difficult — and any thoughts about what to include in the next practice session. After working an exercise for a week, evaluate your progress. You may be ready to add more exercises for posture. Go back to Chapter 3 and find more exercises that work on another aspect of posture, and add them to your practice journal for week two. You can apply this same process for each chapter. Find exercises to begin your technical journey and add new exercises weekly as you progress.

Picking singing exercises may seem more difficult than posture exercises. The same principle is true for vocal exercises: Although you can pick any exercise to practice, you may find it easier to start at the beginning of a chapter and look for the exercises that start at your level. If you've never had any lessons or any experience singing, then you're at the right place. Welcome! I wrote the chapters with your progression in mind. Readers who have some knowledge of singing may start at any point in the chapter that suits their level of expertise. If you haven't done any singing training in a few years, start at the beginning of the chapter and move at a faster pace to refresh your skills.

Consider these big points when you're working on singing exercises:

- ✔ Make sure that you read the instructions enough times so you can work through the exercise and focus on your task.

- ✔ The exercise is appropriate if it's just above your level of expertise. If you've never had singing training, you may feel overwhelmed at first. However, this feeling will subside with practice because you'll gradually understand the terminology — the exercise will eventually become second nature to you. If the exercise gets easier after a week, you're on the right track.

- ✔ Reread the directions and instructions for the exercises often. After working an exercise for a week, you may find something that you forgot when you read the instructions again.

- ✔ If an exercise is confusing, ask a friend to interpret it or practice it with you. Watching other singers helps you discover a great deal about technique. Having to verbally explain an exercise to someone else helps you articulate your ideas.

- ✔ The biggest piece of advice I can offer about singing is that it requires discipline. It's really up to you to find the time to practice and improve your technique. You have many tools in this book to help you, but the tools need a user. Schedule the time, organize your session by choosing the exercises, and have a blast!

Breaking it down

In any given practice session, you need a warm-up to get your body and brain ready to focus and sing. Following the warm-up, work on each area of technique: posture, breath, articulation of vowels and consonants, resonance, and tone production. Choose exercises that work your range, sing through patterns that develop your ear, and find selections that combine acting and singing. Breaking your session into specific areas to work on allows you to grow in each of these areas without chucking your music out the window in frustration.

Also set goals for each practice session. Consider these sample goals for each day's practice:

Monday and Tuesday:

- ✔ Explore two breathing exercises that work on quick inhalation and long exhalation, and then apply that work to your song.

✔ Identify three vowels that you can work in exercises, and then apply that work to your song.

✔ Select three consonants that you can work in combination with the vowels, and then apply that work to your song.

Wednesday and Thursday:

✔ Review the two breathing exercises. If one of those exercises is going well, add a third exercise.

✔ Sing through the exercises from Monday and Tuesday, using the three vowels. If you aren't sure of the shape, review the explanation from the group of exercises in Chapter 8. If your work on one of the vowels is going well, add a fourth vowel.

✔ Review the motion of the three consonants from Monday and Tuesday. Work that motion of the consonants until it's second nature. If your work on those consonants is going well, add a fourth.

Friday and Saturday:

✔ Review all exercises from the past four days. Make a new checklist for adding exercises.

✔ Add to the bottom of the list new vowels or consonants to work this weekend.

Sunday:

✔ Rest.

✔ Start your to-do list for the practicing you'll do in the coming week.

You can choose any day to rest, but be sure to take one day off from practicing each week.

Practicing Correctly

Correct practicing means that you're making consistent improvement. You're applying the technical information that you gather in the book, and your voice feels good as you're singing. Your vocal cords don't have pain receptors, so you can't assume that you'll feel pain if you do something wrong. If you do feel pain, you may be squeezing too hard and constricting the muscles surrounding your vocal cords. Feeling tired after practicing is normal. You may have friends who can sing for hours without feeling tired, but they may have spent many years singing to build up their endurance. If your voice gets tired after a reasonable amount of time singing, don't worry about it. After a month, however, if your voice still gets tired quickly, then you're not doing something right. For help, review the exercises for releasing tension in Chapter 3, breathing exercises in Chapter 4, and especially the onset of tone exercises in Chapter 6.

Recording yourself

Record your practice session each day to monitor improvement. The first time you listen to a recording of yourself, you may not like it. That's a perfectly normal reaction. Performing artists spend big bucks in the recording studio, but they may not sound so perfect at home. The third time you hear yourself on a recording, you'll be used to the sound. Listen for the details, such as the precision of the vowel. Does it sound like an *ah* or *uh?* The two vowels are similar, but you need to be able to distinguish them in the exercise and in the text of the song. Record yourself saying *ah* and *uh* so that you learn to feel and hear the difference. Then go back and listen to the recording. You can also listen for silent inhalation (no gasping for air), smooth transitions between registers, varied sounds that you choose to create a vocal journey in your song, or dynamic variations.

If you have a video camera handy, videotape yourself regularly to check out your body language. (See Chapter 3 and Chapter 18 for information on body language.) Watch the video three times in a row, to get used to your sound on video. You can even watch the video without sound to really focus on your body movement. Video cameras usually have better recording quality than a cellphone, but a phone will work if that's what you have available.

Applying information and exercises

As you read about each exercise in the book, give it a whirl. When you've tried the exercise for a week, *then* you can decide whether it's too crazy to do. Most of the time, you can't see the benefit of an exercise until you've tried it a few times. You won't know what you're capable of until you move out of your comfort zone. Mastering some of the exercises takes some time, whereas other exercises take only a few days to master. The first time you try an exercise, you may be tempted to just skim through the explanation, because you want to test it out. I totally understand. Make sure that you go back later and read the entire explanation and work through each step. The step you skip may be the most important one of the exercise.

For each big concept, I offer several exercises. For those of you who are visual, I offer a visualization exercise. Kinesthetic types (those who learn through movement) can benefit from the movement description. Aural types (folks who learn best using their ears) will be told what to listen to as you practice the exercise. If you don't know which you prefer, try them all!

Using the CD to practice exercises

This book's CD has so many wonderful exercises that progress and gradually get harder. If you're a more advanced singer, skip to some of the later exercises. If you're a beginner, I recommend that you start at the beginning of the book and work your way through each chapter. It may take a while, but you'll have plenty of fun along the way. Keep the CD handy in your practice space. The exercises go in order of difficulty.

The CD may seem boring because it doesn't have many bells and whistles, but the simplicity of the piano and voices allows you to completely focus on your technique. When your technique is really rocking, whip out the Karaoke machine and wow your friends. Until then, use the CD to steadily work on your technique.

Part III
Advanced Techniques to Improve Your Voice

The 5th Wave

By Rich Tennant

"She really knows how to belt out a song."

In this part . . .

The exercises in this part are designed to give you an incredible vocal workout. Your voice has many parts that come together to make one seamless line from bottom to top, and here you get to explore even more exercises to develop your middle voice, chest voice, and head voice. When you need a good challenge and some harder exercises, this part helps you move to the next level by showing you how to expand your range and add belting to your list of skills.

I also discuss the issues of age — young and old — along with the various musical styles. Finally, I round out the part by giving you some tips for locating the right instructor.

Chapter 11

Developing the Parts of Your Singing Voice

*Y*ou have one glorious singing voice made up of three distinct parts or registers: *chest voice, middle voice,* and *head voice.* As you may guess, the notes in the middle part of your voice make up your middle voice, the notes in the lower part of your voice make up your chest voice, and the notes in the upper part of your voice make up your head voice.

To get a better idea of each part of the voice, you have to recognize how each area of the voice relates to the others.

✔ **Chest voice:** The thicker, heavier sound made in the lower part of your voice. It makes vibrations in your chest while you sing.

✔ **Head voice:** The higher part of your singing voice. It makes vibrations in your head or skull as you sing.

✔ **Middle voice:** The bridge between your chest voice and your head voice. It makes vibrations in your mouth and neck. Middle voice feels similar to head voice for many female singers, and similar to chest voice for many male singers. Some people call middle voice a mix because, in this area of the voice, it's neither 100 percent chest voice nor 100 percent head voice. It's a combination.

Specific muscles create head voice and chest voice; these muscles groups work together to produce middle voice. In this chapter, you explore the balance of these muscle groups — middle voice. You then explore the mix you can create from combining the parts of your singing voice. Falsetto is made with head voice muscles but the vocal cords are thinner than in head voice.

Falsetto is the lightest sound the male voice can make. From this light falsetto sound, men can add a faster airflow (which some people call more breath compression) and high resonance, to make the note head voice dominated. The female voice doesn't have a falsetto, so the lightest sound women can make is head voice.

Because the female and male voices are different, not all patterns and exercises in this chapter apply equally to women and men. Some are easier for women than they are for men; likewise, some are easier for men than they are for women. Some even work different areas for women than they do for men. For all exercises you encounter, I provide clear information on how each works for both women and men. Practice all the exercises in this chapter, no matter what part of the voice they work. The ultimate goal is to strengthen all parts of your voice — chest, middle, and head — so that they work together as a team to create beautiful sound.

If you're singing an exercise designed for the other gender, I recommend that you sing it up or down an octave. The distance between one note and the next note up or down of the same name is called an *octave.* For example, the distance between two Cs is one octave: If you start counting at the first C and count eight white notes up on the piano, you find another C.

Finding Your Middle Voice

Your middle voice is the bridge between your chest voice and head voice. For women, middle voice feels like a lighter version of chest voice and a fuller, thicker version of head voice. For men, the middle voice feels lighter than chest voice or head voice and fuller than falsetto. The singers on the CD demonstrate these sounds for you so you can explore the sounds and sensations for yourself. You can explore your middle voice or even build one if yours is missing in action. Continue reading to get an idea of what your middle voice feels like and when to use it.

Noting your middle voice range

The relationship of your middle voice to chest and head voice is the same, no matter who you are. But *how* your middle voice works, *when* it works, and the transitions to watch for all depend on whether you're a woman or a man.

Figure 11-1 shows you the average female middle voice range. In the beginning, your middle voice may be weak as you try to figure out how to reach these notes without transitioning to head or chest voice. Depending on the song, you can take your middle voice as low as you want. If your voice gets too fuzzy or weak on the really low notes, you may need to transition into chest voice. The exercises in this chapter help you figure out how and when to make that transition. When you sense the vibrations in your mouth and throat, you can easily maintain your middle voice sound while you sing.

Figure 11-1:
Female
middle voice
range.

F above Middle C (F4) to the next F (F5)

Figure 11-2 shows you the average male middle voice range. (Exceptions are tenors who may transition into middle voice higher than the range in Figure 11-2.) The men's middle voice range isn't as large as the women's range; you may not notice a huge change when you enter this range. So understanding how your middle voice feels is important, especially when you transition from high notes or low notes. Your middle voice is less thick than chest voice and not light and spinning like head voice; it's a sound and sensation that's in between, vibrating around your mouth and throat. If you try to push up a heavy sound from the bottom, it may take you longer to gain secure control over your high notes. You get an opportunity in this chapter to work out your voice so you can easily maintain middle voice when necessary.

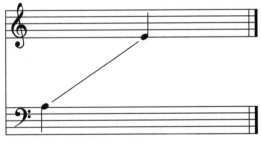

Figure 11-2:
Male middle
voice range.

A below Middle C (A3) to E above Middle C (E4)

Singing in middle voice

The following exercises give you a chance to work your middle voice by itself. Follow along with the CD and get a feel for where your middle voice is and how it feels to sing in middle voice.

On this track, listen to the singers sing the pattern in Figure 11-3. The sound you hear is middle voice. Use the vowels listed underneath to help you find your middle voice sound.

- ✔ **Guys:** Middle voice for a male singer isn't nearly as wide a range as the middle voice for a female. I designed this exercise with the female voice in mind. Sing along with the male voice on the track, but know that you're moving from middle voice to chest voice if you sing the pattern down one octave.

- ✔ **Dolls:** Figure 11-3 was designed specifically with your middle voice range in mind.

Figure 11-3:
Taking it
down.

TRACK 15

*ah*_____ *oh*_____ ooh

Figure 11-4 shows a pattern that helps you explore your middle voice by gradually working your way up to the top of your middle voice.

- ✔ **Guys:** I designed this exercise with the female voice in mind. A male voice sings along so you guys know what to do when you join in. This pattern starts just below your middle voice but gradually works its way into middle voice. Listen to the male voice sing the pattern for you so you know what the male voice sounds like. Notice that the difference in feeling between the notes in chest voice and middle voice is only slight in the first few repetitions of this pattern. You feel a change as the notes get higher in your middle voice.

- ✔ **Dolls:** The female voice demonstrates the sounds for you on the CD so you can hear the sound of a female middle voice. This pattern purposely starts low in your middle voice. Notice how the vibrations change slightly as you move higher in pitch. You sing the pattern to the top of your middle voice.

Figure 11-4:
Descending
by step.

TRACK 16

ee _____ ooh _____

The pattern in Figure 11-5 specifically works the male middle voice range. Ladies, you can work your middle voice when singing this pattern if you sing the pattern one octave higher than what's written in the figure. On the CD, you hear a male singer demonstrate the pattern using his middle voice. Notice that as he gets higher in pitch, he attempts to lighten the sound instead of making it bigger.

- ✔ **Guys:** Your starting note is the first note that the piano plays. The pattern gradually moves through your middle voice range. You can feel that the sound is higher than your speaking voice, but not as high as the sounds you make in the highest part of your range.

- ✔ **Dolls:** Even though the pattern in Figure 11-5 is written down an octave, sing the patterns an octave higher than written to work your middle voice. Listen to the piano play the second note, which is the note you use to start this pattern. This pattern also works your middle voice, but it's written out differently than the patterns in Figures 11-3 and 11-4 so that the men can understand where their middle voice starts.

Figure 11-5:
Gliding through the middle.

TRACK 17

1. moh _____
2. may _____

Listen as the male singer demonstrates the pattern in Figure 11-6 in his middle voice. The sound is lighter than chest voice, but not as high or light as head voice.

- ✔ **Guys:** This pattern sits right in your middle voice range. Notice how the male voice sounds as the singer starts the note solidly in his middle voice. You'll want to open the space in the back of your mouth and throat and take a breath before you begin the pattern.

- ✔ **Dolls:** This pattern is in your middle voice range if you sing the pattern one octave higher than what's written on the page. Use the vowel listed underneath the pattern, just as the guys do.

Figure 11-6:
Moving along the four in middle voice.

TRACK 18

aw _____

Checking Out Your Chest Voice

Chest voice is that thicker, heavier sound in the lower part of your voice that makes vibrations in your chest when you're singing. You may have felt it take over a time or two, whether you wanted it to or not. The trick to singing in chest voice is knowing how and when to use it. If you need to find out how high to take your chest voice — or even how to find your chest voice, if you haven't been introduced — continue reading to learn to have a strong but controlled chest voice.

Zeroing in on your chest voice range

Singing in chest voice can be such a powerful feeling. However, you have to be fair to your middle voice and not let chest voice take over too soon. Explore your range so you know how soon is too soon to transition to chest voice.

In Figure 11-7, you can see the average female chest voice range. Chest voice is a strong part of the female voice — often stronger than the middle voice — and you may want to strengthen your middle voice. You need to know your chest voice range. If you take chest voice too high, you can weaken your middle voice. Remember that you can always switch out of chest voice sooner, but preferably not later, than the range given in Figure 11-7.

Figure 11-7:
Chest voice range for women.

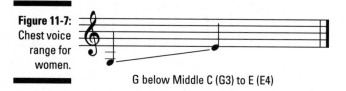

G below Middle C (G3) to E (E4)

Figure 11-8 shows the average range of chest voice for men. Most men speak in chest voice, so they often already have a strong chest voice. You can develop yours if you think it's weak, and explore the difference between your chest voice and middle voice.

Figure 11-8:
Chest voice range for men.

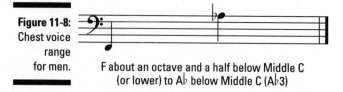

F about an octave and a half below Middle C
(or lower) to A♭ below Middle C (A♭3)

Distinguishing chest voice and belt

Chest voice and belt aren't the same. Chest voice is a thick, strong part of your lower range and has a much heavier and deeper sound than belt. The belt has a brassy sound and may sound like a healthy version of yelling; it may sound like it's dominated by chest voice sounds, but belting should have the ease of middle voice. A good belt is developed from the speaking voice. Most people who aren't fans of belting refer to it as yelling on pitch. But, hey, belting is what you do at home around the dinner table when the discussion of politics gets heated, and it's also what you do when you call out for a taxi to stop.

If you're interested in belting, you can check out Chapter 13 for belting exercises. But don't rush to those exercises unless your middle voice is really strong and you can distinguish between chest voice and middle voice.

Feeling your chest voice

You may already know what's *supposed* to be your chest voice (if not, see the section "Zeroing in on your chest voice range," earlier in this chapter), but maybe you still aren't sure what it actually is. The best way to tell is to feel it. Try some of the following exercises so you can feel those chest voice vibrations.

The pattern in Figure 11-9 gives you your first opportunity to find your chest voice. Listen to the singers on the CD to hear the sounds they make in chest voice. Notice that the sound is full and thick. Identify the sensations in your body and try to feel the vibrations as you sing.

- ✔ **Guys:** This exercise is purposely really low. Some men can sing low, and I want you to see whether your voice can sing low notes. Even if you can't, with time you may find that the notes get stronger. Some tenors may not be able to sing this pattern because it's so low. (See Chapter 2 for more information on the tenor range.) Try it several times — if it's just too low, find other patterns in the chapter that aren't quite so low, or sing up an octave for a few repetitions. Your starting note is the first note that the piano plays.

- ✔ **Dolls:** The first couple of repetitions are low for you. Some women can sing quite low, so the pattern gives you the opportunity to see how low you can sing in chest voice. With practice, you may find that the patterns gradually get easier and that you gain some strength on lower notes. The second note that the piano plays is your starting note for this pattern.

Figure 11-9:
Singing
fourth.

ah - ooh   ah - ooh   ah - ooh   ah

The pattern in Figure 11-10 begins on *ah,* an open vowel, to help you start with a thicker chest voice sound. You can stay in chest voice the entire time you sing this pattern.

✔ **Guys:** Gentlemen, sing the pattern in Figure 11-10 down an octave from what's written on the page. You can hear the male voice on the CD demonstrate for you. The pattern begins low and gradually moves higher in pitch. You can continue working on this pattern on your own and go higher in pitch. If you find the pattern too low for you, sing it as it's written on the page or wait until the pattern gets high enough for you.

✔ **Dolls:** This pattern stays in your chest voice range. If your voice is high, you may find the first few repetitions of this pattern quite low. Try singing it to feel the vibrations of chest voice and gradually widen the space in your throat and mouth as you move higher in pitch.

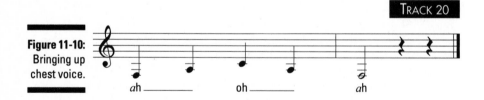

Figure 11-10:
Bringing up
chest voice.

ah _____   oh _____   ah

Aiming High with Head Voice

The higher part of your singing voice is called *head voice* because most people feel the vibrations in their head or skull while singing in head voice. Having a head voice for singing is necessary to access those really high notes in the song. For women, the notes in the middle part of your voice may not feel much different from the higher notes. As you move from the middle part of your voice to your head voice, you want to *lighten up the sound.* In other words, you want to think of head voice as if it's lighter — lighter in the amount of effort or pressure in your throat. You may feel like you open your mouth and the sound just comes flying out.

Finding your head voice range

Just as women struggle with the transition between the chest voice and middle voice, men have a tough transition moving into head voice. With some practice, men can successfully maneuver in this area of the voice.

Figure 11-11 shows the average female head voice range. Ladies, you may not feel much difference between your head voice and your middle voice until you get quite high in your head voice, because the vibrations gradually move up into your head as you go higher in pitch. You also feel a slight change as you descend. You may want to explore some of the patterns that leap around so you can really feel how the vibrations change. Mezzos may have more of a struggle with head voice than sopranos. (See Chapter 2 for more information about the differences between a mezzo and soprano.) At the transition to head voice, you may find some notes unreliable in the beginning. Keep practicing and you'll figure out how to work your head voice, using the suggestions in this chapter.

Figure 11-11: Female head voice range.

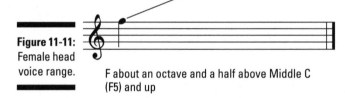

F about an octave and a half above Middle C (F5) and up

Figure 11-12 shows the average male head voice range. For men, working on head voice is important for a good balance when you sing. But I recommend that you work on your falsetto before attempting to push your head voice too high. If your voice feels strained as you work on the higher patterns, working your falsetto (see "Discovering your falsetto" later in this chapter) until you can move in and out of it makes the exercises in this chapter more comfortable. You can also go back to the middle voice exercises until that part of your voice works easily. When you understand the feelings of middle voice, you can more easily understand when you're pushing too hard for head voice in ascending patterns.

Figure 11-12: Male head voice range.

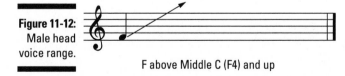

F above Middle C (F4) and up

Feeling head voice

Male and female singers feel the vibrations from singing in head voice in their head or skull. As you explore your head voice in this chapter, place your hand on the crown of your head, which is the top back part of your head. You can also put your hand on the back of your neck to feel the vibrations as you move up in pitch. As you ascend, you may feel the vibrations move from your neck or mouth to your head. When you get really high, you may feel the vibrations on the very top of your head. Singers can feel the vibrations in different locations, but you can explore how the vibrations change places as you ascend in pitch. Also be aware of the sensations in your mouth as you sing in head voice. You may feel sound on the roof of your mouth, on your hard palate, or even in the front of your face. All these vibration locations help you find the sensations of head voice.

A great way to feel head voice is to sing *closed vowels.* When you sing closed vowels, your mouth isn't as wide open. For example, *ah* is wider open than *ee,* so *ee* is a closed vowel and *ah* is an open vowel. (Check out Chapter 8 for more information on vowels.) The closed vowels are helpful for singing in your head voice because the sound is lighter than with open vowels and creates vibrations that are easier to feel. This doesn't mean that you can't use open vowels like *ah* in head voice; it just means that you can explore the sensations of head voice more easily with closed vowels and then take that same ease and feeling of vibrations into your open vowels.

When you sing the pattern shown in Figure 11-13, find the same spin to the tone and feel the vibrations in your head. By aiming the vowels out in front of you, you're more likely to feel the vibrations in your head. Listen to the singers on the CD demonstrate head voice. As you try the pattern, follow these steps to make it easier to sing in head voice:

1. **Find your alignment.**

   See Chapter 3 for tips on finding your alignment.

2. **Take a breath.**

   Check out Chapter 4 if you need more details on breath work.

3. **Open the space in the back of your mouth and throat while lifting your soft palate.**

   Chapter 7 tells you what you need to know about this step.

TRACK 21

Figure 11-13: Working with closed vowels.

1. ooh _____
2. ee _____
3. ay _____

Bobbing for pitches

A common misconception about singing is that you have to move your head up to sing high notes and put your head down to sing low notes. It may work for you in the beginning, but you may look funny bobbing your head when you start singing harder songs. Instead of bobbing your head, allow yourself some time to work on the exercises listed in each of the chapters so the muscles inside your larynx figure out how to do their job. If those muscles have never worked out, they need a little time to learn what to do when you sing high notes. Raising your head tenses your vocal cords because it prevents the thyroid cartilage in your larynx from tilting. The tilt is supposed to happen as you change pitch, but tilting the thyroid cartilage isn't the same as lifting your larynx. The tilt should happen naturally — you don't have to control it. You want your larynx and your head to stay steady as the muscles inside your throat do their job.

Listen to the singers on the CD sing the pattern in Figure 11-14. Notice that the sound is light and high, as if the sound is spinning out of the mouth. If you open the space in your throat and mouth and apply proper breathing technique, head voice often feels like the sound is just flying out of your mouth. If the feeling is heavy and takes much effort, you're using too much weight or engaging the muscles that create chest voice.

TRACK 22

Figure 11-14:
Spinning
out in head
voice.

1. Wee _____
2. Wooh _____

Let's Hear It for the Boys: Figuring Out Falsetto

The male voice has three registers, similar to the female voice: chest voice, middle voice, and head voice. The difference for the male singer is *falsetto* — the lighter part of your singing voice that sounds feminine. The notes in your falsetto are in the same range as your head voice, but the vocal cords are thin, like a stretched-out rubber band. Falsetto feels lighter or higher than your head voice. If you attempt to sing really high notes, you may even flip into falsetto.

Falsetto is an important area of your voice and needs to be developed to strengthen the head voice. Your head voice may be weak in the beginning of your singing training; you can explore sounds on high notes by singing in your falsetto and then later, when you have more strength, work on the same notes using your head voice. When the muscles that create head voice get stronger, you'll be able to sing the same notes in head voice that you originally could sing only precariously with your head voice or in falsetto. Experience the sounds that you can make with falsetto, and strengthen your falsetto. You may hear voice teachers referring to *falsetto* as your *head voice,* but I think using both terms is easier so you know exactly what kind of sounds to make.

Ladies, you can sing the figures in this section by using your middle voice or chest voice.

Discovering your falsetto

If you've ever imitated a woman, by either speaking or singing, you've found your falsetto. Your falsetto may not be really strong, but giving it a good workout for singing is important so that you can strengthen your head voice.

TRACK 23

On the CD, listen as the singer demonstrates falsetto sounds. Notice that the falsetto is light, unlike your speaking voice; it's similar to your voice when you were younger. Now try finding your falsetto by using the following tips:

- First slide around above Middle C. Most men can sing in falsetto from about the A below Middle C up to as high as they're comfortable. The male singer on the CD demonstrates in the correct range for you.

- Allow yourself to just make sounds in your falsetto to get used to the feeling. You don't have to slide high in pitch, but slide around on the *ooh* vowel enough that you can check the position of your larynx as you ascend. See Chapter 5 for help in finding your larynx.

- As in other areas of your voice, keep the larynx steady as you ascend in pitch. Take a breath and check the position of your larynx.

- Keep the soft palate lifted as you slide around in pitch and as you sing the patterns.

- If your larynx moves up as you begin the first note, start on a lower pitch. Remember to open the space as you inhale so your larynx can descend.

Experiencing your falsetto

When you find your falsetto (see the previous section, "Discovering your falsetto"), singing in it gives you an idea of how it's supposed to feel and helps you strengthen both your falsetto and your head voice. Experience how it feels to sing in your falsetto by trying the exercises in Figures 11-15 through 11-18.

Sing through the pattern in Figure 11-15 to explore sounds in your falsetto. Listen to the male singer on the CD demonstrate in his falsetto. Check that your larynx isn't rising. (See Chapter 5 for help finding your larynx.) As you sing the pattern, open the space in the back of your mouth and throat.

Figure 11-15: Checking out your falsetto.

TRACK 24

ooh

Most beginners don't need to sing beyond the octave above Middle C in their falsetto range. You can certainly work it higher if you think you're a higher voice type, to help develop your High C and D. Work on your falsetto for at least three weeks or until it's easy for you to keep your larynx steady and make clear sounds. Then move on to the exercises in the "Descending from falsetto" section, coming up next in this chapter.

Descending from falsetto

The patterns listed in this section help you work from your falsetto down to your middle voice and chest voice. This exercise may seem out of place because you're focusing on your falsetto. However, the goal is to use the easy feeling of falsetto and get your notes in your middle voice to have that same *ease* of sound without pressure. Figure 11-16 allows you to flip out of falsetto down into your chest voice so you can really feel the difference between them. After you experience the flip, you can develop smooth transitions by gliding down from falsetto instead of *falling* down. You may want to visualize the lower note in front of you to prevent the bottom note from falling down and creating a big crack between the notes. When the notes in your middle voice are feeling easy, you want to find that same sensation of moving from falsetto to head voice with ease. The long-term benefit is that you'll be able to easily sing a song or musical pattern that moves from middle voice to head voice because you know how to thin out your rubber band. The shift may be bumpy in the beginning, and that's normal. As the transitions get smoother, you can make the shift more easily. Go ahead and let it bump for now. Preventing the bump entirely prevents you from feeling the difference between the two sounds.

Using the pattern in Figure 11-16, sing from your falsetto and flip down into your middle voice (or chest voice) on the last five repetitions of the pattern on the CD. Let the sound flip and make a noticeable change. You want to allow big changes when you move between the pitches in the beginning. The more you work this transition, the more confident you'll feel making a smooth transition later. When this pattern is easy for you (usually after several weeks of practice), sing the pattern in Figure 11-17 and make a smooth transition to the bottom note.

Figure 11-16: Flipping out of falsetto.

TRACK 25

ooh - ah

In Figure 11-16, you flipped and bumped out of falsetto. In this pattern (see Figure 11-17), sing the first note in falsetto and slide down into your middle voice (or chest voice, on the last three repetitions) on the vowels, as written. You may feel confused in the beginning when you're making the transitions. To help smooth the transition, think of gliding down or sliding between the notes, and gradually open the space in your throat as you slide down. Give yourself some time to explore a smooth transition as you descend in pitch. The more you practice, the more secure you'll feel moving down out of falsetto.

Figure 11-17: Gliding down out of falsetto.

TRACK 26

ooh - oh - ah

Ascending into falsetto

Follow the directions for the exercises and explore the sensations of moving into the lighter sound of falsetto from the heavier feelings of chest voice or middle voice. The benefit of this exercise is that, with practice, you can figure out how to make the transition up to falsetto or your head voice. Your head voice will be stronger because you'll know how to sing the notes without adding heavy pressure or thickness, as if you were pulling a rubber band and it remained thick. Move on to the pattern in Figure 11-18 when you feel confident of your progress in the previous patterns.

Following Figure 11-18, sing the first note in your chest voice and then slide up into falsetto. Keep the slide back down as smooth as possible. It's okay to really slide between the pitches for now. If you feel it bump as you make the transition, keep working and allow the bump to happen. Later you may find that the bump gets smoother as you get more accustomed to making this transition in and out of falsetto. As you slide up into falsetto, you feel the resonance climbing higher in your head.

TRACK 27

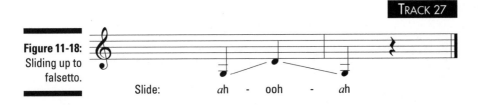

Figure 11-18: Sliding up to falsetto.

Slide: *a*h - ooh - *a*h

Singing songs that use your falsetto

Falsetto isn't just for exercises — you can find songs that allow you to use those sounds. Check out these songs that use falsetto. You can find even more if you want an opportunity to use your newly found falsetto.

✔ "Big Girls Don't Cry" and "Sherry Baby," as sung by The Four Seasons

✔ "Bring Him Home," from *Les Misérables,* by Alain Boublil and Claude-Michel Schönberg

✔ "Buddy's Blues," from *Follies,* by Stephen Sondheim

✔ "Corner of the Sky," and "With You," from *Pippin,* by Stephen Schwartz

✔ "Cryin'," as sung by Roy Orbison

✔ "Maria," from *West Side Story,* by Leonard Bernstein

✔ "Music of the Night," from *Phantom of the Opera,* by Andrew Lloyd Webber

✔ "The Old Red Hills of Home," from *Parade,* by Jason Robert Brown

If you want to listen a performer using a variety of sounds, listen to "Ben," "Billie Jean," and "I Just Can't Stop Loving You," as sung by Michael Jackson. In these three songs, Michael uses a variety of sounds and parts of his voice. He uses his falsetto, a mix, and belt. In "Billie Jean," he uses his falsetto when he says "on the dance"; he uses his mix in the very beginning of the song; and he belts when he says "people always told me be careful what you do."

Making a Smooth Transition

Middle voice is the bridge between head voice and chest voice, so you want to move easily in and out of middle voice. You may always *feel* a transition between the two registers, but the goal is to not *hear* a big change between the two. So you need to figure out where to make those transitions. Comparing the sound and feel of your middle voice to your chest voice and head voice is the easiest way to figure that out. To find out how you can transition smoothly and purposefully to avoid drastic changes in your sound, keep reading.

It may be a little tricky in the beginning to get all the transitions to happen smoothly — keep trying and keep practicing.

Maneuvering in and out of chest voice

Knowing when to make the middle voice transitions can be tricky. As you sing each descending or ascending pattern, notice how it feels — you should be able to feel your chest voice wanting to take over or give up to middle voice. Knowing what's too low for your middle voice and what's too high for your chest voice allows you to figure out where you need to make the transition from middle voice to chest voice. Practicing the exercises helps you make those transitions smoothly.

Descending from middle voice to chest voice

The following exercises work on your transition from middle voice into chest voice. Because you just found your middle voice, you may not be sure what the difference is in the feeling between chest voice and middle voice. The pattern in Figure 11-19 gives you the chance to explore the differences in sound, vibrations, and feeling.

The pattern in Figure 11-19 moves from middle voice to chest voice. The sensations are a bit different, and moving down in scale enables you to feel the changes as you move into chest voice. As you move into chest voice from middle voice, you want to open the space in your throat instead of pressing down. The resonance gradually moves lower as you descend.

  ✔ **Guys:** Gentlemen, this pattern challenges you to sing from your middle voice to your chest voice. The first time you hear the pattern played, you sing the first two notes in your middle voice and then move to chest voice. As the pattern gets lower, you can move into chest voice sooner.

Notice the slight difference in feeling between the notes in middle voice and the notes in chest voice.

✔ **Dolls:** Sing the first repetition of this pattern in middle voice. Make the transition into chest voice on the bottom note. As the pattern gets lower in pitch, you may need to switch to chest voice sooner. No matter how low the pattern goes, always sing the top note in your middle voice.

TRACK 28

Figure 11-19: Smoothing the transitions.

oh ————   ah ————

Ascending from chest voice to middle voice

The exercise in this section moves from chest voice back up to middle voice. This may be difficult for you in the beginning. Just as it's easier to gain weight than to lose it, moving from middle voice to chest voice is often easier because it's like getting thicker and gaining weight. Moving from chest voice to middle voice is about losing weight. Practice the middle voice patterns until you're confident of the sounds and feelings of middle voice. You can then work this exercise, which moves from middle voice to chest voice. When you're really confident, try the exercise in Figure 11-20.

Remember what it felt like to make that transition from middle voice to chest voice? The feeling gradually got thicker as you went down the scale. The reverse happens in the pattern in Figure 11-20. You need to gradually lighten the sound as you ascend in pitch — the vowels listed help you move from a heavier chest voice sound and lighten up as you ascend into middle voice. If you find a lighter chest voice sound that moves easily from the bottom into middle voice, you've found the gold mine. If you aren't sure what it should sound like, listen to the singers a few times to hear the differences.

✔ **Guys:** The first two repetitions of the pattern are in chest voice. The third repetition moves from chest voice to middle voice on the top note. Allow the sound to lighten or use less pressure as you ascend.

✔ **Dolls:** The first couple of repetitions start in chest voice and move to middle voice on the top note. As the pattern gets higher with each repetition, you can transition to middle voice sooner. Try to sing the top notes lighter than the bottom notes.

Figure 11-20:
Creating a
legato line
in and out of
chest voice.

TRACK 29

1. oh _____
2. ah _____

Transitioning in and out of head voice

Ascending to head voice means that you have to let go of the thick weight of chest voice or middle voice and lighten up the sound. You may have to go overboard at first to lighten the sound without squeezing your throat. The key is to feel the sound vibrating higher in your head. (See the "Feeling head voice" section, earlier in this chapter.)

Ascending from middle voice to head voice

Taking the middle voice too high keeps the head voice from getting its fair share of the workout. It also strengthens your middle voice while weakening your head voice. The transitions in your voice also become more difficult if you try to push a middle voice sound too high. The transition notes won't be dependable because you'll try to sing them heavy, and maintaining that heavy sound can be tricky. You can make a choice of when to change to head voice in a particular song, but in the exercises, you want to keep the head voice strong by switching as early as possible.

Work the exercise in Figure 11-21 to help you feel the transition from middle voice to head voice. Notice that the pattern has rests in it for you to detach the notes. Make sure that you transition into head voice instead of carrying up middle voice. Notice, too, that the vowels are laid out so that your sound is thicker at the bottom and gradually lightens as you ascend.

- ✔ **Guys:** This pattern starts in your chest voice, but you definitely move through your middle voice on your way up to head voice. As you ascend in pitch, you may be tempted to sing a full, heavy sound. Instead, feel the vibrations changing as you ascend and allow the sound to lighten, with less pressure in your throat on the higher notes.

- ✔ **Dolls:** Sing this pattern moving back and forth between middle voice and head voice. With each repetition, you can change to head voice sooner. As you descend in the pattern, notice how the middle voice feels heavier than head voice.

Figure 11-21: Working from middle voice to head voice.

ah _____ oh _____ ooh _____ oh _____ ah

Descending from head voice to middle voice

When moving from head voice to middle voice, the sound and sensations gradually thicken as you move down the scale. Taking head voice too low creates a light sound, and if the sound in the middle part of the voice is too light, it's harder to make yourself heard. Try the exercises in this section to smooth that transition from head voice to middle voice.

In the pattern in Figure 11-22, you start on the high note of the pattern and work your way to the bottom. Find the spinning feeling of head voice on the first note, and gradually let the sound grow thicker as you descend. You may even feel the sound moving from your head to your mouth or your neck as you descend. That's just fine. The pattern starts slowly and gradually gets faster. Take your time. You may need to repeat the first few slower patterns to get accustomed to making the transition before you tackle the faster patterns.

  ✔ **Guys:** As you descend in this pattern, you land in chest voice. It's a great pattern for you to sing moving from your head voice down through your middle voice. If the top notes are too high for you right now, start in falsetto. Later, when you're more confident, you can start in head voice. (See Chapter 13 for help with falsetto.)

  ✔ **Dolls:** This pattern moves from head voice to middle voice. Some of the later repetitions move to your chest voice. If the first few repetitions are too high, join in whenever you can as the pattern descends.

Figure 11-22: Spinning down.

1. oh _____ ah
2. ee _____ ah

Mixing It Up

Mix is a sound commonly used in contemporary music that you hear on the radio or in musicals. If middle voice is a transition between chest voice and head voice and uses a balance of those muscle groups, then mix occurs when you choose to vary the balance. If middle voice is a 50/50 balance of head voice and chest voice, the mix may shift those percentages. For example, you may want to use 70 percent chest voice and 30 percent head voice, to create a sound that is fuller or thicker than middle voice. Other times you may want the mix to be 40 percent chest voice and 60 percent head voice; with more head voice mixed in, this sound is lighter than chest voice but fuller than head voice. You create these variations by changing the combination of resonance, weight, and breath compression. Mix is appropriate for almost any style of singing, but it isn't as commonly used in classical music.

The terminology can be confusing, but I want you to know the phrases you may hear from other singers:

- A heavy mix or a mix that has more than 50 percent chest voice is often called a **chest-dominated mix** because it feels full like chest voice and sounds similar to chest voice. The difference is that it isn't pure chest voice; it has some head voice mixed in.

- Likewise, a mix that's lighter or has more than 50 percent head voice in it is often called a **head voice-dominated mix.**

No measuring scale can tell you the percentages; you discover how to hear the amount of weight or resonance in a sound and know that it's a mix.

Make the most of your mix, man

Men, as your falsetto gets stronger, it's time to mix it up to strengthen the notes that were once purely falsetto sounds. In the male voice, when the muscles that create chest voice and head voice work at the same time, it's called a *mix*. If you use a blend of 50 percent chest voice and 50 percent head voice, you're describing what happens in the middle part of your voice. You can also vary that percentage to use more chest voice or head voice, or mix up the percentage. Depending on where you are in your range, the mix can be more head voice dominated or chest voice dominated. In singing just one note, you can start in falsetto and then add faster airflow and a high resonance to make the note head voice dominated. This head voice–dominated mix is more common at the higher end of the male voice; a chest voice–dominated mix is more common in the chest voice range. If you add some weight or thickness as you sing the note and keep the resonance low, you move into a mix that is chest voice dominated. Mix for the male voice is similar to mix for the female voice because you can vary the amount of weight and resonance you use when you mix.

Mix requires you to find a balance of the muscles that create head voice and chest voice. If the muscles that help you create chest voice are too active while you try to sing high notes, the sound becomes heavy and may even break or crack. Allowing the muscles that create head voice or chest voice to engage at the appropriate time ensures smooth transitions from the top of your voice to the bottom.

Remember that you can sing the exact same notes two different ways: You can sing the F just above Middle C in your falsetto or in your head voice. Having the strength to make either choice gives you a chance to decide what kind of sound you want to make in each song.

Listen while a male singer demonstrates the pattern in Figure 11-23, which moves from falsetto into a mix. Notice that as he descends, he drops into a sound that's not heavy. The sound is lighter, yet has fullness just like head voice. The feeling is of less pressure in the throat.

TRACK 32

Figure 11-23:
Sliding into a mix.

ooh _____

Get into the mix, gals

Ladies, you can explore the female mix in this section. The female mix is a sound that you can use when you want to make a thicker sound in the middle part of your voice. Mix is appropriate for almost any style of singing but isn't as commonly used in classical music.

You can use the female mix when you want to make a thicker sound in the middle part of your voice, so you want to work your middle voice until it's quite strong. Work on the speaking voice exercises so you have command over the onset of tone, and then tackle mix. (See Chapter 13 for more on your speaking voice.) Using mix is appropriate when you don't want to use a belt sound (see Chapter 13) or when you want to explore different sounds to express the text of your song. Some songs don't need a heavy chest voice sound, but instead need a sound that's rich and full, like a mix.

To find your mix, try the opposite of what you normally do to sing in middle voice. To sing from middle voice to head voice normally, you gradually lighten the sound as you ascend in pitch. To strengthen your mix, I want you to avoid lightening the sound into head voice as you ascend.

Gentlemen, the patterns in Figures 11-24 and 11-25 are fine for you to sing. You can sing the patterns in your falsetto if you're just getting the hang of your falsetto. If your falsetto is pretty secure, you can sing the patterns in a mix.

Listen to the singer demonstrate the pattern in Figure 11-24, using a mix. Notice how she ascends in pitch and how the sound vibrates in the same place in her body. As you sing through the pattern, think of singing straight out. Allow the tone to move out in front of you and not rise higher in your head as you ascend in pitch. This feels odd at first, but you'll gradually sense the sound getting wider as you ascend in pitch. You can also think of your chest opening wide as you move up in pitch. I pretend that I'm swimming into the tone. As you swim toward the tone, open your arms and your body to move into the sound. You can also imagine your chest and throat opening to make more room for the sound. Because you normally allow the resonance to move higher as you ascend into head voice, you want to keep the space open so the resonance stays down as you move higher in a mix. Keeping the resonance down (instead of allowing it to rise to your head as you normally do when you ascend) makes it sound as if you ascend and stay in chest voice.

Figure 11-24:
Mixing it up.
1. ee ————
2. ay ————
3. eh ————

Mixers

You can hear some pretty terrific women demonstrate a mix. Listen to Mary Martin sing "Why Shouldn't I?" or Barbara Cook sing "Chain of Love." Barbra Streisand is another famous mixer. Listen to her singing "Memory," from *Cats*. In the very beginning of the song, she's mixing; later in the song, you can hear her belting. Dionne Warwick uses her mix in "Walk On By." Listen closely to the sound she uses when she says "walk on by." That's the sound of her mix. Linda Eder uses her mix at the beginning of the song "When I Look at You," from *Scarlet Pimpernel*. In the beginning of the song, she alternates between a chest voice–dominated mix and a head voice–dominated mix. Listen to the difference in the weight of the sound.

The chest voice–dominated mix sounds a little heavier. You can also listen to Rebecca Luker, whose work you may know from Broadway shows such as *The Sound of Music* or *Mary Poppins*. Listen to her song "River" on her album to hear her using her mix. If you want to try out some songs to explore your mix, try these two: "I Don't Know How to Love Him," from *Jesus Christ Superstar,* and "It Might As Well Be Spring," from *State Fair.* Because of the story, the first song requires a chest voice–dominated mix and the second song requires a head voice–dominated mix. Develop your registers and then work on the mix exercises in this chapter.

Wicked high notes

Have you ever heard a woman sing notes that sounded higher than any note on the piano? Those wicked high notes that females sing have several different names: *flute register, bell register, flageolet,* and *whistle register.* I use the term *whistle,* because in the beginning, you feel that the sounds are squealing out of your body like a whistling teakettle. If you're a really low female voice, your voice may not be able to make these sounds — the notes above High C may be just too high for you right now. That's okay, because you have plenty of notes below High C to play with. Singing in whistle feels as if the notes are turning over into a different register at the very top of head voice range — it feels out of control, really high and small, and you may feel the sensations on the top of your head. These notes may not feel big and strong, like chest voice or even middle voice. It's similar to what Mariah Carey did in her first few recordings. Not everyone can make those funky high sounds, but you can try if you want.

Singing in a mix is a choice that you want to consciously make. As you explore the mix, continue to work on your middle voice transitions into head voice so that you can still make the sound gradually lighten as you ascend in pitch when you choose to do so.

The pattern in Figure 11-25 alternates between a chest voice–dominated mix and a head voice–dominated mix. Listen to the singer demonstrate for you. The first and second times she sings the pattern, it sounds like she's singing in her head voice even though she's not in her head voice range — she's using a head voice–dominated mix. The third and fourth times she sings the pattern, she uses a chest voice–dominated mix. She made this change by thinking of the third pattern as heavier and dropping the resonance lower. After you listen to her demonstration a few times, play the track again and sing along.

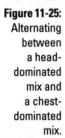

Figure 11-25:
Alternating between a head-dominated mix and a chest-dominated mix.

TRACK 34

There are times when I just want to mix it up.

Chapter 12

Expanding Your Vocal Flexibility and Range

In This Chapter

▶ Shifting gears with your voice

▶ Singing throughout your range

▶ Running 'round your range: Pop

Singing throughout your range while making successful register transitions further fine-tunes your vocal skills. *Range* is the highest and lowest pitch that a singer sings and all the notes in between. The *vocal registers* are chest voice, middle voice, and head voice; as with shifting gears in a car, you switch registers as you sing through your range. (See Chapter 2 for more information on range and Chapter 11 for information on registers, which you may know as the different parts of the voice.)

Your overall singing goals are to extend your range, make your highest and lowest notes stronger, and increase your singing agility. In striving to meet these goals, then, your range for practicing and your range for performing are different. For example, I practice singing high notes, but I may not sing all those notes in public. Instead, I stick to singing the strongest notes in my range in public, but I keep practicing to extend it and make my singing voice more *agile* — able to move quickly between notes.

In this chapter, you have an opportunity to extend your own practice range so that your notes grow stronger and your voice becomes more agile. You even work on some riffs to make your pop style really hot. As you listen to the CD, remember that you don't have to sing every exercise today. Work a few patterns until you're comfortable and then move on to some of the harder ones.

Tactics for Tackling Register Transitions

If you haven't had a chance yet, check out Chapter 11 for information on where to make transitions in your voice. Knowing where to make transitions makes it easier to figure out how to successfully sing a song. When you know the transition points, you can choose tactics, such as the following, to help you sing through the transitions when you practice:

- **Choose friendly vowels to sing.** Closed vowels, such as in the words *me, may,* and *to,* are often easier to sing than open vowels such as *ah.* (See Chapter 8 for more information on vowels.) The vowels I list next to each exercise are the vowels that help you the most when you first sing the patterns. If you're having trouble singing the pattern, go to Chapter 8 and find some other vowels to help you sing through those transitions.

- **Imitate a siren to feel the change in the vibrations as you go higher in pitch.** That same sensation of the vibrations rising higher in your head applies to your singing. Head voice requires a higher resonance, so the resonance or vibrations should move higher into your head as you go up the scale. See more information about sirens in Chapter 5, and check out Chapter 7 for information on resonance.

- **As you descend the scale, allow the resonance or vibrations to drop.** It may feel like the vibrations are going down a ladder on your face, gradually stepping down each rung as you go down the scale. The resonance should move lower as you descend in pitch. Middle voice requires a lower resonance or vibration than head voice. Chest voice uses even lower vibrations or resonance than head voice.

- **Go gently into chest voice.** When you descend into chest voice, you want to drop smoothly into it instead of falling down into it. You can experiment by singing a higher note and sliding down in pitch. Try this slide twice. As you slide down the first time, allow the sound or sensations of the vibrations to just fall. This creates a big clunk into chest voice. Then try the same slide again, but think of opening the throat and body as you gradually descend. You'll make a much smoother transition into chest voice. See Chapter 11 for more information on chest voice.

- **Open the back space as you ascend.** You can read about opening the back space in Chapter 6. As you ascend, you want the space in the back of the mouth and the throat to open to give those high notes plenty of room to sing. You also get better results by dropping your jaw, not just dropping your chin. You can read more about dropping the jaw in Chapter 5.

- **Keep your breath steady.** In general, you want to keep the movement of breath steady and flowing as you sing. If you're ascending in pitch, your breath has to move faster. You don't have to blow more air, but the speed of the airflow must increase. You can read more about breath flow in Chapter 4.

✔ **Keep energy flowing in your body.** Singing requires a lot of effort, and you want energy to be flowing in your body. You can read more about energy exertion in Chapter 13. Move around as you sing to feel that your entire body is involved in making the sound, especially on the higher notes.

As you sing patterns throughout this chapter, use these tactics to help make smoother register transitions.

Working On Your Range

Figuring out how to sing in each of the registers in your voice is the first big step in singing. The next big step is moving between the registers smoothly, and the final step is extending your range in both directions. Because most singers already have lower notes just from speaking lower in their range, singing exercises usually focus on singing high notes. Ninety-nine percent of singers who ask me for help want to focus on singing high notes, so in this chapter I offer you exercises that work your higher range. Working on high notes can even help your low notes to strengthen; you may find that your range will expand in both directions by working for higher notes. You can explore singing lower notes by working on the exercises on chest voice in Chapter 11; those exercises give you an opportunity to develop lower notes if your voice is capable of extending downward.

Taking your range higher

A great way to increase your range upward is by singing *staccato,* which means "short and detached." Singing shorter, lighter notes helps you in singing higher notes, because you're not using as much heavy weight. To sing staccato, keep your larynx steady and keep the muscles in your neck still. If they flex or tighten, sing the staccato notes lighter, with less weight or pressure; that technique helps you figure out how to work the muscles inside your neck in your larynx. Make the notes light and short, and keep them connected to your breath. If the sound is airy, too much air is escaping. Find a clear sound on a longer note and then gradually sing notes that get shorter to maintain that clarity.

Figure 12-1 gives you the opportunity to explore staccato sounds as you skip notes along the scale. As you ascend in pitch, allow your back space to open. You have to open this space fast because you're moving quickly in the pattern, so think ahead as you're singing. The singer on the CD demonstrates the pattern, singing staccato. You may feel your abs move as you start each note. That's normal: You want your breath to connect to each note. Blowing too much air makes it harder to sing lightly. On the other hand, if you connect just the right amount of air, the notes bounce along the scale. Use the *ee* vowel at first to keep the sound light and dominated by head voice. As your staccato gets easier, you can explore other vowels.

Figure 12-1:
Skipping
around on
staccato.

TRACK 35

fee fee fee fee fee fee fee fee fee   fee

Break this exercise into steps: Open the space, send the breath, and then make the sound. Hopefully, it all happens at the same time, but concentrate on the individual steps if you're having trouble getting it all coordinated.

Varying the dynamics

You've probably heard singers control their voice beautifully, whether they're singing loudly or softly. As your flexibility increases in your upper register, you want to figure out how to vary the *dynamics* (volume). The exercise in Figure 12-2 is called a *messa di voce,* which means "placing the voice." In a *messa di voce* exercise, the singer begins the note softly, gradually gets louder, and then grows soft again. Working on the *messa di voce* helps you get comfortable singing loudly or softly on any given note. Allow the vibrato to happen as you work on the exercise. If you aren't sure about vibrato or how to find yours, check out Chapter 6.

The singers on the CD demonstrate the *messa di voce* exercise in Figure 12-2. You can try this exercise, starting on any note. Just follow these steps:

1. **Start singing the note as softly as you can manage.**

2. **Continue singing the note while gradually getting louder — *crescendo.***

    Maintain a steady flow of air as you grow louder. You want the sound to grow louder because of the increased airflow, not because you're squeezing your throat.

You may feel a bump or wiggle as you grow louder. Don't panic: Your muscles need time to adjust to this new skill. Use a consistent flow of air to eliminate the wiggle.

3. Continue singing the note while gradually getting softer — *decrescendo*.

Keep the airflow constant as you grow softer. You can pretend that the note begins floating, to help you gradually decrease the volume.

As you work through this exercise, you may find that you can start the tone even softer and grow even louder. You'll gradually improve this skill with practice — sing only as softly or as loudly as you can manage for today.

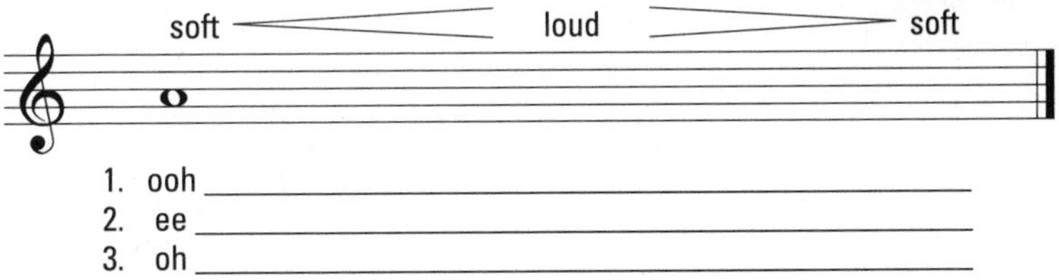

Figure 12-2:
Messa di voce.

Moving between registers

If you want some specific information about each register, check out Chapter 11, which describes each of the areas of your voice. Most of the patterns in the earlier chapters are slow patterns with notes right next to each other; they give you a chance to focus on every sound and sensation as you sing. When you have those specific areas down pat, you'll want the challenge of moving between registers to improve your technique even more. The patterns just ahead move faster, involve larger intervals, and require you to quickly make smooth transitions between registers as you move up and down your range.

If the patterns are too high for you right now, wait until you're more comfortable singing high notes. Listen to them and get used to all the notes so you're ready to sing them when your voice can handle the higher notes. Make sure that you keep practicing, because you want to be able to sing the higher notes and not just avoid them.

The pattern in Figure 12-3 starts on the top note and keeps returning to that top note. Always sing the higher notes in this pattern in head voice. Remember to maintain a steady larynx as you ascend to the higher notes. You also need a steady airflow to make it all the way through the pattern. If you're having trouble singing from start to finish, use your lip trill or tongue trill to work on your breath and then go back and sing the pattern on the vowels.

TRACK 37

Figure 12-3:
Descending.

1. ooh___ oh_____ ooh___ oh_____ ooh___ oh_____
2. ee___ oh_____ ee___ oh_____ ee___ oh_____

The pattern in Figure 12-4 ascends over an octave, which gives you a wonderful opportunity to move among chest voice, middle voice, and head voice. As you ascend, take care in making the transitions between the registers. To make the transitions into head voice, you want to allow the resonance to rise higher as you ascend. Look over the list of suggestions under "Tactics for Tackling Register Transitions," at the beginning of this chapter, for a review. You can also drop down an octave if this pattern is too high for your voice.

Figure 12-4:
Stepping
between
registers.

TRACK 38

ah_____ oh _____ ooh _____ oh _____ ah

Taking Your Agility to New Levels

Not every song you sing is slow, and you need to be comfortable singing both fast and slow songs. Singing fast scales develops *agility* — the ability to change notes quickly and easily. Agility is important no matter what kind of music you plan to sing. If your voice can move easily *and* quickly, you're much more likely to enjoy singing faster songs, because you can sing them well.

Some voices are designed to sing fast. If your voice happens to love only slow songs, be disciplined and work through these agility patterns. Later, you may be glad you did. Agility is especially important for singing classical music and upbeat pop songs. To advance your vocal agility, work through the rest of the exercises in this chapter.

Moving along the scale

The patterns in Figures 12-5 to 12-7 begin by moving quickly among just a few notes. Take your time getting used to all the notes. The patterns get progressively harder and longer and include more notes as they go. In addition, the tempo starts slowly and gradually speeds up. This gives you a chance to settle into the pattern before it starts moving too quickly.

Figure 12-5 moves along a pattern and repeats a few of the notes along the way. Notice that the first two notes are repeated as are the highest two notes in the pattern. This gives you flexibility; you don't have to try to control every note in the pattern. Be sure to notice your breath connection: You want your breath to move the voice along, not bounce your jaw or your larynx.

Track 39

Figure 12-5: Flexing on five notes.

1. ee _____
2. ee _____ oh _____

Picking up the pace

By practicing scales or patterns that move quickly, you can develop better agility. The pattern in Figure 12-6 helps you sing at a faster pace up and down a scale. This pattern is a full scale plus one extra note on the top. It's often called a *nine-tone scale,* in technical terms. On the CD, the pattern starts slowly and gradually speeds up. These tips can help you sing this track:

✔ Try to feel the pivot points or accents on the fifth note and the top note. You can see a line over the pivot notes. If you aim for these pivot notes, you can feel the pattern in two sections instead of one long, run-on pattern.

✔ Make sure that your jaw stays still as you sing the pattern and that your larynx doesn't bob up and down. Use a mirror and check the movement of both. Keep your fingers on your larynx if you can't see it in the mirror. Review Chapter 5 if you don't remember how to find your larynx.

✔ If you have trouble getting all the notes, add a consonant — for example, add *L* or *D* to sing *lah* or *dah.* By inserting the consonant, you feel the movement of your tongue as you sing each note, helping you land more confidently on each note. Later you can take away the consonant and sing just the vowels.

Track 40

Figure 12-6: Sliding up the scale.

ee _____

Figure 12-7 shows the same five-note pattern that you explore in other chapters (such as Chapter 8), but I added a few notes. Try to hear that familiar five-note sequence and think of those notes as your pivot notes. You can see a line over the pivot notes.

You really have to let go of control to sing this pattern. Watch yourself in the mirror and make sure that your jaw isn't bouncing with each note. If you find yourself trying to change the rhythm, sing half of the pattern each time it plays so that you can really focus on the first few notes to release the tension in your throat or jaw.

Figure 12-7: Tripping along the scale.

TRACK 41

Skipping through the intervals

Most of the patterns you've worked in the book move in stepwise motion — the notes don't jump around. However, not every song has notes that are right next to each other. You may have to hop all over the place, which requires agility; your voice can do that easily if you practice the following exercises.

The patterns in Figures 12-8 and 12-9 aren't easy. I want the CD to be beneficial to you for quite some time, so I added some hard patterns. It may take a few times listening to the CD to get used to these bouncing patterns. Just keep listening and humming along while following the patterns in the accompanying figures, until you get the patterns straight. After that, you can tackle the patterns, using all the information and skills you've been developing throughout the chapter.

As you sing patterns that hop around, keep your larynx steady. If you feel your larynx bobbing around, go back to some of the easier patterns from the beginning of the CD. When you can do those patterns with your larynx steady, come back to this section. Review the suggestion in "Tactics for Tackling Register Transitions" at the beginning of the chapter.

Check out the spunky dotted rhythm in Figure 12-8! You've been singing mostly smooth eighth notes, but now it's time to spice them up. Because the notes jump around so quickly, be positively sure that you're not bouncing your jaw or your larynx to change notes. Remember that the note changes inside your larynx, not from your jaw bopping around.

TRACK 42

Figure 12-8: Spicing it up with dotted rhythms.

1. oh _____
2. ee _____

Notice that as the singer sings the pattern in Figure 12-9, the sound is smooth, even though the pattern is bouncing around. Feel the momentum of your breath to keep the line moving, but try not to let the notes jerk as you leap around on the intervals.

TRACK 43

Figure 12-9: Bouncing on thirds.

1. dah ___ dah ___ dah ___ dah ___ dah ___ dah ___ dah
2. mee ___ may ___ mee ___ may ___ mee ___ may ___ mee
3. mah ___ moh ___ mah ___ moh ___ mah ___ moh ___ mah

Improvising for a Better Pop Sound

When you listen to pop singers on the radio, they sound like a million bucks. After all, they have all those instruments and backup singers behind them. At home, you probably don't have a professional sound engineer to record you every time you sing. So how do you get your voice to sound like a million bucks without an engineer? You figure out the style of pop music and add your fabulous technique that you've been developing.

One of the key ingredients in a good pop sound is a flexible voice. Pop music offers a freedom of movement and sound that's unlike classical music. When you sing classical, you sing what's on the page with musical precision. With pop music, however, you sing the lyrics with your own take on the music — called *improvising*. Singers who can move their voices easily have a much easier time singing the riffs and licks in pop music. *Riffs* or *licks* are short pieces of music, commonly in pop songs, that move quickly in a specific pattern and are often improvised. The singer adds notes that express a unique version of the song. I have notated some basic patterns that you can find in pop music. Naturally, you still want healthy technique as you sing cool pop sounds.

Mastering patterns in pop music

The patterns in Figures 12-10 and 12-11 are short, but they give you a chance to sing some basic riffs that you often hear in pop songs. One of the characteristics of pop music is freedom of sound: You can move along the melody line uninhibited. Try to find a free flow of the musical line as you sing.

As the singers demonstrate the pattern in Figure 12-10, they easily move without trying to sing a huge sound. You explore big sounds in the other chapters, but now you can explore a sound that's a little more casual.

TRACK 44

Figure 12-10:
Checking
out pop riffs.

Try the descending pop riff in Figure 12-11. Notice that it begins with the same basic notes. After you try this one, experiment on your own to create an ascending riff. Just make them funky to sound like pop music. You're precise in other exercises, but now you can spice it up.

TRACK 45

Figure 12-11:
Descending
pop riff.

Singing pop riffs with chords

The patterns that you sing in Figures 12-10 and 12-11 help you explore a pop sound. Those patterns often arise in pop songs, so you can now sing them on your own with the chords you hear on track 41 on the CD. The first couple of times you try this, you may feel frustrated. Just keep trying. Each time I try this with students who aren't used to singing pop music, they try to sing it *right*. Singing notes that don't blend with the chords is okay — laugh it off and try again. You can even try singing along with a familiar song and adding a few notes yourself; you hear people do that all the time.

TRACK 46

On Track 46, you hear a chord played and singers singing an improvised melody. They practiced the patterns listed in Figures 12-10 and 12-11 and then combined some of those musical ideas to create their own sequence of patterns. The singing is totally improvised. I simply played the chord and let them sing. After you listen to their improvisation, try it yourself. You can sing what they sang, or you can make up your own riff. After the singer demonstrates the riffs, the next few chords are for you to try to improvise by yourself. Be brave and make up something simple in the beginning. As you get better at it, you can make up longer patterns. As long as what you sing blends with the chord, you're right on target.

TRACK 47

On Track 47, you hear the background track to a pop song. You hear the singer improvise a melody and then call out for you to try it. You can make up your own melody by using the riffs you've explored. Listen to the track a few times to get the feel of it, and then try your hand at improvising. The first few times, you'll feel lost, but you'll get better at it.

TRACK 48

On Track 48, you hear the background track to another song. This time, the singer gets you started, but you get to sing the rest of it by yourself. Listen to the track a couple of times to get used to the sound. You then can make up your own pop tune with riffs.

If you just aren't sure about pop riffs, try this. Sing through your favorite song as you always do. Now sing through the song and add some riffs — embellish the melody to make it sound like a pop song. The first time you try it, add a few extra notes to the melody. Next time, add more extra notes to the melody. The more notes you add, the more flexible and agile your voice has to become.

Chapter 13

It's a Cinch: Belting Out Your Song

In This Chapter

▶ Resonating new sounds with your speaking voice

▶ Figuring out how to apply good singing technique

▶ Discovering how to belt

*B*elting is such an exciting sound for a singer. Belting is the high-energy sound that singers make in pop, musical theater, and rock music. It's similar to yelling on pitch, but with more of a singing tone than yelling.

Many different styles of music use belting. You've undoubtedly listened to the sounds of belting — you just may not have known how to define it. Belting (or belt) is a combination of forward resonance (see Chapter 7 for information on resonance) and mix (see Chapter 11 for information on head voice, middle voice, and chest voice). In mix, the sound isn't totally head voice or chest voice — it's a combination of the two. It's the sensation you may have already explored in Chapter 11 while working on the middle voice. In this chapter, you use your mix and add forward resonance to create a belt. This chapter offers a lot of information about belting and exercises for you to develop your belt.

The first step in learning to belt is to discover how to properly use your speaking voice. Belting is such an exciting sound that some people want to jump right in and learn to belt before they develop their singing skills. I encourage you to work through the exercises in the order they're listed in the chapter and work slowly to successfully create your belt sound. Take your time and discover that belting uses all the skills you've been exploring throughout the book. If you haven't worked through Chapters 11 and 12, I encourage you to check them out before you explore belting.

When you find a really resonant speaking voice, you can fill an entire room with little effort. For years, I didn't know how to use my speaking voice properly, and I became really tired after speaking for short periods of time. Now that I've discovered my optimum speaking pitch, applied the same breath that I use when I sing, and found resonance in my speaking voice, I'm able to chatter all day without nearly as much effort and with no strain.

By working the exercises in this chapter, you can discover a variety of resonant speaking pitches and range to make your speaking voice clear and commanding. After you work on your speaking voice, you get the chance to finally try some belting exercises. But check out the exercises *after* you've worked on your speaking voice. You need to have a healthy speaking voice that's ready for the high-energy work of belting.

Working the speaking voice helps you to feel the middle ground in your singing voice. Many people, especially women, speak on a low pitch to sound tough. That's fine, but you can also speak in your middle voice range and command attention. Men usually speak in their chest voice. If you happen to have a high speaking pitch, you may still be in chest voice. You can work the exercises in this chapter to explore variations in pitch and get your speaking voice on track by using resonance and breath coordination.

No matter what sound you explore with your speaking voice, remember to apply your knowledge of breathing from Chapter 4. You may be tempted to squeeze your throat to make some of the tones, but that won't help in the long run; you still have to release that tension later. Keep exploring tones with an open throat, consistent airflow, and an abundance of gusto.

Playing around with Pitch

To get the most benefit from the speaking voice exercises in this chapter, I set up the following sections to work out your speaking voice so you go through each of these steps:

1. **Explore the tones and pitch you currently use when you speak.**

   You need to know what sounds you currently can make before you can explore other sounds and pitches with your speaking voice.

2. **Explore chanting to find an optimum speaking pitch.**

   Your optimum speaking pitch is the pitch that resonates and sounds the best in your voice.

3. **Apply that same vibrant speaking tone of your optimum speaking pitch to other pitches.**

   Being able to make vibrant tones on a variety of pitches is the precursor to handling spoken text in the middle of your song or just before your song starts. Those vibrant tones also make you sound great when you have to make a presentation at work or give a speech.

4. **Work on high-energy speaking and resonance to prepare for belting.**

5. **Explore belting.**

Because your speaking voice is so important to the health of your singing voice, the steps are detailed. To keep you speaking and singing well every day, try all the exercises in the chapter — but try them in the order they're listed to get the most benefit.

Talking to yourself

Before you explore the speaking voice exercises in the upcoming sections, record yourself speaking and listen to the tone. Just listening to yourself talk involves a different sound than when hearing your voice from a recording. When you play a recording of yourself, you can hear the tone of your speaking voice from an outside source. You can even listen to your message on your voice mail. Notice whether the pitch of your speaking voice is low or high and whether your tone is bright and forward or covered. You can also record yourself during a conversation discussing some happy event in your life: Your speaking voice may have more pitch variety because of the excitement of your emotions.

Everyone has a central pitch that they return to when speaking. You can change your central speaking pitch to find one that helps you get the most ringing and resonant tone from your speaking voice. Explore the following exercise to explore a resonant speaking voice and then find which pitch sounds the best in your speaking voice.

Chanting and speaking

To understand what I mean about resonant speaking voices, I want you to explore chanting, which is like speak-singing. Exploring chanting helps you understand the close relationship between a resonant tone for speaking and a resonant tone for singing. To explore chanting, you sing some pitches, chant the same pitches, and then speak the same pitches.

This exercise uses the opening three notes to "Three Blind Mice." You may want to sing a bit of the song just to refresh your memory before following these steps:

1. **Sing the first three notes of "Three Blind Mice" and notice the feeling in your throat.**

    Make sure that your version of the song isn't really low in your chest voice. Your optimum pitch isn't the lowest note you can sing or speak. It needs to be higher to find the most ring and resonance.

2. **Speak the opening words "Three Blind Mice."**

   Aim for a pitch that's in the vicinity of Middle C or a little higher for women and around an octave below Middle C and higher for men. You can explore higher pitches if you think that you're speaking too low.

3. **Sing the first three notes of "Three Blind Mice" again.**

4. **Chant the first three notes of the song on one note.**

   Chanting means to speak-sing the pitches, as you hear monks doing in monasteries. To speak-sing the pitches, you hold out vowels when you speak, similar to what you do when you sing. Chanting may feel silly because either it seems like you're working to get someone who's hard of hearing to understand you or it feels like singsong.

5. **Speak the first three words of the song again (speaking naturally this time) and see what pitches come out.**

   Keep the sensations of resonance similar in your singing, chanting, and speaking all on the same pitches. Remember to connect your breath to the speaking voice just as you do for singing.

You can also choose to sing "Three Blind Mice" on higher pitches, and then chant and speak into those pitches.

You may feel strain or pressure when doing this exercise. If so, follow these instructions:

- ✔ **Women:** If you feel strain, you're probably using your full chest voice to create the tone. Try speaking again, but use a tone more similar to your *middle voice* (a balance of muscle groups that create head voice and chest voice working together instead of just chest voice), or find a pitch that's a little higher and doesn't use as much chest voice.

- ✔ **Men:** If you feel pressure when you're speaking, it may be because you're not maintaining a consistent airflow as you're speaking. The feeling of pulling up weight from the bottom means you're actively engaging your chest voice. If the tone is too wispy and light, you're not connecting your body to the higher pitch. Your whole body should be ready to help you make the sound. You can pretend that you're about to leap up and dance like Billy Elliott or Mikhail Baryshnikov, to help you feel the commitment from your body. You can also explore the exercise in the section "Using body energy to find clarity of tone," later in this chapter. Try again and open your throat, find your breath, and aim the tone right in front of you.

Finding your optimum speaking pitch

In the previous section, you find that you can move from singing to chanting to speaking and apply your same breathing technique and tone production when speaking or singing. In exploring chanting, you find the pitch that sounds the best in your voice, called the *optimum pitch*. Your optimum speaking pitch, or the central speaking pitch that sounds the best in your voice, is usually where you say, "Uh-huh." The pitch on *huh* works the best for most people. If someone asks you a question and you answer without thinking about what you're doing, you probably make the tone on a pitch near your middle voice if you're a woman and near chest voice if you're a man. This is good. The tone of the optimum pitch is important, not just the pitch itself.

To find your optimum pitch, follow these steps:

1. **Say "Uh-huh."**

   Notice the second pitch that you sound for the *huh* of "Uh-huh."

2. **Say "Uh-huh" a few times and then move right into speaking by saying your name immediately after the *huh*.**

   Notice the pitch when you said your name. Was it one of the pitches in "Uh-huh," or was it lower? If it was lower, try again and say your name on the same pitch as the *huh*.

Your optimum speaking pitch helps you find prominent vibrations and easy carrying power to your speaking voice. You can then take that to other pitches. If you aren't sure what sounds best, ask a friend to listen or record yourself and listen back. It's okay to explore different pitches; that's the objective of the exercise.

Listen for the pitches that really buzz or really vibrate as you speak. The best speaking pitch isn't the lowest or highest note of your range; it's somewhere near the middle voice range for women and the chest voice range for men.

Increasing your speaking range

The next step in your quest of a belt is to practice speaking with a tone that uses forward resonance and high energy on various pitches. Please don't try this exercise until you explore the exercise in the previous section, "Finding your optimum speaking pitch." By knowing your optimum speaking pitch and exploring that sound and feeling, you'll be more prepared for this exercise, because you'll understand the pitch in your speaking voice. When you're ready, try this:

1. **Try being monotone.**

   Find your optimum speaking pitch, and practice reading a recipe or an article from the newspaper in a monotone on the optimum pitch. That means saying every word on one pitch and not varying as you do when you normally speak.

2. **When the monotone is quite easy, vary your reading by alternating between two adjacent pitches.**

   Use only two pitches for now so you can connect the breath and feel the sensations in your body and face.

3. **When you're feeling confident, move up to a slightly higher pitch and repeat Steps 1 and 2.**

   On the higher pitch, you want to maintain the resonant tone of your speaking voice that you had on the previous pitch. Just as in the singing exercises, the resonance needs to move higher as you ascend in pitch. You also want to maintain a mixed sound and not flip into head voice.

4. **Each time you're confident of the pitch you're speaking, play the next-higher note and use that as the central speaking pitch when you repeat Steps 1 and 2.**

Women, after you get to the F just above Middle C, you'll feel like you can't speak any higher. You can. Find a middle voice sound, not chest voice, and continue speaking. After you try the exercise and explore a few pitches, listen to Track 49 on the CD to hear a female demonstrate how to move up the scale to increase her speaking voice range.

TRACK 49

On Track 49, you can hear a female singer demonstrating the sound of speaking "Give that back!" and moving higher in pitch. She starts near Middle C and gradually works her way up the scale. Notice that as she moves up the scale, her speaking voice stays strong. The first few times you try this exercise, you may feel comfortable going up only a few steps. When those few steps are solid in your voice, try moving up a few more steps. The singer demonstrating on the CD has worked on this exercise for quite some time and is confident moving quite high with her speaking voice. Notice how the resonance moves higher as she ascends. You want the resonance to move higher even though you're not going into head voice.

Using body energy to find clarity of tone

Using body energy is really helpful to get a clear speaking or singing sound, especially for belting. By *body energy*, I mean that surge of energy in your body that helps you make the sound, such as when you're about to lift something heavy or when you yell. When you apply this same kind of movement or energy to singing, you can take advantage of that purposeful flow of air to create clear tones on a specific pitch. So connecting this idea to speaking means finding your alignment from Chapter 3, finding the breath from Chapter 4, finding some energy from physical movement, and then making the sounds with your speaking voice. You find that your speaking voice can make plenty of noise just because of the breath and energy surging in your body. The surge of energy must come from the center of your body.

- ✔ As you sing part of your favorite song, rock back and forth from one foot to the other or swing your hips from side to side to feel the surge or connection of energy for your whole body.

- ✔ You can also bounce in place just to get your legs in motion or engage an imaginary fencing partner.

- ✔ Using a *plié* from your ballet class is another way to engage your upper and lower body. *Plié* means "to bend." In this case, you bend your knees as you gradually move toward the floor and then back up.

- ✔ You can also just hold on to something heavy as you sing. Don't go lifting the pool table, but lift a heavy book as you sing. Notice that, as you lift the book, the tone of your voice responds to the energy moving, which probably makes the tone clear. Keep your breath moving as you experiment with lifting objects.

You want your breath to keep moving. It's possible to really squeeze and make clear tones, but you know what tension feels like by now and you know that it won't help you in the long run.

To pump up the volume and make a louder tone, use a faster flow of air and add more energy. To gradually get louder *(crescendo)* as you speak or sing, speed up the flow of air and exert more energy. See Chapter 4 about breathing for singing. Practice speaking through some dialogue from a song or a monologue; start the tone softly and then gradually get louder to practice this idea of a consistent energy flow. Belting requires a lot of effort; you want your body — not your throat — to make the effort.

Defining Healthy Belting

Because your speaking voice is so closely related to belting, using the speaking voice to develop a belting sound allows you to use a balance of muscles to create the sound instead of just using full chest voice.

Belting is controversial among singers and voice teachers. The most common statement you hear is that belting is dangerous and can ruin your voice. Of course, any type of bad technique can hurt your voice, including bad technique for belting.

Healthy belting is possible if you take the time to really work on your speaking voice to prepare you for the high-energy sounds. Good technique prevents you from having to use a heavy chest voice to make the belting sounds.

When you're just beginning to work on belting, you may think the sound is too intense. The feeling shouldn't be too tight, but the sound may be intense because of increased vibrations around your face from nasal resonance. Keep reading to experiment with resonating qualities and understand nasal resonance. (See Chapter 7 for more on resonance.)

If you're not a fan of belting, you can pass up this section and head straight to Chapter 14 for information about training for different styles of singing. If you really want a chance to explore belting, please work on the speaking voice exercises and then come back to the belting exercises.

The steps to making a healthy belt require that you find some high-energy speaking sounds before using your singing voice. You'll have a harder time figuring out how to correctly make the sounds if you jump right to the belting on the CD. If you're an advanced singer and have some experience with belting, you can explore the exercises at a faster pace.

When you do return to these exercises to begin belting, take some time to practice some singing exercises to warm up your voice before you begin the belting exercises. You'll have an easier time making the sounds if your voice is warmed up.

When you figure out how to belt, move back and forth between your different styles of singing so you don't get stuck. Singers often like to belt so much that they neglect the rest of their voice. The top part of your voice — head voice — still needs a good workout to stay in shape so you're able to move back and forth between your other styles of singing.

For a beginner, I strongly suggest that you work on your singing voice by using exercises in another chapter, such as Chapter 11, and then return to this chapter. When you begin this chapter, you need to really focus on your progress in each exercise before you can move on to the next. Most beginner singers need a year or more to work on their singing voice, and then another six months to a year to belt successfully.

Comparing belt and chest voice

Belting is similar to a strong mix rather than a full, heavy chest voice. Save the heavy chest voice sounds for the bottom of your voice.

Belting can be detrimental to your singing voice if you don't take the time to gain strength in your middle voice (see Chapter 11) and work on your speaking voice to prepare your voice for the high-energy sounds you need to make. (Use the exercises in the earlier section, "Playing around with Pitch.")

TRACK 50

On Track 50, listen to the female singer demonstrate the difference between a belted sound and a chest voice sound. The chest voice sound she demonstrates is 100 percent chest voice, a heavy chest voice sound. The sensation she felt was that her chest voice was much heavier than the belt sound. By working on her speaking voice, she was able to develop her belt without engaging her full chest voice.

Knowing your limits as a beginner belter

Belting is like any other singing skill; it takes time to master it. If you're just beginning to belt, make it part of your daily routine — but not the only part of your daily routine. You don't go to the gym on the first day you buy the membership and spend the entire day on the treadmill. Give yourself time to build up the muscle strength to make the sounds in a healthy way.

If you find yourself pushing or feel tired at the end of a work session, go back and check your technique. If all the points on your checklist are in good working order, shorten the amount of time that you work on belting at your next practice session. Continue to also work on your speaking voice to keep it in good shape. Be sure to work on all areas of your voice after you discover belting. You want to keep your technique balanced and build strength in all areas of your voice.

Noting the difference between the sexes

Belting is different not only between women and men, but also for different voice types. Keep reading to discover the differences for yourself and develop a healthy belting technique, custom designed for your voice.

Women

A healthy belt for the female voice means using a consistent flow of air, high resonance (especially nasal resonance), and a strong speaking voice sound that sustains into sung tones. When the belt is right, belters say it feels like middle voice but sounds like chest voice. Belting is going to be easier for the lighter sopranos than for mezzos. I'm not saying that you mezzos shouldn't try it, but you may have to work a little harder to figure it out.

Men

Belting for the male voice can be fun. It's not a huge technical feat for men to change the sound enough to create this style of singing. To create a belting sound, you need to find a forward resonating sound and a fullness of tone as you ascend in pitch. The fullness of tone can happen from using nasal resonance. Using forward resonance may feel smaller to you, but it sounds full in the room to your audience. Because this sound is so much harder for the female, the CD has only one example of a male voice belting. If you're feeling left out, Chapter 11 devotes more time to the male voice and falsetto. The exercises in this chapter are in a great range for you, too, so feel free to sing along even though the demonstrator on the CD is female.

Most men allow the sound to roll back as they ascend in pitch. This is a perfectly normal action to take when singing classical music. When the sound moves back, it's called *cover*. In other words, the sound moves back (or uses more resonance in the throat) and the vowels slightly modify. To make a distinction between your classical sound and your belting sound, you want to keep the sound rolling forward or use more nasal resonance. All resonators are used for singing, but for belting, the prominent resonance comes from the nasal resonator.

TRACK 51

On Track 51, you can hear a male voice belting. The male singer sings, "Listen to me wail!" so you can hear the sounds of a high, male voice belt. Notice that the notes are in the head voice range, yet the sound is different from the other sounds you hear the male singers make on the CD in the falsetto and head voice examples.

Introducing mix belt

Some people use the terms *belt* and *chest voice* as if they're the same. Belt and chest voice may be related, but they're not the same. Belt uses some chest voice, but it's not pure chest voice. Mix just means that you're mixing or combining registers — combining or using head voice and chest voice at the same time and using qualities of both. The exercises in Chapter 11 help you explore the middle part of your voice, a combination of head voice and chest voice called mix. Two primary muscle groups help create head voice and chest voice. When you sing in the middle part of the voice or mix, you're using both of those muscle groups at the same time.

If you sing in chest voice, you're using only one of the muscle groups; the one that helps you create chest voice. One of the reasons the term *mix belt* has become popular is to help people understand that belt is not pure chest voice — it's a combination or mixture of registers used at the same time. Mix belt is exactly what you explore in the exercises in this chapter; you explore how to use some chest voice and a lot of forward resonance to create a belt. So whether you call it *belt* or *mix belt,* continue reading and exploring the exercises to create a fabulous belt.

Coordinating breath and energy

When you're making belting sounds, you must maintain a consistent flow of air. If your air isn't flowing quickly, you may find yourself squeezing or tightening to make the sounds. You must also increase energy flow as you make more intense belting sounds. The flow of energy you need to create belting sounds may be greater than the amount of energy you need in your chest voice or middle voice. Move around the room to connect your whole body to your singing, as you did earlier in the chapter in the section "Using body energy to find clarity of tone." Taking coordinated breath and energy to the next level for belting is one of the goals of this chapter.

Preparing for Belting

To feel the vibrations necessary for belting, you need to explore taking speaking voice sounds higher than you normally speak and explore some tones that aren't very pretty. Belting isn't about making pretty tones. Belting sounds like yelling on pitch. I don't think of yelling as a bad sound: Beginner belters often like the belt sounds of other singers but dislike the sounds in their own voice. Singing in head voice–dominated sounds is very different from belting. You may grow to love the sound of your voice belting, but you may not think it's pretty at first. The sounds are exciting but not pretty.

Being confused about belting in the beginning is normal. Many singers aren't sure whether they like the sound right away. Knowing that the first sounds aren't the finished product, continue to explore the sounds. As your skill develops, you can play with the tone to find a quality that you can live with. Remember that the first few songs you sing to practice belting need to be spunky, feisty characters. (Appendix A contains a list of belt songs.)

Speaking in a mix

You can use a mix not only for singing, but also for speaking. Using a mix when you speak helps you understand what you need to do when you sing. You can go back to the earlier exercises in the chapter to explore your optimum speaking pitch and then take that optimum sound to more pitches. If you explored Chapter 11, which describes the registers of the voice, you can apply that same registration work to your speaking voice. Speak some text and use a pure chest voice. It's going to feel really heavy. Speak the text again and allow it to be head voice dominated — you likely sound very young. Knowing what is chest voice and head voice when you speak allows you to now explore a combination — mix — in the following exercise.

Try the following exercise to explore the mix when you speak. Later exercises in the section "Moving Resonance to the Front" help you add forward resonance to your mix to create a mix belt. (See the nearby sidebar, "Introducing mix belt," for more information.)

TRACK 52

The exercise on Track 52 ("I Wanna Know!") allows you to explore speaking on a variety of pitches. Listen to the singer demonstrate for you. Notice that the sound of her speaking voice is chatty and conversational. As she moves higher in pitch, she maintains the chatty sound and the resonance moves higher. The sound is a mix — neither chest voice nor head voice but a combination of both. After you listen to the track several times, play it again and join in.

Calling out to a friend

Making high-energy speaking sounds, such as calling out to a friend or making demands of an imaginary foe, helps you find nasal resonance and coordinate breath and energy.

Pretend that your friend is across a noisy room. Try to get his attention by calling out, "Hey." Use your knowledge of breath and energy to connect to this sound. Your imaginary friend doesn't respond, so call out "Hey" again on a different pitch. Remember that it's okay to explore different pitches with your speaking voice. You can also modify this exercise: Call out phrases such as "Give me that back!" or "Back off!" or "Never!" or even try to sell your friend something. Many of the vendors at the ballpark are belting and don't even know it. Try selling some apples, oranges, or popcorn to an imaginary crowd. Use your knowledge of resonance from Chapter 7 to get the tone vibrating in your face to find nasal resonance.

TRACK 53

On Track 53, you hear the singer demonstrating high-energy speaking sounds. The speaking quality that you use to work this exercise feels nasal. It doesn't *sound* nasal, but it may *feel* nasal. This is perfectly legal belting. The wide-open, dark, resonant sounds are good for your classical music. This twang sound that's spoken is perfect for helping your belt. If you've never explored the type of speech I'm describing, get out the CD and listen to the example before you attempt this exercise.

Moving Resonance to the Front

When you sing, you may not be aware of resonance. You can read Chapter 7 about resonance and how it varies in different styles of music. In this section, you explore resonance in different ways and locations so you know how to move it forward when it's time to belt.

Exploring vibrations of resonance

For this exercise, you divide your head into three segments. It's not as painful as it sounds. To really feel the vibrations of resonance in the front of your face, you want to explore the vibrations made in the very back, middle, and front of your face and head. Read on for an explanation of the sounds and sensations in the back, middle, and front of your head, and then listen to the examples on the CD.

- ✔ **Back:** Pretend that you're very proper and pompous, and say, "Oh, darling!" When you say it, you want to feel the vibrations of sound only in the back of your head or mouth. You can imitate the speaking voice of a very proper queen or royalty. Knowing what the vibrations feel like when they're really far back helps you understand when they move forward. To be sure that you understand the sensation, you want to open the back of the mouth and throat and keep the sound back there. It's as if your mouth is in the back of your head and you're sending the sound out the back of your head.

- ✔ **Middle:** Finding resonating sensations in the middle of your head allows you to feel where the vibrations are when they're halfway to the front. You can pretend that you're out with your mates at the local pub and say, "Fights like that are not for me." It may feel like the sound is going straight up from the middle of your head. The space in the back of the mouth or throat is similar to the space you use when you speak, as opposed to the space you open to create full resonant tone for classical music. Pretend you're Crocodile Dundee or Hugh Jackman for a moment, and speak to your mates. Imitating this speaking voice may help you find the sensations in the middle of the head.

- ✔ **Front:** For this segment, you want to feel the sound in your face and not at all in the back of the head. Pretend you're a kid on the playground cheering with friends, or imitate the sounds of a boisterous and overbearing relative — you know, those relatives who make a lot of noise when they speak. They tend to shout even when you're standing next to them. You want that same kind of resonance for this exercise. Choose one of the previous examples and say, "Yeah, that's what I want." If you aren't sure whether you felt the vibrations in the front of your face, try all three again — back, middle and front — to feel the vibrations gradually moving forward as you explore all three segments of your head.

TRACK 54

After you try the three types of resonance in this exercise, listen to the examples on the CD on Track 54 to hear the sounds demonstrated for you. For belting, you want to use the front vibrations that you just explored.

Being bratty to feel resonance

To help you feel that forward resonance needed for belting, I want you to imitate a little kid who's about to tattle on his big brother or sister. You know that taunting, singsong sound, *nya-nya-nya-nya-nya.* Be a brat for a few minutes and find that tattletale sound — feel the vibrations as you make the sound. If you didn't feel the sensation in your face, try again and be even more of a brat. Let the bratty sound buzz in your face, but with no squeezing in your throat. When the sound is right, you feel vibrations in the front of your face or just behind your face. You want the sound to be buzzing behind or beside your nose, but not in your nose. If you think it's too nasal, hold your nose and make the sound. The sound stops if it's "in your nose," but it continues buzzing if it's just behind your nose. If the vibration is in the front of your head or face, you're on the right track. The vibrations aren't in one single area; you may feel your whole face, especially your cheeks or forehead, vibrating. Some people like to call the area behind their face "the mask." If that's a term you're familiar with, you're trying to create tones that generate plenty of vibration in the mask.

TRACK 55

On Track 55, you can hear a female singer demonstrate the *nyah* sound for you. The sound needs to really buzz in your face or behind your nose — not in your nose as in *nasal,* but behind your nose to take advantage of nasal resonance. When you find the *nyah* sound, speak some text from a belting song in this same manner. As you make these sounds, keep plenty of breath moving so you don't push in your throat. The sound may not be your favorite in the beginning, but you may grow to like it.

Combining Resonance and Registration

To belt successfully, you want to use both high forward resonance and mixed registration. With mixed registration, you use some chest voice and some head voice. (Check out the mix description earlier in the chapter in the sidebar "Introducing mix belt.") If you've been practicing the exercises earlier in the chapter to help you with registration and you've explored some really forward resonance, you're ready to work on increasing your belt range. As you belt higher in pitch, the sound or resonance is going to roll higher in your head, similar to what you do as you're singing up the scale moving from middle voice into head voice. The difference is that you keep some chest voice instead of turning over into head voice as you ascend. You may feel the vibrations from the resonance climbing higher in your head, as if you have a ladder on your face that the vibrations of sound gradually climb.

Increasing your belt range

Some people think that you can belt only to a certain pitch because that's how high they can take their chest voice. You can read throughout this chapter that belting is a combination of forward resonance plus mixed registration. Because not every voice is the same, some singers have an easier time with belting and increasing their belt range, whereas other singers find it tricky.

Higher sopranos and tenors have an easier time belting and belting high in their range. Mezzos and baritones may struggle a little more to figure out their belt. You can read more information in Chapter 2 about voice types and their range. If you're a mezzo or baritone trying to increase your belt range, you want to work slowly and deliberately. Spend about a month working on the speaking voice exercises earlier in the chapter. Work for another month or so on the forward resonance. That forward resonance may be harder for you than for your soprano or tenor buddies. Your voice tends to be darker and heavier, so finding forward resonance is going to take you a while. Be patient. If you rush to increase your belt range, you may end up pushing and making a harsh sound. If you can find the forward high resonance, you'll understand the difference between when you're using too much weight and when it's just right so you can sing higher belt songs.

On Track 56, illustrated in Figure 13-1, the singer on this track sings a short belt exercise, "That Ain't It Man." You want to use your belt sound for this exercise. If you haven't explored the exercises earlier in the chapter, you may find this exercise hard. Go back and explore the bratty resonance exercise and mixed registration explanation in the sidebar "Introducing mix belt." Work on "That Ain't It Man" until you're comfortable singing it before moving on to track 57 just ahead. This exercise on Track 56 helps you use a chatty sound in a narrow range.

TRACK 56

Figure 13-1:
That Ain't
It Man.

That ain't it ___ man! That ain't it ___ man! That ain't it ___ man! That ain't ___ it man! ___

Belting up the scale

As you belt higher in pitch, you want to combine your high resonance and mixed registration. If you physically understand how to combine high forward resonance with mixed registration, then you can belt right up to the top of the staff. Try the next exercise to practice combining mixed registration and forward resonance to belt your way up the scale. It may seem like you're just talking on pitch higher and higher up the scale. That's a good thing. Remember that belting is extended speech. If you use your speaking voice for this exercise, you're on the right track to becoming a proficient belter.

The exercise in Figure 13-2 allows you to climb the scale and feel that resonating ladder I talk about in the earlier section, "Combining Resonance and Registration." Think of speaking on pitch, using some chest voice no matter how high you go, and allow the resonance to climb higher as you ascend.

TRACK 57

Figure 13-2:
Not Now.

Not   now!

Advancing Your Belt

Belting is really fun but you have to get your body coordinated to make advanced belt sounds. The chatty sounds you explored earlier in the chapter help you figure out resonance and registration. Before continuing on to the exercises in this section, do the following:

✔ Review the information earlier in the chapter about exerting energy when you sing or speak. You want some serious energy moving when you sustain the belt sounds in these next exercises.

✔ Review the information about breathing (especially the exercises at the end of Chapter 4) that describes sustaining the breath. You also want really consistent breath control to help you sustain belt sounds.

✔ Review the exercise from "Moving Resonance to the Front," earlier in this chapter, to figure out how to find forward resonance. You can also review the mix exercises in Chapter 11 to move back and forth between a chest voice–dominated mix and a head voice–dominated mix. When you're confident that you understand mix and know the difference between a mix and a belt, practice rolling back and forth between the two. Advanced belting often requires you to move from a mix into a belt. The belt sound is going to use much-more forward resonance than the mix, so you want to be confident that you can roll back and forth between the different uses of resonance.

Try the exercises ahead to explore more advanced belt sounds and sustained belt sounds.

TRACK 58

On Track 58, the singer sings a short belt song, "Take Shelter! I'm a Belter," that gives you an opportunity to take your belting skills a little farther. Listen to the track a few times to get used to the sound. Be sure you're warmed up before you try singing this song.

Sustaining belt sounds

Developing your belt sound takes time and patience. If you've been working on the exercises throughout the chapter, you may be ready to explore sustaining belt sounds. To sustain a belt sound, you need a lot of physical exertion in your body. If you don't use physical exertion, you may end up pressing in your throat, and that's not good.

Belting requires a lot of effort, so you want the effort to come from your body, not your throat. Using physical exertion means moving energy in your body. Go back to the exercises earlier in this chapter that explore coordinating breath and energy (see the section "Using body energy to find clarity of tone"). Work on those suggestions and explore how to really use your entire body to make sound. Not only do you want this physical exertion when you sustain notes in your belt song, but you want to make sure that you're not pushing in your abs at the beginning of the phrase.

Review the exhalation exercises in Chapter 4. Using a hard push of your abs at the beginning of a phrase pushes out too much air. Your throat closes down to prevent all the air from blowing by, and you end up starting with a tight tone. Physical exertion isn't about pushing in; it's about opening your body or gradually letting the abs, ribs, and sides of your body move back in when you exhale.

Try the exercise shown in Figure 13-3 to explore the exertion required for sustaining belt sounds. You want to find the high resonance that you explored in earlier exercises and use some chest voice — but not pure chest voice. Review the mixed belt information if you aren't sure how to use some chest voice, but not 100 percent. The first word intentionally has a *TH* at the beginning. Allow your tongue to move forward for the *TH,* and allow the air to move over your tongue when you say the *TH.* This movement forward helps you release the back of the tongue and also propel the resonance forward. When you say *that's* the second time, you sustain it. You want to feel your body opening out — your sides, your ribs, your hips, your back — instead of pushing in. If you feel yourself pushing in, go back and cough or laugh to notice how your body moves out on the sides to create the sound. Then try the pattern again, opening your body to sustain *that's.*

Figure 13-3: That's Mine — That's Mine.

TRACK 59

That's mine! That's mine!

Exploring different vowels

You may have noticed that the belt exercises in this chapter use the vowels *ay* (the *ay* sound as in *day*) and *a* (as in *cat*). Those two vowels help you find the forward resonance you need for belting. Of course, you have to sing more than those two vowels in belt songs, so you want to find the same resonance on other vowels. You can find that same resonance a couple of different ways:

- ✔ The first option is to modify the other vowels so they're similar to *ay.* This suggestion is good to try when you're first beginning to belt. Modifying the vowels means that you're trying to find the same resonance on all vowels that you got when you were singing the *ay* or *a.* If the phrase you're about to sing is "I'm not at all in love," you want to pretend that the words look more like *aaah'm naaat aaat aaaal aaaan laaaaav.* That combination of letters makes no sense unless you understand that you're pretending that the vowels you're singing in that phrase use the vowel *a* as in *cat* or are really similar to the *a* vowel. When you find the same height of resonance that you had when singing the *a* vowel, you can sing the actual vowels within the words and keep that high resonance. If you find *ay* more helpful than the *a* vowel, pretend that the vowels in your phrase are all similar to *ay.*

- ✔ The second option to help you maintain high resonance on a variety of vowels is to speak the sound *nyah* to feel the high resonance. You can go back to Track 55 on the CD to hear this sound demonstrated for you. When you feel the high resonance of *nyah,* say the words of your song and try to keep the same height to the resonance. When you can speak the words and keep the high forward resonance, sing the words of your song and try to find the same height when you sing. If you're having trouble belting, you're likely having problems with the word right before that troublesome note. For example, if you sing the phrase "I'm not at all in love," you may have trouble with the word *all.* If you focus on getting the right resonant sound for the word *at,* you can maintain that same forward resonant sound on the word *all.* It's tempting to open the space in the back and allow the *aw* sound in the word *all* to fall back into a very open and head voice–dominated sound. Instead, you want to keep the sound in the front of your face. A visual that may help is pretending that you have a Jim Carey mask on your face that can expand as you belt higher. The mask is a visual of your face lifting up or expanding in the front of your face.

When you're more skilled at belting, you'll be able to sing the real vowels in your words without having to modify or change them. You still want the high resonance, but you'll be able to sing the real vowel in the word. For now, keep modifying until you're confident that the resonance is both high and forward. You'll also find later that you don't need to use the forward resonance all the time when you belt. You'll be able to roll the sound forward when it's appropriate. Listen to the belters in the later section, "Belters and Belt Songs You Should Hear," and listen to the different colors they use when they sing an entire song. They don't use the really forward sound all the time; they use it only when it's appropriate to the portion of the story.

TRACK 60

On Track 60, the singer sings a short belt song for advanced belters called "Let's Celebrate." This is a more advanced belt song because the range is wider, the notes stay higher, and you have larger leaps. Continue working on the exercises in this chapter for belt strength and endurance. If you feel fatigued after singing this song, go back to the first belt song and practice it until you feel that your technique is solid. As you listen to the singer, notice how high and forward her resonance is, even when she changes vowels.

Belters and Belt Songs You Should Hear

Listening to some technically savvy belters can be helpful when you're figuring out how to make the sounds described in this chapter. In Appendix A, you can find some great suggestions of belt songs to try for yourself.

Male belters

For some skillful male belters, listen to

- Chuck Berry singing "Roll Over Beethoven"
- Elton John singing "Philadelphia Freedom" or "I Guess That's Why They Call It the Blues"
- Bobby Lewis singing "Tossin' and Turnin'"
- John Cougar Mellencamp singing "Hurts So Good"
- Rod Stewart singing "Tonight's the Night" or "Do You Think I'm Sexy"

You may not think of those guys as belters, but they're using the same qualities you explore in this chapter.

Female belters

For female belters, listen to these ladies:

- **Kristin Chenoweth:** She demonstrates her belt versatility in "Popular," from *Wicked,* and "My New Philosophy," from *You're A Good Man Charlie Brown.*

- **Linda Eder:** She provides great examples of moving back and forth between different sounds and colors in the voice. You can listen to her recording of "Bridge Over Troubled Water," where she moves from her head voice and on to a belt.

- **Sutton Foster:** She uses her belt effectively in "Show Off," from *The Drowsy Chaperone.*

- **Beyoncé Knowles:** She effortlessly shows off her belt in "Listen," from *Dreamgirls.*

- **Ethel Merman:** Her tone is an example of very forward resonance, especially in selections such as "Some People," from *Gypsy,* and "There's No Business Like Show Business," from *Annie Get Your Gun.*

- **Barbra Streisand:** She demonstrates how to mix belt especially in her recording of "Memory" from *Cats.* You can compare Streisand's sounds to some of the other recordings of "Memory," where you hear singers using really heavy chest voice.

Belt songs

You may notice that belt songs tend to start out in a mix and then gradually move into a belt. Some songs stay in the belt sound the whole time, but not all do.

Consider these examples of songs that are commonly belted for the entire song:

- "Girls Just Want to Have Fun," as sung by Cyndi Lauper
- "Joy to the World," as sung by Three Dog Night
- "Some People," from *Gypsy*
- "You Can't Get a Man with a Gun," from *Annie Get Your Gun*

Is belt the same in all styles of music?

Students often ask whether belt is the same in all styles of music. That's a very good question. The answer: Some differences do exist.

Rock: For rock songs and a rock belt, the resonance is forward and almost harsh. You get that harsh rock belt by using straight tone, keeping the screaming sounds that rockers make in the front of your face and not letting the sound spread and press in your throat, and sliding or falling off the last note of a phrase instead of holding it out. Normally, when you sustain a note in most styles of music, you use vibrato. For a rock belt, you don't use much, if any, vibrato.

Pop: A pop belt is similar to the belt sounds that you explore in this chapter. Early pop music, called doo-wop, uses a lighter belt sound compared to more contemporary pop music.

Musical theater: For musical theater, the belt changes in contemporary material. The more traditional musical theater songs have high belt notes — but not as high as some of the newer shows, which require that females belt to the top of the staff (normally head voice territory). You have to be a pretty skilled belter to use this kind of sound on a daily basis in a show. The newer musical theater shows are also influenced by other styles, such as rock and pop.

R&B: For R&B, singers often use more chest voice in their belt. If you choose to use a heavier chest voice sound in your belt, try to use it only in some parts of the song, not in the whole song. Varying the amount of weight keeps you from getting as tired as when you use a heavy chest voice throughout the song, and you can keep the balance of registration so that all parts of the voice stay equally strong.

Country: For country, singers use a lot of twang in their belt, from a really high speaking voice sound that has forward resonance. Modern country music is similar to pop music, and the sounds the singers make also are quite similar. Both styles interchange the belt and mix throughout songs.

Examples of songs that use both belt and mix:

- "Faith," as sung by George Michael
- "Hot Stuff," as sung by Donna Summer
- "I'm Going Back," from *Bells Are Ringing*
- "I Wanna Dance with Somebody," as sung by Whitney Houston

Chapter 14

Training for Singing

*T*he training requirements for singers can be confusing. Every singer needs a basic healthy technique, but knowing what to do with that technique depends on what kind of music you want to sing. In this chapter, you find out what it takes to sing your favorite style of music, when to begin that training, and whether singing in the choir offers the right kind of training for you.

Training for singing means developing singing technique. The information about technique throughout the book is designed for all singers, not just one type of singer or style of material. So explore the rest of the book for foundational information, and read on to understand what specifics are required for different styles of music. After reading this chapter, you'll know what to polish in your practice sessions.

Defining Training Requirements

No matter what type of music you want to sing, you need a healthy technique for a long life of singing. If you're interested in singing a specific type of music but you're not sure what it takes to sing those songs, check out what kind of sound you should be shooting for. (I also provide a list of talented singers in each genre.)

Crooning as a country singer

Country music has the good ol' boy songs about whiskey and women, as well as heartfelt ballads about lost love. The artists put on quite a show at their performances and use a variety of sounds when they sing. The biggest common denominator in country music is the story being told. It describes how the singer feels, in a sound that's similar to a speaking voice.

- ✔ **Sound:** Country music is slowly and surely becoming more similar to pop music. For now, you can assume that country music focuses on sounding like a real person and telling a story with simplicity in the voice. Generally, country singers use a microphone, so they don't need to carry the hall like classical singers. Country music also has more twang than you hear in the opera house. Singers create the song from their speaking voice — they think of singing as an extension of speaking. For this reason, they don't need wide, open spaces (in their mouth and throat) and round, rich tones like classical singers. You may have this ability, but you probably won't use it when you sing country.

- ✔ **Healthy technique:** You don't want to sound cultured when singing vowels in country songs. (See Chapter 8 for more on pronouncing vowels.) You want to be specific with your articulation so that your audience can understand you, but you don't want to sound like you're in class with Professor Higgins in *My Fair Lady.* Figuring out how to create healthy belt (see Chapter 13) is also a good idea, because many singers use a beltlike quality when singing their songs. Knowing the difference between a belt and chest voice helps you keep your voice in balance.

- ✔ **Naming names:** Clint Black (twang and cry of country), Johnny Cash (great storytelling, similar speaking and singing techniques), Reba McEntire (easy belting, good storytelling, some twang), Trisha Yearwood (strong legit sound and belt, good storytelling ability, combination of emotions and voice to create interesting sounds).

Jazzing it up

Familiar jazz songs are sometimes arrangements of songs from other styles of music. When jazz singers create an arrangement of a musical theater standard, they usually change the notes and rhythms from the original music. Jazz singers create their style with rhythmic flexibility, and the singer and pianist don't always have to be together note for note (called *back phrasing*).

- ✔ **Sound:** The world of jazz is similar to the other contemporary fields in that the singers have to make a variety of sounds. The sounds in jazz are often more about using the voice like a musical instrument than making big vocal sounds like you hear at the opera. The singer often sings syllables or rhythmic sounds in place of words.

- ✔ **Healthy technique:** Jazz singers need to have a good ear, because their music is often improvised and changes with each nightly performance. The singer also has to know how to *scat,* which is using doo-wop kinds of syllables, while singing a variety of notes that may or may not be written on a page of music. The jazz singer needs a great sense of rhythm, because the musical instruments are often playing background music while the singer offers his own melody line.

✔ **Naming names:** Some jazz singers who apply great jazz technique include the famous scat queen herself, Ella Fitzgerald; the laid-back, sultry sounds of Diana Krall; and the man who uses his voice like an instrument, Bobby McFerrin.

Making your mark in musical theater

Unlike the opera, the musical theater production is about the story first. Singing is high on the list of priorities, but it doesn't rank first. Musical theater performers aren't cast just because they sing well (although singing ability does count!); they're cast because they look the part, can dance or move well, and can both act and sing. Musical theater singers also need to know how to make a variety of sounds.

✔ **Sound:** With musical theater repertoire, you want the sound to be conversational, not oversung. The simplicity of the voice allows the singer to portray the text, which is most important. Musical theater singers do have to make beautiful sounds, but the sound should reinforce the text. Many musical theater productions use microphones, and singers need to understand how to adjust their technique when using a hand-held mic or wearing a body mic. Those adjustments include not punching consonants (such as the T), because doing so results in a popping sound, and trusting your feeling while you're singing instead of relying on the sound to come back from the monitors or echo in the theater.

✔ **Healthy technique:** A healthy musical theater technique involves making the beautiful open, round sounds called *legit* (open space and round head voice–dominated sound). This technique is similar to the opera singer's, but it also includes belt. Belting is making sounds like Ethel Merman, Kristin Chenoweth, and Idina Menzel. The sound is brassier, more forward, sometimes nasal, and similar to a high chest voice. You make this sound by working to combine the sounds of your speaking voice and singing voice. See Chapter 13 for help with your belt. Musical theater productions tend to be scheduled close together, and performers need solid technique to handle back-to-back performances. On Broadway, performers often do eight shows per week. Performing that much sounds like fun, but it requires stamina and skillful technique.

✔ **Naming names:** Joel Grey (conversational, high belt), Mary Martin (legit sound and belt), John Raitt (rich, round, almost operatic sound), and Gwen Verdon (great dancing skill, ability to make many different sounds with her voice to create her character).

Performing pop-rock

The lines in the music industry are starting to blur, and rock music is connected with pop. The styles are similar vocally, both use a wide range, more belt than head voice, and tone that ranges from funky to pretty. Rock singers have heavy guitars backing them up and make a variety of sounds, from screams to moans. Both types of singers need to know how to keep their singing voices healthy for their demanding music. Healthy technique means making sure that your voice will last over time.

- **Sound:** Because you have a microphone, you don't need the same kind of intensity and clarity when singing pop-rock as you do when singing opera. Having a fuzzy tone is okay, as long as that's your choice. Your microphone can help carry the sound if your tone isn't clear and focused, but you have to have some clarity to amplify. Because the lines and phrases may not be as long and drawn out in this repertoire, you also don't need the intensity of long, legato lines, as opera singers do.

  The latest technology in sound systems can instantly correct a singer's wayward pitch. Newer karaoke machines and microphones use this technology, as do some famous singers. They don't want you to know that their mic is correcting their pitch, but it's true. A live performance of someone singing without the aid of pitch-correction technology shows imperfections or minor fluctuations, whereas a studio recording is perfectly mixed to add reverb to simulate resonance and edit out any minor slips of tone. You want solid technique so that you sound great without the aid of pitch correction.

  Choosing to delay the onset of the vibrato is also perfectly legal. You can sing with a straight tone and then allow the vibrato to happen later or at the end of the phrase. As you ascend in pitch, you can allow the sound to flip into another register or yodel. You can also allow the sound to get lighter as you ascend instead of growing stronger, as you may in opera or musical theater. Using a mix or a stronger middle voice sound is a choice that female singers make; guys can choose whether to use falsetto or head voice. (Chapter 11 tells you more about voice sounds, including head voice, falsetto, and middle voice.) You may not need a wide space in your mouth and throat as you do with other styles of music, such as classical music.

- **Healthy technique:** When singing pop-rock music, you want a basic, solid, healthy technique, but your abilities need to blossom when it comes time to strut your stuff onstage. Pop singers are expected to dance *and* sing, so you need to be in shape (or be famous enough that you can choose not to dance). Try dancing and singing along with your favorite video, and you find that it takes skill to sing well when you're dancing full out. Because the sounds rock singers make are often scratchy and close to screaming (think Meatloaf), rock singers need to be aware of how to keep making the funky sounds that fans adore without causing damage to their voice. Screaming too much for too long in concerts can tax the voice and cause fatigue, strain, and tone changes. To prevent damage, singers can use resonance to create sounds that they normally make by screaming. See Chapter 7 for an explanation of resonance, and see Chapter 13 for suggestions on working with resonance in the speaking voice and belt.

✔ **Naming names:** Karen Carpenter and Carly Simon (classic pop singers); Billy Joel, Elton John, Bonnie Raitt, Rod Stewart, Tina Turner, and Ann Wilson (classic rock singers); Katy Perry and Kesha (more contemporary pop-rock singers).

Opting for opera

If you're interested in training to sing opera, you have plenty of territory to cover. Training for opera usually requires a long process of lessons or study, which isn't necessarily bad. Studying singing for a lengthy period isn't a punishment: It gives you the opportunity to master your voice. For many singers, the long process of studying also means starting early in life. Review the following list to see what you may experience as you train for opera.

✔ **Sound:** Singing opera requires you to sing long phrases, sing loud enough to be heard over an orchestra in large halls, and sing material that's musically demanding. For opera, the performance is about the sounds the singer makes. The sounds are consistent and not as varied as they are in jazz, musical theater, and pop-rock.

✔ **Healthy technique:** When singing opera, the focus of the performance is on the singing technique. Opera technique is *bel canto* technique, which literally means beautiful singing; as you may expect, the space in your mouth and throat needs to be wide open. Endurance for long operas is an issue for singers. You want to practice enough that you can sing well for the length of the opera, which can be two to four hours.

✔ **Language:** Opera singers often sing in Italian, French, German, or Russian. You don't have to be fluent in all these languages, but you want to be familiar enough with them that you can easily sing and sound like you're fluent in them. You can work with a teacher or coach when training for each aria or opera, or you can take classes (called *diction classes*) to help you see the words and pronounce them correctly. You also want to be able to translate what your scene partner says so you know the difference between "I love you" and "I love those satin slippers." You can't react appropriately if you don't know what your scene partner said.

✔ **Naming names:** Some familiar names in the opera world include Olga Borodina (mezzo with warm, round tones), Renée Fleming (soprano with luscious tone and a flexible voice), René Pape (bass with deep, rich, dark sounds), and Bryn Terfel (baritone with fine diction and a good actor).

Showing your range with R&B

The sounds of the R&B singer vary from agile riffs to high belt. Finding a voice teacher willing to work technique and apply it to this material is tricky. Most teachers insist on working classical or musical theater material to build technique. The basic technical skills the R&B singer needs are the same as any other style: solid alignment, great breathing coordination, facile articulation, and balanced registration. These skills are all addressed throughout this book. If these skills are solid, the R&B artist can seek a coach to help polish their style and material.

- **Sound:** The R&B singer uses vibrato on the sustained tones in ballads but a lot of phrases are conversational and don't require vibrato. The lyrics are very important and the sounds of the voice need to vary to reflect the message. R&B singers use a microphone, so projecting the tone isn't as crucial as in the opera.

- **Healthy technique:** R&B singers have to be versatile artists. An agile technique is a must to sing riffs and belt into the top part of the range. It's tempting to use full chest voice to sing this style, but balancing the weight of chest voice is crucial for your long-term vocal health. See Chapters 11 and 13 for information about balancing the weight of chest voice. The ability to be understood without overarticulating is also crucial to the fast-paced stories in R&B songs.

- **Naming names:** Beyoncé Knowles (remarkable solid technique and versatile artist), Maxwell (comfortable showing off his falsetto and mix), Rihanna (powerful singer, comfortable singing in her head voice and then moving right into a belt), and Usher (comfortable creating luscious tone as well as facile articulation).

Training to Sing at Any Age

If you can speak, you can sing — and you can enjoy singing no matter what your age. I've had students in their 80s take classes, and they loved it. As long as you're ready for the work it takes to develop a healthy technique, you're never too old to begin singing. However, to develop and foster a healthy singing technique, understanding how your voice may change with age is essential. Keep reading to find out the best way to train young singers (under the age of 12) and teenagers, and get some insight into a few voice changes that you may encounter at the different stages in life.

Recognizing differences between young singers and teens

Music preference may be the most obvious difference you encounter between a young singer and a teenager, but other differences exist. Young singers and teenagers are different in the following ways:

- **Range:** Young singers have a limited range; they need songs with a narrow range that focus on subjects they enjoy. Teenagers need music that's a little more hip and cool, yet still not incredibly taxing vocally, because their voices are still developing. For teenage males who've recently experienced some voice changes, lower sounds may be new and temporarily unreliable. A young singer probably has a range of fewer than 8 notes, and a teenager likely has a range of between 8 and 16 notes.

- **Training:** Most young singers can benefit from singing in a choir or joining a group singing class just to explore music. If your youngster joins a choir or group singing class, make sure that the class focuses on sounds appropriate for his or her age. Really young singers often can't make much sound when they sing because their larynx is still growing and developing. However, plenty of sound is usually the first thing a novice director asks for. If your child ends up pushing or is really tired after rehearsals, explore other choirs or classes that work at a more appropriate level.

Many young singers want to sound just like the latest pop star. They don't really realize that the pop star has all kinds of equipment and sound engineers helping make the sounds. The more you can expose your young singer to singers of the same age, the better. Take young singers to elementary-school music concerts or junior-high concerts so that they can hear their peers sing live and know what voices their age sound like.

Some teenagers with mature voices are ready for lessons and training. As long as the teacher is quite good with adolescents, lessons can be beneficial. If the teacher doesn't allow the students to choose any songs, or if the students aren't allowed to pick anything fun to sing, they may lose interest. Watch for consistent progress. You don't have to know a lot about singing to help your child. Keep asking questions, as you probably do about any other subject you aren't familiar with, and listen to your child talk about the songs (not wanting to practice is a good sign the teenager doesn't like the music) and enthusiasm for the next lesson.

Some teenagers are more ready to take direction and constructive criticism than other teenagers are. If your child's ego is still a bit delicate, you want to hire a teacher who can make positive changes in the teen's voice with humor and enthusiasm.

Developing long-term technique in teenagers

Most teenagers want to know only what they can do today to sound fabulous. They may not know the long-term benefits of healthy technique, and they may not have the patience to listen. However, using healthy technique and training their ears for singing is important for maintaining long-term technique.

Pushing the voice too far, too fast doesn't help in the long term. This concept is important for both parents and teachers to know. By pushing the voice, I mean making big sounds, such as singing material that requires a big sound before teenagers have the technical skill to support the sound. Working on chatty sounds is fine at a young age, but making pressed or pushed sounds may make producing healthy sounds more difficult later.

Having a healthy technique means singing within your range. An adult may have a wide range, but a 13-year-old may have only an octave range (see Chapter 1), which is about eight notes. Range develops with time, and pushing the singer higher offers no benefit in the long run. When the voice is ready, the singer can make huge sounds for the rest of his life. Make sure that your young teenager is aware of the advantages of using breath and resonance to help him find a variety of sounds. Let him know that he can shoot for the big guns later.

Something any singer, especially young singers, can work on to boost long-term musical life is developing his ear. Matching pitch is a skill you can read about in Chapter 4. If the youngster can match pitch but also sing a series of pitches after hearing them for the first time, he is more likely to quickly conquer new songs. Ear training can also benefit singers who end up in the choir. Singing the top soprano part may be easy because it's on the top, but those middle parts can be tricky to hear. If the youngster already has exposure to intervals and chords, the middle part — or any part — can be a snap.

Understanding that voices change with age

All voices change with age, whether you sing or not. That's why, on the phone, you can easily tell whether you're speaking with a younger or older person. The following list describes a few types of voice changes that may affect singing and offers tips on how to work around them.

  ✓ **Puberty:** Letting young men who are going through puberty sing is okay. But because you really can't predict what their voice is going to do, puberty isn't a good time for them to make a big debut. Being in an all-male choir at that age can give the singer comfort because he knows that the rest of the guys are going through the same thing. Allow his voice to wriggle and crack, and know that it's going to become much more steady in time. The female voice also changes during puberty, but the change isn't as extreme.

✔ **Menstrual cycle:** One big physical aspect that affects the female voice after puberty is the menstrual cycle. Not all women experience the same symptoms during their menstrual cycle. Some experience a sluggish feeling, as if the voice is really tired or the cords are swollen. Some experience difficulty with high notes or produce low notes that feel really heavy. Other singers experience no change whatsoever.

Track your cycle so that you know the symptoms you experience right before, during, and after your cycle. You may find that knowing the timing of your cycle allows you to plan the concert or audition on just the right day of the month.

✔ **Menopause:** After menopause, women may experience a little more stiffness in their singing. This stiffness is the result of a loss of elasticity in their muscles after estrogen production slows. Menopausal women may be able to keep their voices flexible with regular workouts. Continuing to practice specific exercises for different areas of the voice increases the chance of maintaining stamina in each particular area.

✔ **Aging:** One common occurrence with aging is the wobble. You may have heard older singers' voices wobble when they sing. The wobble is a result of a lack of muscle toning, specifically in the singing muscles. Working your singing muscles on a regular basis can help keep that wobble at bay. Getting lax with your breath is another common factor that may contribute to a wobble in your singing. If your breath backs off, your voice is more likely to flounder or wobble. A steady flow of air helps keep the rate of the vibrato steady. You can also continue working on exercises that move back and forth from straight tone to vibrato, to help maintain your ability to support the vibrato.

Vibrato and a wobble aren't the same. *Vibrato* is the normal undulation of pitch when you sing. You may feel the slight shaking feeling in your throat as the vibrato happens, and that's normal. Wobble happens when the vibrato rate is much slower than normal vibrato, which is about five to eight pulses per second. See Chapter 6 for exercises that explore vibrato.

Training with a Choir

As an individual singer, you want to stand out and be unique. You want your voice to carry the hall or resound so every person in the audience hears you. Because having a resonant sound that projects is desirable in solo singing, you may want to focus your attention on projecting your voice. However, when singing with a choir, you may find the director holding his hand in front of your face to get you to sing more quietly and blend in with others.

In this section, I discuss the benefits of training with a choir. I also tell you about the differences between singing as a soloist and singing in the choir. If you decide that training with a choir is up your alley, I give you tips on how to select a great choral director. (If you decide to sing as a soloist instead of with a choir, check out Chapter 15 to find the right voice teacher for you.)

Enjoying the benefits of singing in the choir

Many people thoroughly enjoy being in a choir. You get a chance to sing different kinds of music, and you get to be around others who share your interest in music. Making music with a group of people may give you just the balance you need between practicing alone at home and singing with a group.

The following list details some of the benefits you gain from singing with a choir.

- **You discover how to listen carefully.** When singing in a choir, you have to listen so that your voice blends with the voice of the person next to you, as well as with the sounds of the particular type of song you're singing. If the music requires a specific style of singing, you have to work to make sure that you're making the appropriate sound with healthy technique.

- **You discover how to monitor your sound based on how it feels.** If you can't hear your voice standing out, you have to rely on the feeling to determine whether your technique is still in good shape. Monitoring how your voice feels is a good idea because each room is different — you can't rely on the sound bouncing back to you.

Sometimes choral singers cup their hand around their ear to hear their voice. You can try using this technique to direct the sound of your voice back to your ears. Just make sure that the person next to you doesn't think that you're trying to block out the sound of their voice.

- **You get an opportunity to work on your ear.** Picking out your part when the other voices of the choir are surrounding you is a good work-out for your ear. Solo singers may not have someone else singing different notes in their ear. The choral singer may be mixed up with other voices singing other parts and may have to rely on her ability to read music or really listen for her note in a chord.

- **You get a chance to work on your social skills.** In choirs, you often find people who like similar music or are inspired by beautiful music. You may feel right at home around people with similar interests, which can boost your sense of belonging.

✔ **You get to travel with the choir.** You may have to raise money to go on trips, but traveling with fellow musicians who enjoy making music in beautiful concert halls can make it worth your while. Teenagers and young singers often enjoy going on the road with the choir because they get to travel around doing what they enjoy: singing with their peers.

✔ **You can work on reducing your performance anxiety by singing with a group.** Onstage with your peers, you may find that your anxieties about performing dissolve. If you feel comfortable within a group, you may be able to transfer that comfort level to your solo singing. If you suffer from anxiety about singing in public, slowly work your way from singing in the choir to auditioning for one of the solos with the choir.

The challenge and joy of singing in a group may be just the lift you need at the end of a long week of work. Singing is a wonderful release and opportunity to express your thoughts and feelings through music and singing. Joining a choir may give you that regular opportunity to enjoy singing if you just don't have the time to practice on your own.

Singing in the choir versus going solo

Depending on how you want to explore your own singing voice, singing with a choir may or may not be for you. Because the choral singer has different needs, before you join a choir, you may want to explore the differences between training with a choir and going solo:

✔ **You may frequently be asked to sing without vibrato when singing with a choir; going solo, you often sing with vibrato.** If you can make the change in the sound without pressure, singing without vibrato need not a problem. The sound without vibrato can be free and loose and supported. (See Chapter 6 for an exercise that helps you to move between straight tone and vibrato.)

✔ **You need to find a part that works for your voice and for the choir director; going solo, you can sing songs within your range.** The notes may stay pretty high or low when you sing certain parts in the choir. If you're a low female voice, you may even be asked to sing with the tenors. You can agree to sing tenor once in a while, but the part was designed for the male voice, not the female voice. Good musicians who sight read well may also be asked to sing a particular part to help the choir even though it may not be appropriate for their voice. If you feel tired after singing, you may want to ask whether you can switch to a different part or ask the director for advice on how to prevent fatigue.

✔ **You may be asked to sing quite loudly in the choir if few people are on your part.** Use this opportunity to rely on your knowledge of resonance so that you don't push too hard. If you find yourself tired after singing loudly, you need to take it easy for a while during the rehearsal so you can rest up a bit, or talk with the choir director about how your voice feels after rehearsal. Singing alone means that you can work at any volume, without worrying about having to lead others with your voice.

✔ **You may be asked to stand for long periods of time when singing in a choir; while rehearsing by yourself, you can rest whenever you need to and give your legs a break.** Having to stand for a rehearsal can provide a good opportunity to practice standing with your weight evenly distributed on both legs. If you find this tiring, explore your options with the director.

✔ **You need to be aware of your facial expressions when moving back and forth from choir to soloist.** Sometimes choir directors tell you to raise your eyebrows or smile to keep the pitch steady. You can do this as long as you know that, when you sing alone, you need to put your eyebrows back down. You can keep the pitch steady by keeping your breath consistent and by making sure that your vowels are precise. Keeping your breath moving at a steady rate and singing precise vowel sounds is easier than trying to move each pitch up or down. The smile can also be deadly to a soloist: Smiles don't work for sad songs when you're a soloist. The smile also can cause tension inside your mouth when you try to open the *back space* (the space in the back of your mouth and throat). Find enjoyment in singing from the joy inside your body, and let it reflect on your face without the tension of a frozen smile.

Chapter 15

Finding the Right Voice Teacher

*F*inding the person who's just the right voice teacher for you can be tricky. The different types of instructors available may be confusing. You may have no idea how to select a voice teacher or what to expect from the lesson itself. No matter what your level of understanding is, this chapter gives you insight and advice on selecting a voice teacher. This chapter also helps you know what to expect from the voice teacher, the lesson, and yourself.

Searching for the Best Voice Teacher

Regardless of your level of singing, if you want to improve your singing by taking voice lessons, you need to do your homework to find the one who best suits your needs. I provide you with some ways to find a voice teacher, as well as some questions to ask both yourself and the prospective teacher before you even step into the studio.

Finding a prospective voice teacher

You can track down a voice teacher in many ways. The following list makes finding a good teacher simple.

- ✔ **Get recommendations from friends who take voice lessons.** Keeping in mind that no teacher is perfect, ask your friends what they like and don't like about the teacher. Compare their preferences with your own.

- ✔ **Ask for suggestions at the local music store.** The store may even have someone on staff who can work with you. If not, the staff is probably familiar with at least a few local voice teachers.

✔ **Look for ads in the local newspaper or trade paper in print or online.** Before you give the person a call, have your list of questions ready. If you feel uneasy during the conversation, just say that you want to think about it.

✔ **Call the music school at the college nearest you.** Many graduate students make great voice teachers. They're often in the heat of their training and want to share all the juicy information they've gleaned. They may not have years of teaching under their belt, but that may work well for you: The two of you can explore singing together.

✔ **Search online.** You can also find voice teachers online. I recommend starting at `nats.org` (the National Association of Teachers of Singing, Inc.).

If possible, get input from current or former students about a particular teacher before you make contact. Although no teacher is perfect for everyone, if you hear one bad review after another, heed the warning that this teacher probably isn't the best choice.

Identifying what you want

You can't get far choosing a voice teacher if you can't identify what you want out of your lessons. You may have questions for prospective voice teachers, and they may also have some for you. To be prepared, consider the following questions before you begin chatting with prospective teachers.

✔ **What exactly do you want from lessons?** If you want to improve your technique, sing higher notes, hold out phrases longer, or make yourself understood, discuss these goals with your prospective voice teacher. Your prospective voice teacher can tell you what she focuses on and how a lesson may be structured around your goals, and you can see whether that fits your wants and needs.

✔ **Are you doing this for fun or are you interested in developing a career or exploring some major singing?** If you're looking for a singing career, your teacher may move you through your lessons at a faster pace and make more demands on your practicing; on the other hand, if you're taking lessons for fun, your prospective teacher may assign you different kinds of songs or not worry so much about the business aspects of singing. You may be interested in being pushed a bit harder, even if you're singing just for fun, and you want to be sure that she's willing to adjust the pace to meet your needs.

✔ **How much time do you want to spend practicing?** If you're really busy and can't spend much time practicing, discuss this availability with your prospective voice teacher. Find out whether she's flexible enough to provide lessons every other week to give you enough time to practice between lessons.

✔ **What do you want to sing?** Check out Chapter 16 if you aren't sure about your options. When you know what you want to sing, talk it over with the teacher to see whether she teaches that style of music. Some teachers teach only classical music and prefer that their students not sing pop music or jazz. Working on classical music has great benefits, but that may be the wrong choice for you.

Interviewing a prospective teacher

Finding out basic information about a prospective voice teacher, such as qualifications and costs, is just as important as identifying what you want from a voice teacher.

Really good voice teachers are probably busy and quite booked with students. They may not have time to answer all your questions. If that's the case, you may want to try a few lessons and find out the answers during that time. Either way can work quite well.

If you call a teacher and start quizzing her as if she's being audited, you may not get a good response. Treat the topics in upcoming sections as suggestions for steering the conversation to get the answers you need. After all this questioning, if you get a good feeling about the teacher, give it a try.

Unfortunately, lessons cost money. You don't want to get stuck adding up costs at the last minute only to find out that you can't afford them. The following sections include questions to help you get a grasp on how much money you're gonna have to fork over. In addition, I tell you how to get some answers about a prospective voice teacher's background.

Experience

One of the first questions you want to ask a prospective teacher is "How many years have you been teaching?" You want to find out whether this person has been teaching more than just a few years. But don't automatically assume that you don't want to work with a teacher who's just getting started. Consider the following:

- ✔ Some brand-new teachers are really great because they've recently had so many lessons themselves. A newer teacher probably charges less than someone with more experience and may have more options for lesson times or may be more open to working on contemporary music, such as pop or rock.

- ✔ A more experienced teacher may know how to address the type of vocal problems you want to focus on. He may also have years of experience explaining how to do something and may have a variety of ways to explain the technique so you're sure to understand. If the prospective teacher has been around for a while, you're also more likely to find some current or former students who can tell you about his strengths.

If you have some serious vocal health problems, such as nodes or severe acid reflux (see Chapter 23), I recommend finding an experienced teacher who is familiar with rehabilitating voices.

Avoid teachers who promise remarkable results in a very short period of time, claim to be the expert of a particular teaching method, offer only a few exercises that are supposed to fix all vocal problems, and promise that only they can give you the information that you need.

Education

Be sure to ask where the teacher studied or got her singing education. You want a voice teacher who's had years of performance experience or years of lessons or training in a degree program that focuses on the voice. The teacher doesn't have to have a degree from an Ivy League school to be a good teacher. She just needs to know a great deal about singing and know how to pass on the knowledge of singing to her students.

If you're interested in singing classical music or choral music in other languages, find out during your conversation whether this teacher has knowledge of foreign languages. You can discover this answer by asking what kind of songs the students sing.

Choir directors and piano teachers commonly also teach voice. As long as this person knows quite a bit about how the voice works and how to help when something goes wrong, it's worth a try. If you do take lessons from the choir director, find out how much of her training was about individual singing. Many degree programs allow choral directors to graduate without any knowledge of how the voice actually works. They spend many hours coaching choirs to make lovely sounds, but how to make those sounds is important for voice lessons.

Music styles

Find out whether the teacher focuses on different styles of music. For example, does the teacher understand belting and how to teach it for musical theater? You want to find out whether the teacher is interested in the same kind of music you enjoy. If he only assigns songs and doesn't allow the student to choose, think about how you feel about his preferred style of music before you commit. If you need help with a specific type of voice, such as a countertenor (see Chapter 2), or if you want specific kinds of help with styles of singing, such as jazz, pop, or belting, make sure that the prospective teacher can work with your voice type or the particular style of singing you're interested in pursuing.

Accompaniment

Ask whether the teacher plays the piano or has a pianist play. Keep in mind that you're seeking a voice teacher, not a pianist. Most voice teachers don't play the piano that well; they spend their days training the voice and may have skipped the piano lessons. However, you want to ask this question, because many voice teachers who don't play the piano well hire a pianist to accompany their students. You need to find out whether the cost for this extra person is already figured into the cost of your lesson. Most times, it is. If it's not, however, you need to decide whether you're willing to take on the added expense.

If the teacher doesn't play and doesn't have a pianist available, find out what kind of system she has for working on music. Many teachers use accompaniment recordings for the students to sing along with. Your teacher also may have a keyboard with songs already programmed into it. You may also consider finding a rehearsal pianist to record songs for you so that you can take a recording to your lessons and sing along.

Location

Where the teacher conducts lessons is another consideration. The teacher may hold lessons in his home, at a studio, at a school, or even at your home.

If the teacher is willing to come to your home, that certainly may be your most convenient option. However, keep in mind that you may have to pay more for this convenience. (See the later section, "Cost.")

Just as important, you need to know where the teacher's students perform. The teacher may tell you how many of his students are performing in local productions or other local venues. Asking this question gives you an idea of how familiar the teacher is with local performing venues, and you'll get some idea about the variety of students within the studio.

Cost

The cost of voice lessons varies depending on location. The price of voice lessons in New York City or San Francisco may be $100 and up for an hour-long lesson, but you may pay only $50 for an hour's instruction in a small town in the Midwest. You may also want to ask the teacher whether you can opt for a half-hour lesson (or an hour lesson every other week), if that fits your budget better.

If you're a beginner, you may prefer taking a half-hour lesson anyway. Your muscles are just figuring out what to do, and your voice and brain may be quite tired after a half hour of work. When your skills improve, you can increase the time.

The fame of the voice teacher can also affect the cost. Voice teachers who've had successful performance careers or famous students charge more than teachers just starting out. The famous teacher may be able to help you with contacts in the business as your technique advances, but high prices don't guarantee better results or a better teacher. You have to try some lessons to know whether it works for you.

The price of lessons doesn't guarantee the best or worst teacher. You may find a young teacher just starting out who has terrific rates but doesn't know anything yet about teaching. The famous teacher who charges more than your rent may not be the right teacher for you, either, if you resent having to shell out the dough for lessons. Shop around and ask plenty of questions.

Payment policy

Ask about the teacher's payment policy. If you agree to set a specific lesson time each week with a teacher, the teacher may require that you pay in advance. This policy is common with teachers who have large studios. Other teachers may allow you to set up a lesson whenever you find enough money. Ask about scheduling during your initial conversation so that you don't encounter any surprises.

You also want to ask about the method of payment. If your teacher requires cash, you need to make sure that you hit the ATM before lessons. Checks are usually acceptable, and many teachers accept credit cards in their studio or via an online account. If you pay in advance, keep track of the number of lessons. Most teachers are good about keeping up with lessons, but you want to know when that next payment is due.

Cancellation policy

You need to know the cancellation policy. You don't want to be surprised when you call in sick and the teacher requires you to pay for the missed lesson. Most teachers require that you give 24 hours' notice if you plan to cancel a lesson. Other teachers require that you make up a lesson within a certain period of time to avoid being penalized. Teachers who have very full studios may not even offer a cancellation policy. Be sure to ask so that you know going in whether getting sick can cost you big bucks.

Knowing What to Expect from a Teacher

A voice lesson is usually a time when you're alone with one person, so you want to feel comfortable with that person and also feel positive about the work you're doing on your voice. To evaluate how well you work with your teacher, you need to know what you can expect from her. This section gives you an idea of what type of interaction to expect in your lessons.

You may need three to six months to really grasp the concepts in voice lessons and hear changes in your voice. You want to hear changes within the first month, but the big concepts and tough technical exercises may take awhile to gel. Enjoy each lesson with the understanding that you're on a journey that you can't make in one day.

Feeling good when you leave the lesson

Feeling good about your lesson is a two-way road. The purpose of a lesson is to gain more information about singing, so you want your teacher to focus on the work. However, you need to able to shoulder criticism well.

During a voice lesson, you're doing plenty of singing, and your teacher needs to give you feedback on the sounds you're making and offer suggestions on ways to improve those sounds.

Constructive criticism is about your singing technique and isn't directed at you personally. If you feel that your teacher isn't giving you positive feedback, ask for it.

Focusing on the work helps you see the teacher's constructive criticism as a means to get you to the next level. If you expect your teacher to do nothing more than gush over your talents, you're going to be sorely disappointed. Any teacher worth his salt isn't going to shy away from telling you what you're doing wrong (or right).

If you find a teacher who does nothing but praise you, you're wasting your time, because that type of lesson doesn't help you improve.

To feel confident at each lesson, you need to know what to practice. During your lesson, your teacher needs to suggest exercises for you to practice to help you improve your technique. He then needs to help you apply those concepts to songs that you're singing. If you aren't sure about what to practice, you can ask your teacher to clarify which exercises to focus on for the next lesson.

Working with imagery and other tools

Because you can't see your voice, you need some tools to help you make changes. One way to obtain these tools is to make sure that your lesson involves working with a variety of techniques, such as imagery.

The teacher may use images to help you understand how to make the best sounds. The teacher may ask you to notice the sensations as you sing, give you something to visualize as you sing, or give you something to listen for. All three approaches can work beautifully for you as you work on your voice. You may also find that one approach works best for you. Knowing your preferred approach is good because you can translate what your teacher says into your own language. For instance, if your teacher describes something to you and explains the anatomy of why that worked, you may remember what it felt like when you made the best sounds. If you enjoy working with images, you can find a way to visualize the sound to enhance your experience.

Don't fret if a teacher wants to explain physically what's happening. You may not want to know in the beginning, but later you may be glad that you understand why a particular image works.

Applying tried-and-true singing methods

Teaching people to sing is an old profession. If you encounter a teacher who claims to have a "never-before-revealed, life-altering system of teaching," be wary. You want a teacher who bases her teaching on facts, not just experiments. Your voice may be very different from your teacher's voice. That's not a problem if your teacher has been teaching for at least five years. Hopefully she's encountered different vocal problems and figured out a way to work with them.

If you discuss lessons with a prospective teacher and she doesn't have a "system" of teaching, that's okay. Many great teachers combine all the information they've encountered into their own method.

Knowing What to Expect from Yourself

Yes, you do have to take some responsibility for creating your own singing success. Although knowing what to expect from your teacher is important (see the previous section for details), understanding what you need to be doing in and out of your lessons is just as important.

Developing your own practice process

You may have a weekly lesson with your voice teacher, but you have to practice between lessons to apply the techniques discussed each week. Practice leads to improvement. (For more details about practicing, check out Chapter 10.)

The best way to create a practice routine that works for you is to record any lessons and practice sessions and to keep notes in a journal. You want to record the lesson so that you can listen to it to hear the changes you make during that time. Taking notes as you listen to the tape helps you figure out how you made those changes so that you can make them again on your own.

The concept and purpose of an exercise is more important than the exercise itself. For example, you can find many ways to work on breath, but the principle of moving breath is more important than one exercise. So when your teacher assigns you an exercise, make sure that you understand what it's for and how to use it. Simply doing an exercise isn't going to help you improve if you don't know what to do or what to listen for.

At the end of each voice lesson, I recommend that singers recap what they need to practice before the next lesson. If you recap the big concepts that you intend to focus on, you and your teacher both have a list of goals. Your goal is to do the work, and your teacher's goal is to listen to you sing at the next lesson to determine whether you need to continue in the same direction or expand your work.

Avoiding overworking your flaws

In your lesson, you want to focus on the entire voice and find a good balance of skills in all areas. If you spend too much time on the "flaw," you may get discouraged and feel like you can't do anything. Find a balance for your practice session and your lesson so that you work on techniques you do well and others that you don't do well. Hopefully the list of what you don't do so well grows shorter with each practice session.

If you find that your teacher is focusing so much on your flaws that you're becoming discouraged, ask your teacher for feedback on what you're doing well. Don't be shy about asking for positive reinforcement in lessons. Your teacher may assume that you know what you're doing well and may not be telling you as often. If you call this to his attention, he can offer you some needed words of encouragement.

Making Your First Lesson a Success

If you've never had a voice lesson, you may be nervous during your first lesson. The teacher knows that the first lesson is a little bit scary and may encourage you to be brave and try to make some new sounds. Admit that you're nervous and know that feeling this way is perfectly normal.

After you choose a voice teacher and know what to expect from the lesson, check out the following list to get a few tips on how to make your first lesson go smoothly.

- ✔ Before your first lesson, ask the teacher whether you need to bring your recorder. She may have one that you can use at the studio. If not, you want to bring one.

- ✔ Bring along a bottle of water to keep your throat moist during all the singing.

  Don't set the water on the piano unless your teacher tells you that it's okay. Pianos are expensive, and spilling your water into the baby grand makes a really bad (and expensive) lasting impression.

- ✔ If the lesson is in a school or other location without supplies, you may also want to bring along a small mirror. Check out the list of supplies that you may need for practicing or lessons in Chapter 10.

- ✔ Ask how many copies of the music to bring. Some instructors want you to bring an extra copy of the song for them or the pianist. See Chapter 16 for ideas on locating sheet music.

Part IV
Preparing to Perform

"Very nice audition, Vince. Let's talk a minute about that little thing you do at the end with the microphone."

In this part . . .

This part packs in plenty of information. If you're itching to choose some songs, check out the list of suggestions about choosing songs and finding the sheet music. I also offer a step-by-step process to help you get a new song under your belt in less time and more effectively than trying to cram all the details in one session.

One of the great joys of singing is adding acting skills. You get performance pointers to add to your dependable technique to help you look good and give your audience a reason to watch you sing.

If you're interested in the bright lights of Broadway or an audition in your hometown, you also get advice on overcoming stage fright, as well as tips for a great audition. It's time to take your technique beyond the practice room!

Chapter 16

Selecting Your Music Material

*I*n this chapter, you discover how to choose an appropriate song and where to find the music. I show you how to choose the right style and key, find a song at your level, and show off your strengths. Knowing whether to buy the original score, a *fake book* (a book with only the melody line, chord symbols, and words), or sheet music makes your shopping experience so much easier. When you've narrowed your choices, you can look for the right music in your local music store or download the music digitally.

Choosing the Song

Starting a new song can be so much fun. Digging into the phrasing, the story, and the vocal challenges of a new song can provide hours of entertaining work. But the process of choosing the song can stump many singers. Keep reading for some tips on how to select the right song for you.

Finding songs at your level

Your level of expertise and technical ability at this moment in time is the primary determination when finding music to sing. Choosing a song that's too hard for you is sure to frustrate you. On the other hand, selecting material that's too easy for you may give you fun songs to sing, but it won't help advance your singing technique.

Choosing songs at your level requires you to balance your current abilities with what you want to accomplish. To advance your singing technique, you want to choose songs that are just a little outside your comfort zone. Selecting a song to sing for a performance is different from selecting songs to practice and songs that help you develop technique. Songs for a performance need to highlight your level of ability at the time of the performance. For example, you may choose to perform a song that was once a little difficult for you but that you practiced long enough to master the technical challenges.

The following list includes the three basic song levels you want to choose from. (For more info, check out Appendix A, which lists songs in different styles of music for beginner- and intermediate-level singers.)

- **Beginner:** *Beginner songs* have simple rhythms, a narrow range, an accompaniment part that plays the singer's melody, a melody line and accompaniment that are the same, and simple articulation opportunities.

  Examples of a beginner song include "The Sound of Music" and "Edelweiss" from *The Sound of Music.* "The Sound of Music" has rhythms that are fairly easy to count, and the range isn't too extreme. "Edelweiss" also has easy rhythms, a narrow range, and smooth lines to help you work on phrasing.

  Other beginner songs include the following:

  - The folk ballad "Greensleeves"

  - The Old Scottish Air "Auld Lang Syne"

  - The traditional air "Drink to Me Only With Thine Eyes," by Ben Jonson

  - "In The Gloaming," by Mete Orred and Annie F. Harrison

  - The spiritual "He's Got the Whole World in His Hands"

  - "Killing Me Softly," as sung by Roberta Flack

  - "You Light Up My Life," by Joe Brooks

  - "Love Me Tender," by Elvis Presley and Vera Matson

- **Intermediate:** *Intermediate songs* have harder rhythms that test you a bit beyond your current level. If you're an intermediate-level singer, you can opt for a wider range, a few high notes to test your top notes, more difficult intervals that challenge your ear, and opportunities to explore more detailed articulation. The piano accompaniment may not follow the melody note for note.

  Some intermediate songs include "Over the Rainbow," from *The Wizard of Oz,* and "My Favorite Things," from *The Sound of Music.* "Over the Rainbow" is an intermediate song because the rhythms are a little more complex and varied than in a beginner song, such as "Edelweiss," and the leaps are much wider than in songs that move in stepwise motion.

"My Favorite Things" moves quickly, with more variety and more complex rhythms than "The Sound of Music" from the same show, and the articulation of text has to be much faster. After you get some experience working on slower songs, such as "Edelweiss," to get your articulation fluid, a song like "My Favorite Things" offers you the challenge of articulating faster.

The following is a list of familiar intermediate-level songs that you may recognize:

- "Crazy," by Willie Nelson

- "You're So Vain," by Carly Simon

- "You Oughta Be Here With Me," from *Big River*

- "Desperado," by Don Henley and Alen Frey

- "O sole mio!," by E. di Capua (tenor)

✔ **Advanced:** An *advanced* song is a song that really tests your skills. The melody you sing may be completely different from the accompaniment and have intervals that don't always blend with the piano music. You may be confronted with long notes that require breath control, several high notes that demand skill in execution, a detailed story that requires you to make the journey of the text as you use your technical skill, text that enables you to portray the height of the story, and an opportunity to convey the specific style appropriate for the song, such as high belt, classical legit, or the twang of a country song. I discuss training for different styles of singing in Chapter 14. See Chapter 13 for more on belting. You know your voice well by the time you're an advanced singer, so I don't include songs for advanced singers in Appendix A.

A list of advanced songs you may know include the following:

- "Take Me or Leave Me," from *Rent*

- "Miss Independent," by Kelly Clarkson

- "Habañera," from the opera *Carmen,* by Bizet (mezzo)

- "I Know That My Redeemer Liveth," from *The Messiah,* by Handel (soprano)

- "Se vuol ballare, Signor contino," from *The Marriage of Figaro (Le Nozze di Figaro),* by Mozart (bass)

The upcoming sections can help you figure out your level of expertise.

Considering your range

If your range is about eight notes, a beginner song works for you. An intermediate song has a range less than two octaves, and an advanced song may have a range wider than two octaves. For more on musical notation, see Chapter 1.

An *octave* is eight white notes on the piano, and two octaves are 16 white notes apart. To go up an octave from a black key, find the next black key in the same pair of two or three black notes.

Making leaps

How comfortable are you singing big leaps in a melody? Many beginner songs move in *stepwise motion,* which means that the notes in the melody are right next to each other. An example you may know is "Mary Had a Little Lamb." Yes, it's a nursery rhyme, but try singing it — you'll notice that most of the notes are right next to each other, and that's stepwise motion.

Intermediate songs have bigger leaps of skipping five or six notes, and advanced songs can have leaps up to eight notes, or an octave. Wider *intervals* (the distance between two notes) challenge your ear. Spend some time working the larger intervals in a song to make sure that your throat stays open (see Chapter 6), your breath is flowing consistently (see Chapter 4), and your larynx stays steady (see Chapter 5). Singing wider intervals also makes you listen more. If you figure out the wider intervals, you're more likely to repeat that sound when you see the same interval in your next song.

Climbing higher

What's the highest note you can sing successfully? Suppose that your highest note is F5, or the top line on the treble clef staff (see Chapter 1 for an explanation about staff and F5). Then consider these strategies:

- ✔ If you're a beginner, you want to choose a song that has most notes below D5 or E5 and maybe only one F5.

- ✔ If you're an intermediate singer with the same range, you want to choose a song that has one or two opportunities to sing that F5.

- ✔ If you're an advanced singer, you know your voice well enough to determine how many times you can sing that F5 with ease. A soprano may sing her highest note four to five times in an advanced song, but a mezzo may want only one or two repetitions of her highest note. The same is true for a tenor and a baritone or bass; the tenor can handle more repetitions of those high notes than a baritone or bass. (For more on voice types, see Chapter 2.)

Battling fatigue

What causes you to get tired as you're practicing? Many singers tire when they sing a song in which most notes stay at the top of their range. Even if the song doesn't have many repetitions of your highest note, if the majority of the notes sit near that top note, you may get tired. Think of singing as similar to lifting weights. You can lift a weight several times, but how long can you hold it up? When you're staying near the top part of your range, you're holding up the weight — in other words, you're using quite a bit of body energy to maintain that physical exertion. If the high notes come at rapid-fire pace, that may be just the thing to get you singing the notes without worrying about it, but it can also be quite a challenge.

The more you practice and get to know your singing voice, the better you can answer this question.

Speeding along

What is the song's speed? A song's speed may cause you to spit out words at the speed of lightening. If you've been working on articulation (see Chapters 8 and 9), you can spit out those words easily without getting tense from the constant movement of your *articulators* (tongue and lips).

- ✔ Beginner songs are often slower, so you can articulate and really notice the movement of your lips and tongue.
- ✔ Intermediate songs may move at a faster pace and have tougher combinations of sounds.
- ✔ Advanced songs may be quite fast and require you to make your words understood as your melody bounces along the page.

Following your accompaniment

How confident are you singing with a piano or other musical accompaniment?

- ✔ A beginner song usually has the melody line played by the piano and in an obvious way.
- ✔ An intermediate song may have the melody line in the piano part, but the chords may be thicker and your melody may be harder to pick out.
- ✔ An advanced song may have an accompaniment that is totally different from the melody written for the singer.

Paying attention to detail

How comfortable are you at combining multiple details when singing a song? When you look at a song or hear it for the first time, you probably need to hear it a few times to get a feel for it.

If you have to listen for a few weeks to get the notes right, the song is too hard for you right now.

By breaking down the details when you figure out a song (see Chapter 17), you're more likely to get all the pieces of the song working faster. If your ear picks up a tune pretty fast, you may assume that you can take on harder songs. Give yourself some time to work on songs and master a variety of technical details, such as breathing, articulation, and storytelling, before you jump to more advanced songs.

Telling a story

How familiar are you with acting and singing at the same time? Actors on television or stage make it look so easy, but acting and singing at the same time is a skill to make the song sound good and look good at the same time.

- ✔ Beginner songs often work for either gender and have easier stories to tell.
- ✔ Intermediate songs often contain more detailed lyrics.
- ✔ Advanced songs often are written for a specific gender, with a through-line in the story.

See Chapter 18 for more on acting and singing.

Picking up the rhythm

How comfortable are you with rhythms? Some singers can pick up rhythms quickly, whereas others struggle to hear the difference between sounds.

- ✔ Beginner songs often have simple rhythms to allow the singer to focus on one or two types of rhythms.
- ✔ Intermediate songs have a wider variety of rhythmic combinations.
- ✔ Advanced songs may have complex rhythms.

For more help with rhythms, check out *Guitar For Dummies,* 2nd Edition, by Mark Phillips and Jon Chappell, or *Piano For Dummies,* 2nd Edition, by Blake Neely (both published by Wiley). If you know a bit about rhythms, you can look at the song and determine whether the piece is complicated musically.

Determining the appropriate key for you

You may hear a great song on the radio and rush out to get the sheet music so you can sing it at home. The trick is to read music well enough to know whether the song's notes are within your range. You don't have to know everything about what's on the page; you just need to know enough to discern the difference between the right key for you and the wrong key.

When a singer says, "I need this song in a higher key," he means that he wants the notes of the song higher. After looking at the song, you may also determine that you want the notes to be lower — that is, you need to sing the song in a lower key. A song's *key* just means that the song is written with one note as the *central note,* or *tonic.* That central note is the name of the key. If Middle C is the central note, you regularly return to Middle C in the song. You don't have to know all about reading music, but you need to know whether you want the song four steps higher or two steps higher. Wanting the song in a higher key means you want the song to sit higher in your range.

Sometimes singers ask, "What's my key?" when they actually mean, "What's my range?" Not every song that has Middle C as the central note has the same range. You want to be able to describe your range (see Chapters 2 and 12) and to know whether you need the song in a higher or lower key.

Selecting a suitable song style

You may love to listen to operatic arias but aren't yet able to sing one. Your voice may be suited to belting out show tunes, even though your car radio is set to the country music station. If you're choosing a song to sing for fun and for your own listening pleasure, settle on a song in a style that you like but that also challenges you to use your knowledge of technique. You can choose some songs to sing for fun and some that make you work a little harder on your technique.

Chapter 20 helps you choose an audition song that works for you. Other styles of music require similar thoughts. If you're going the classical route, make sure that the music is appropriate for your voice type. If you're a mezzo-soprano, opt for arias written for that voice. Arias written for the mezzo voice often have the same range as arias written for sopranos, but the notes in the soprano aria stay higher than the mezzo arias. Read Chapter 2 for information about voice types and how to determine yours. For pop, folk, country, and other styles of singing, see Chapter 14 for more information about singing different musical styles.

Singing to your strengths

You want to emphasize your particular singing talents whether you sing at your cousin's wedding, at a family gathering, for an audition, in church, or as part of karaoke night at a local pub.

The following list highlights skills and strengths you can emphasize. If your strength is

- ✔ **A lovely tone,** choose a nice ballad that enhances your tone. Examples of songs that showcase a lovely tone include "A Dream Is A Wish Your Heart Makes" from *Cinderella* and "To Make You Feel My Love" by Bob Dylan.

- ✔ **Acting,** choose a great story song with a conflict that you work through as you sing the song. Examples of good story songs include "I Can't Make You Love Me," by Mike Reid and Allen Shamblin (female); and "Long Cool Woman in a Black Dress," by Allan Clarke, Roger Cook, and Roger Greenaway (male).

- ✔ **A strong head voice,** sing a song that has some high notes, such as "Oh, Holy Night," by D. S. Dwight and Adolphe Adam, in the high key.

- ✔ **An ability to sing notes quickly and easily,** sing "Rejoice" (female), from *Messiah,* by Handel.

- ✔ **Proficiency in switching quickly between registers,** sing "The Lonely Goatherd" (female), from *The Sound of Music,* by Richard Rodgers and Oscar Hammerstein.

- ✔ **A strong chest voice,** sing "Ol' Man River" (male), from *Showboat,* by Jerome Kern.

- ✔ **A strong range from top to bottom,** sing "Crying" (male), by Roy Orbison and Joe Melson.

- ✔ **Your great sense of humor,** poke fun at yourself and sing "Great Balls of Fire" (male), by Otis Blackwell and Jack Hammer.

Shopping for Sheet Music

When you finally know what you want, you have to go shopping to get it. Choosing music may be the harder of the tasks. You have the choice of walking into a store and looking at the music or letting your fingers do the buying online or over the phone. You may be able to check out sheet music at your local library and purchase it later, if you like it.

Finding retail outlets

If you like to hold music in your hand before you make a decision to buy, search online or look in the phone book for your local music store. You can call the store to ask whether it carries vocal music before you hop in the car. If the store doesn't carry your song, it may offer to order it for you. Ask the clerk whether you have to purchase it if you decide you don't like the key or that particular arrangement of the song.

Some stores allow you to browse online or call and ask for advice. Most large bookstores carry music, and if they don't have your music, they can order it for you or you can call the customer service department and order it.

Several music distributors have online catalogs that you can browse, and some offer help online or over the phone. The following list offers some of the more useful Web sites and their specialties.

- ✔ **Hal Leonard** is the world's largest publisher of printed music. You can browse the company catalog online at www.halleonard.com or write Hal Leonard Corporation, P.O. Box 13189, Milwaukee, WI 53213. You can't buy music directly from the company, but you can get your local store to order it for you or follow links at the Web site to find a retailer.

- ✔ If you're looking for classical music that's a little tricky to find or for some help finding your song, check out **Classical Vocal Reprints,** at www.classicalvocalrep.com. The owner, Glendower Jones, is happy to help you in your quest to find that favorite classical or musical theater song. Call him for some advice at 800-298-7474 in the United States.

- ✔ You can browse a huge catalog of songs at the **TIS** Web site at www.tismusic.com, order online, or call 800-421-8132 (or locally at 812-355-3005) to purchase by phone.

- ✔ **Amazon.com** also sells songbooks and sheet music. You can't get individual answers to your questions if you need to call, but you can easily browse the collection of music to find your song in sheet music form or in a song collection book.

Downloading sheet music

Online sheet music stores enable you to search a Web site for a specific song — sometimes even in the specific key you want. You may have to download software from the site to read the song, but this option is worth exploring, especially if you prefer to shop online. Type *sheet music* or *digital sheet music* into your favorite search engine, or try these Web sites:

- ✔ www.musicnotes.com allows you to see page one of the music and use its software to hear samples of the music.

- ✔ www.sheetmusicdirect.com enables you to download free software to hear, view, and transpose the music before printing and purchasing.

- ✔ www.sheetmusicnow.com lets you view a sample of a classical song before purchasing.

Web sites that offer cheaper prices may be selling a fake book, which doesn't include the piano part. A *fake book* has just the melody, chord symbols, and the words. If you choose this copy, your accompanist has to make up the accompaniment. Some accompanists are good at this; others aren't.

Flipping through compilation books

As you shop online, you have the choice to buy the song in a single sheet of music or in a *compilation book,* which contains a collection of songs that usually follow a theme, such as movie theme songs, love songs, pop hits of a certain decade, or a particular artist's songs. You have to decide whether you want to pay a little extra to have a few more songs or just get the song in the exact key you want for a smaller fee.

As you look through a compilation book, check the key of the songs that you like to make sure that they're in your range. Songs are often printed in keys that are easy to play on the piano, which doesn't mean it's the best key for your singing voice. Know your range and your comfort zone for singing before you shop. If you buy the book online, you won't know which key each song is printed in. You may have to explore the book in a music store or a bookstore that sells songbooks to decide whether the collection is for you.

Checking out music at your local library

The library is a great place to search for music. It's free, and you can check out the book to try the song at home at your own pace. If you find that it's not in the right key, you save yourself a few dollars and some frustration. You can even take the music to a pianist to play through it for you if your music-reading skills are still pretty new. If you decide that you like the song, jot down the name of the songbook, along with the name of the publisher and edition of that publication. Some books are republished and songs are added. Ask before you purchase so you aren't disappointed.

If you own the original sheet music, making a photocopy of the song for your own use is legal. For more information about making a legal copy of your music, visit www.copyright.gov or type *copyright music* into your favorite search engine.

At musical theater auditions, taking along a photocopy of the song is okay. At most classical auditions, taking an original is customary. You may be able to use a photocopy for the audition, but at competitions involving classical music, you're required to own the original. The reason? Songwriters deserve to make a living by selling their music.

Chapter 17

Mastering a New Song

. . . .

. . . .

Mastering a new song is tough. In this chapter, you discover how to take the song apart and study it step by step. I even work through a song with you to give you hands-on practice. After reading this chapter, you'll be ready to master a new song by yourself.

Tackling a Song in Steps

Getting a new song is so much fun. The new melody and new words make you want to just burst out singing.

Many singers try to conquer all the details of a brand-new song in one session. But picking up an unfamiliar song and getting the words, rhythms, and melody right at the same time may take more than one session. The process goes much quicker if you take some time to scan the song, break it down into manageable pieces, and then conquer it one piece at a time.

By *scanning,* I mean checking these musical details:

✔ **Direction of the melody:** A melody can move up or down in stepwise motion, meaning that the notes are right next to each other or just one step away from each other, or in leaps, called intervals. The more you look at your music, the more you get used to seeing the notes on the page and knowing what the distance between those two notes sounds like.

✔ **How the rhythm and the words work together:** The melody may have one note for every word or syllable, or you may have to sing two or three notes for every syllable.

- ✔ **Repeating sections:** Sometimes music is written with no repeats; other times, certain sections repeat. Look at the music for signs to indicate what you're supposed to repeat.

- ✔ **Speed:** Tempo, or speed, markings usually appear at the beginning of the piece. Sometimes the words describing the tempo are in Italian. Look up the word so you know the speed the composer intended.

- ✔ **Volume variations:** In music, volume (degree of loudness and softness) is called *dynamics*. Dynamic levels are also often written in Italian.

If you give yourself time to absorb these details one at a time, you can master the song much more quickly than if you try to cram it all into your head. Read on to find out how to create steps in your discovery process. To sing a song as the composer intended, you need to understand these notations. See *Music Theory For Dummies,* by Michael Pilhofer and Holly Day (Wiley), for more help with reading musical notation.

Follow the song in Figure 17-1 as you read through the following sections.

Memorizing the lyrics as text

Look at the lyrics as a monologue or a story. Write or type the words, including the punctuation, so you can examine the lyrics apart from the melody and take a look at the big picture. If the song has words that you don't know, look them up. Find the meaning and the pronunciation of all the words in your song. Notice the punctuation, because you can breathe at the punctuation marks in a song. (See the section "Paying attention to punctuation," later in this chapter.)

Read the lyrics out loud so you can hear the inflection of the words. As you read the lyrics, look for the *operative words* — the words that you emphasize in normal, natural, everyday speech. Operative words are nouns, verbs, adjectives, and adverbs. The rest of the words in the sentence are important but aren't usually emphasized. Keep reading the text aloud until it sounds conversational.

If you keep forgetting the words, speak through the text quickly until you no longer stumble on the words. You can also use key words in phrases to help you remember what comes next. Create a system to help you remember the order of each phrase's key word. Just knowing whether the list has some common characteristics can help you remember key words to get to the next phrase.

Sometimes when you read poetry or lyrics for the first time, they don't make complete sense. The more you read them, the more you're able to understand the meaning behind the words. When you really have a grasp on the words, memorize them. You may find that it takes only a short time to memorize the words.

Tapping out the rhythm

Even if you don't read music well, you can tap out the rhythms. Just look at the rhythms on the page and try to tap them out without worrying about words or speed. The first time you try, it may be difficult, but after some practice, you get accustomed to certain rhythm patterns and can quickly master them.

Lucky for you, only a few rhythms need to be worked out in the sample song "Simple Things" (refer to Figure 17-1). The rhythm in this song is a great example of what I mean by a beginner song. (Chapter 16 has more information about beginner, intermediate, and advanced songs.) I chose a beginner song for you to explore so you can feel totally confident about figuring out rhythms.

For more help on reading rhythms, pick up a copy of *Piano For Dummies,* 2nd Edition, by Blake Neely (Wiley).

After you tap out the rhythm of your new song, try speaking the words in rhythm. Speaking the words in rhythm can help you solidify some of the rhythms and divisions of syllables.

Reading the time signature

To figure out a song's rhythms, you have to know a little about reading music. At the very beginning of a song, you can find some numbers that look like a fraction. This fraction, or *time signature,* tells the singer how to divide the beats between each bar line. As you look at the music in Figure 17-1, notice the single vertical line between the words *simple* and *feeling* at the beginning of the song. That line is called a *bar line.* In that bar, or measure, the time signature indicates that you find four beats: The top number of the time signature 4/4 indicates how many beats you find in each bar; the bottom note indicates what kind of note gets one beat. (4/4 is also notated as C, which means *common time.*) Because the top number is four, each measure has four beats. The bottom note is also four, which means the quarter note gets one beat.

Simple Things

Words and Music by
Martha Sullivan

Figure 17-1:
Sample
song —
Simple
Things.

Knowing how long to hold notes

In "Simple Things," the song in Figure 17-1, you find three kinds of rhythms: eighth notes, quarter notes, and half notes. The duration of notes is similar to math.

The first two notes in "Simple Things" are eighth notes, and because quarter notes get one beat, eighth notes get half a beat each. When you see a note with a dot next to it, you hold the note for the full duration of the note plus half of the original value. For example, the quarter note with the dot next to it at the word *are* indicates that you hold the note for one beat plus another half, for a total of one and a half beats.

TRACK 61

On Track 61, the singer taps out the rhythm of "Simple Things" and says "Tah" for each note. Listen to the track several times until you can distinguish between eighth notes and quarter notes.

Even though listening to a recording to get a song in your ear is easy, try to avoid that method. You may want to hear your favorite artist singing the hit song you've chosen to sing, but most recordings differ from the music as it's written. Of course, if you want to hear and sing a song just for fun, by all means, get out the recording and sing along.

Singing the melody (without the words)

Sing the melody without the words. This may seem like strange advice, but singing the melody without having to worry about whether you're getting the words right helps you fix the melody in your mind and also focus on your breathing technique (see Chapter 4), back space (see Chapter 6), and legato line (see Chapter 6). Add the words after you have the melody down.

TRACK 62

On Track 62, you hear a singer singing the melody line on a single vowel. You can sing along while watching the melody line of the song in Figure 17-1. You know the rhythm, so add the melody to the familiar rhythm.

Defining musical elements in different styles

Music written on the page is the same for any style of music. The notation is the same, but how the music is performed isn't the same. In opera and classical music, singers sing exactly what's on the page. They memorize all the words, notes, musical directions, and markings. That's a lot to memorize and to get exactly right. Classical singers have to be good musicians, because they have to follow the road map exactly as the composer intended.

In musical theater, the singer follows what's on the page, especially for earlier, more traditional songs. In later musical theater songs (material influenced by pop and rock), a singer may sing the basic notation on the page but take liberties with the rhythm and timing in the measures. Singers often back phrase, or take liberties with the rhythms and timing while the piano continues playing what's on the page. The singer and pianist end up back together in the next measure.

For pop, rock, R&B, and jazz, the singer takes a lot of liberties with both the melody and the rhythms written on the page. The R&B singer adds notes to the melody, commonly called riffs. Riffs are musical improvisation on the melody written on the page. In Chapter 12, you can practice some of the most common riffs you hear in songs. The pop singer also riffs, but not as much as the R&B singer. The phrasing in these styles of music is more casual than in classical music, and it's more common for the singer to not hold out notes at the end of phrases, even though a long note may be written on the page. The jazz singer improvises with the pianist. The pianist may improvise a segment of the music, and the singer joins in when the piano finishes. The singer may also improv on the melody while the pianist follows along. Jazz singers need a good ear for music so they know when to come back in based on the chord progression they hear.

Putting words and music together

Are you ready for the last round? It's time to put all the puzzle pieces together. Because you already know the words, rhythm, and melody, singing the words with the melody is a breeze.

On Track 63, listen to all the parts put together. The first time through, the singer sings the song with you. The second time through, you get to sing by yourself.

TRACK 63

Notice how long the musical introduction lasts so that you're prepared when you sing by yourself. If you're not sure what to do during this introduction, check out Chapter 18 for some ideas on acting.

This same step-by-step process can lead you to great discoveries of new songs. Take your time when you find a new song and get all the steps down. With each new song, you get faster and faster. Pretty soon, you can get a song down in no time. Have fun singing along.

Using Vocal Technique in Your New Song

When you begin a new song, the first thing you probably want to do is sing it over and over. That's fine, as long as you take some time to apply some work to your singing technique. You can sing along with the exercises on the CD, which helps you advance your singing technique, and then you can apply that technical skill to songs. By breaking down your game plan for a song, you can work on technique and a song at the same time.

Giving voice to vowels

Working on single vowels in the exercises on the CD is a great way to make sure that you know how to make distinct vowel sounds. When you know the sounds of each vowel (see Chapter 8), you can apply the same work to your song. Taking the time to focus on which vowel sounds you make in each word helps you improve your technique in singing vowels with each practice.

Singling out one vowel

As you explore the melody of a new song, sing it on a single vowel to find a *legato* (smooth and connected) line and work on your breath moving smoothly through long phrases. You can apply this idea as you sing along to the CD with the melody of "Simple Things" (refer to Figure 17-1) on a single vowel. See "Singing the melody (without the words)," earlier in this chapter, to find the correct CD track to sing along with.

Streaming through the vowels

You can also sing the song on a *stream of vowels*. The stream of vowels in a song is the vowel sounds in the words minus the consonant sounds. When you can successfully speak through the vowels in one continuous stream of sound, apply that stream of vowels to the melody: Sing straight through the song without pausing between each vowel sound. This exercise helps you really listen to each vowel to make it distinct. Adding the consonants back in allows you to make those specific vowel sounds followed by very clear consonant sounds.

Making the song your own

Preparing a song for an audition means understanding how to read the sheet music a little. When you know what's written, you can work on making the song your own.

For example, if you listen to a famous singer, you may sing the song exactly the same way. At an audition, however, the music director wants to hear *you,* not a carbon copy of someone famous. Find out what's on the page and then make it yours by following these techniques:

✔ Varying dynamics

✔ Plotting tempo changes

✔ Looking for *operative words* — words that you emphasize in natural speech

✔ Choosing some acting objectives from Chapter 18

The composer has put some really great ideas into the music — you just need to know how to find them. See the later section, "Using Musical Elements to Create Your Arrangement," for more ideas on how to make a song yours.

Look at the words of "Simple Things" in Figure 17-1. Speak through the text without the consonants. When you get used to pronouncing the stream of vowels without the consonants, sing that stream of vowel sounds with the melody. When you feel confident that your vowels are top notch, put the consonants back in. You may be surprised by how clear your vowels are now that you've given them your undivided attention.

Backing into phrases

Another good way to improve your technique is to work the phrases backward. No, I'm not telling you to sing the song backward — just work from the last phrase you find difficult and gradually add the preceding phrases as you master the hard one.

Sing the last few measures of a song until your phrasing is solid. When you can do that easily, make another grouping with the preceding few measures. So imagine that your text is, "The loud cows aroused the sows. The sound of the hounds resounded all around."

1. **First, practice the last phrase, "resounded all around."**

2. **When that phrase sounds good, work through "The sound of the hounds resounded all around."**

3. **When that phrase is smooth as glass, add the preceding phrase, "aroused the sows."**

4. **Then work through the whole enchilada: "The loud cows aroused the sows. The sound of the hounds resounded all around."**

The phrasing and breath flow likely are more polished now. You can apply this same idea to "Simple Things" (refer to Figure 17-1). By working some of the phrases from the last few words, you gradually practice your breath control so you can make it through the entire phrase. In "Simple Things," you can work the phrase "These are the simple things that I would celebrate in song" by starting at "I would celebrate in song." When you can successfully sing that phrase, go back and add "simple things." When that much of the phrase is easy to manage, go back and sing the entire phrase, "These are the simple things I would celebrate in song," and see whether you can tell the difference in your breath control.

Breathing heavy: Fogging up the windows

You probably already figured out that you have to pay attention to your breathing when you sing. In fact, proper breath control can make the difference between singing successfully and failing. This section tells you how and when to breathe properly in order to sing properly.

Knowing how to breathe when you sing is a great skill. Taking your breathing to the next level in a song means breathing with the intent to say something when you sing. For each phrase that you sing, you need to plan the amount of breath that you need to complete that phrase or thought. That concept sounds like a big one, but it's what you do every day in your conversations. As you're deciding what to say next in a conversation, you take in air and then express those thoughts.

Try taking a breath and saying, "I have some bad news." Your breath was probably slow and deliberate because you knew something unpleasant was about to follow. Take a breath and say, "I won the entire jackpot in the lottery." Wow! That breath is certainly different than your bad-news rendition. When you sing songs, you want to know clearly what you're trying to say so that you take the appropriate breath for each line and express a specific thought.

Knowing where to breathe is also helpful. In a song, you can breathe in the following locations:

✔ Anytime you see a rest in the music

✔ Anywhere you see punctuation, such as a comma or period

✔ Anywhere that makes sense with the musical phrase and the lyrics

Marking the places where you intend to breathe gives you an opportunity to try that breath and see whether it works for you. The place to breathe may seem logical, but then when you try the breath, you may not feel confident. Just choose another place and try again. The more you practice singing through songs and plotting out the breaths, the better you get at figuring it out.

Refer to Figure 17-1 to read through "Simple Things" again and notice the punctuation. You can breathe in a lot of places because the song has quite a few commas.

Paying attention to punctuation

The punctuation in a song tells you where the big thoughts are. As with written and spoken text, periods indicate complete thoughts and commas point to lists and auxiliary phrases. Punctuation indicates an opportunity to take a breath, so a song's punctuation can help you with phrasing and interpretation.

A series of questions in a song provides you with a different task than a series of commas. In your everyday speech, the inflection of your tone of voice usually goes up when you ask a question and goes down when you make a statement. In singing a song that has a list with a series of commas, you want to reflect that continuing thought. You can practice this by taking a breath in the middle of a sentence when you're speaking. Notice how the inflection of your voice stays up. That same idea happens when you sing; the inflection of your voice tells the listener that you're continuing on the same train of thought. In contrast, a period needs a sense of finality. Say the following two sentences: "You did that." and "You did that?" Notice the change in the tone of your voice when you read the question. This difference of inflection helps the listener know that you've just made a statement or asked a question while singing.

Breathing in a series of commas takes a little planning. You can breathe after every comma, but you may not need to. You can take a slight pause, just like you do in speaking when you pause in the middle of a sentence but don't take a breath. A series of questions is similar: Breathe where you need to, and use a slight pause in places where you don't need a breath.

You can breathe after a comma as long as you remember that your train of thought doesn't stop as you take the breath. The same train of thought continues, just as when you take a breath between phrases in a conversation.

The places where you don't want to breathe are between syllables in a word, in the middle of a grammatical phrase that needs to be kept as one thought, and between a noun and modifier. Look at the text to determine where you take a breath while speaking the words. If it doesn't sound logical to breathe at that point when you're speaking the lyrics, try to find another place to take the breath when you sing.

If you're struggling with a phrase because you need a breath, cheat the last note of a phrase instead of trying to hurry in on the first note of the next phrase. If the last note is a half note, you can cut the note off a half beat early to catch your breath. In "Simple Things" (Figure 17-1), you can take a little time away from the word *me* to make sure that you have enough breath to sing the next phrase.

Catching your breath

If you're singing an up-tempo song with quick-moving words, you have to know exactly how to get the breath in quickly to make the next line come out clearly.

Remember that the release for the next breath has to happen quickly. Open your body to allow the breath to drop in quickly and exhale slowly. Opening the throat quickly prevents gasping. Gasping doesn't allow you to get the air in as fast, and it feels more like a struggle. For more help with breathing, see Chapter 4.

Timing your breathing from the beginning

Look at and listen to your musical introduction, or prelude — the part before the lyrics come in. Before you sing that first note, you need to be ready — you need to time your breath. Sometimes timing your breath just right so you can begin the first phrase with enough air is tricky.

The best way to get the breath is to practice breathing two beats before you sing. Get your song's tempo in your head. When you have that tempo set in your mind, count one, two, breath, breath (breathe for two counts), and then begin to sing. If you find that's too much time for breath, practice taking the breath in one count. You don't want to take the breath, hold it for a few counts, and then sing. Holding your breath may get you locked up in your upper body. Remember that breath is always in motion. (See Chapter 4 for an explanation of how your body moves for breathing and singing.) For "Simple Things" in Figure 17-1, you want to start taking your first breath about two beats before you sing the first word, "Sometimes."

Changing the tone for each section

Each section of a song must have a distinct feel or tone. To convey different tones in different sections, you need to make a change of thought to create a change of tone. In "Simple Things"(refer to Figure 17-1), you have an opportunity to change your thought as you begin the second verse. Look through your song and determine how many sections it has. You know it's a new section because one of these things happens: A piano interlude (a solo section for the piano in between the vocal section) often leads to a new section, the music changes and adds different rhythms or moves to a new key, or the text changes and a new topic arises.

You can compare this study of your music to studying poetry. Each *poem,* or grouping of words, has a certain rhythm to it, called *meter.* When you know the meter, you can look farther to find the rhyme scheme. Knowing the rhyme scheme gives you a clue to how many sections the piece has.

The form of a song tells you how many sections you can expect to find.

- ✔ **Strophic,** which is similar to a hymn, means that the same music is repeated for each section of text, or each *stanza.*

- ✔ **Two part AB** means that two main sections may occur in order as AB or ABA, with the first section repeating. An example of an AABA song is the *Flintstone's* theme; an AB example is "(Baby You Can) Drive My Car," by The Beatles. You may think of other songs that fit because they have a verse and a chorus.

- ✔ **Through composed** means that the entire piece is new, with no repeats of any sections in any stanza. Examples of through composed songs include "Yesterday," by John Lennon and Paul McCartney, and "Stairway to Heaven," by Led Zeppelin.

If a section repeats, speculate about what made the composer or lyricist repeat those words. What reason necessitates saying the same words again? Exploring those reasons may help you discover how to create changes in your tone by changing what you're thinking. You need to sing a repeated part differently the second time than you did the first time. (And if it repeats a third or even fourth time, each repetition needs to be distinct from the others.)

Finding the minimum number of sections to a song tells you the minimum number of changes.

Using Musical Elements to Create Your Arrangement

When you start working on your new song, how do you create the arrangement that works for you? How do you make the song yours? You can start by listening to other arrangements to see and hear the elements each artist used to make the arrangement their own. If you look at the music for "Hound Dog" as sung by Elvis Presley, the music on the page may look bland compared to the sounds that you hear on the recording. Elvis used a variety of sounds with his voice to create a fun song. You can use variations in musical elements, such as dynamics (volume) or tempo (speed), or you can change the colors of your voice or vary the articulation. (If you want to know more about Elvis and his music, check out *Elvis For Dummies,* by Susan Doll, PhD [Wiley].)

You want to think of the song as a journey of music and lyrics. If it's a journey, you want changes and variations in that journey. If you repeat the same lyrics over and over, it may be fun, but it's not a journey for the listener and that's not the kind of song to choose for an audition or competition. Musicians talk about the hook in the song. The *hook* is the recurring and memorable part that gets the listener hooked. When you're searching for just the right song to arrange and make your own, remember that the hook can be the repeating rhythm, melody, or lyrics. You want a hook, but also a story to tell. Making only fun sounds may not be interesting enough to keep your audience listening for the three minutes it takes to sing the song.

You may have seen television shows such as *American Idol* or *The X Factor* that ask singers to bring in their own arrangement of a song or to sing a song they don't know. Because you sometimes have to sing a song a cappella, you want to know how to make it interesting without relying on the instruments. Using these suggestions on how to make the song your own, as well as what to explore to create your own arrangement, may come in handy when you're put on the spot and have to master and perform a new song in a short period of time. Build your technical skill so you can confidently apply it.

Comparing songs

"Get Down Tonight," recorded by K.C. & The Sunshine Band, is a great song for dancing, but the lyrics repeat a lot and it doesn't have a strong story. It's also a song that may sound boring with just the piano and no other instruments. "Simply Irresistible," as recorded by Robert Palmer, and "Lollipop," as recorded by The Chordettes, are two more examples of songs that have a great hook but may not have great stories or work without the instruments. They're fun songs, but not great choices to sing by yourself or without a major arrangement with your backup band.

On the other hand, "Desperado," as recorded by The Eagles, has a great story and simplicity that lends itself to a solo with piano. "Lipstick on Your Collar," as recorded by Connie Francis; "Blue Moon," written by Richard Rodgers and Lorenz Hart; and "Respect," as recorded by Aretha Franklin can also be arranged so that you sound great singing with a piano. These examples are just a few of the songs that have a great story, sound good with a piano, and work well for a one-person performance. The songs listed in Appendix A also make great story songs to sing as a solo and are appropriate levels for read-ers of this book.

You don't have to spend a lot of money paying a musician to arrange a song for you; you can experiment with some familiar songs to get the hang of making a song your own. Think of a familiar song that you know very well. You can use the hymn "Amazing Grace" or familiar tunes such as "Happy Birthday," "Old MacDonald," or even the song in this chapter, "Simple Things."

Articulation

Sing through the song as you normally do, noticing the articulation and flow of the melody. Now sing the song again and change the articulation. Make the consonants super crisp and really precise. When you articulate like this, you're most likely inspired to make precise sounds with your singing voice, similar to classical music. When you sing the song again, change the articu-lation so that the consonants and vowels are correct but not so crisp and precise. This laidback articulation is similar to what happens in a pop song or other contemporary songs that you hear on the radio. You can choose the best articulation for the type or song you're singing based on how you want to express the story of that song.

Dynamics

When you sing the song this time, sing it loudly. The meaning of the song may change when you sing it loudly. Now sing the song again, but softly. The third time you sing the song, vary the dynamics, singing some sections loudly and others softly. You want to gradually change the volume so your song builds toward the climax.

Tempo

The next element to explore is the tempo. Sing through the song slowly, and then sing through it at a fast tempo. When you've explored fast and slow, sing through the song and gradually change the tempo of the song. You can start slowly and gradually speed up, or vice versa — start fast and gradually slow it down. You want to explore which segments in the song make sense to sing faster and which sections make sense to sing slower. The changes in tempo don't have to be drastic — just change them enough to keep the song evolving.

Explaining prelude, interlude, and postlude

The *prelude,* or introduction, is the beginning of the song. The accompanist plays it on the piano before you start to sing. A prelude is important because the first word and note grows out of the musical introduction.

The *interlude* is a segment of music in between sections of a composition. In songs, the interlude usually occurs between segments of the song, and the pianist plays alone.

The *postlude* is the song's ending that concludes the musical and dramatic thoughts. The song isn't over until the pianist releases the last note of the postlude.

Using vocal variety

You can change the colors of your voice by using the information in Chapters 11 and 12 about the registers of the voice and resonance. You can sing the first phrase of your song in a head voice–dominated mix, the second phrase in a chest voice–dominated mix, and the next phrase using belt. That progression may happen more slowly in your song, but using variations in registration and resonance offers you a variety of sounds in your song. If you make the same exact sound throughout the song, it sounds repetitive after the first few phrases. Gradually changing the vocal sounds shows off your versatility and provides a changing and flowing journey of sound throughout the song.

You may choose to sing softly and use your head voice or falsetto. If you speed up the tempo, you may want to belt the song. To know which sounds work really well, record yourself singing and listen back. You may have to experiment for a while and record yourself several times before you really find the sounds that fit your new version of the song. Singers often tell me that it feels weird to change registers when they sing a song. Somehow they think that they're supposed to sing in the same register throughout the song. The singers you hear on the radio shift registers, and so can you. Unless a spunky dance beat requires you to belt it out for the entire song, you'll want variety in your sounds. Practice moving between registers in the exercises in Chapter 12 so you're ready to incorporate those transitions into your song.

Style

When performers arrange a song, they often sing through the song and change the style. They sing familiar songs but change them to sound different from what you normally hear. For example, you can sing "Amazing Grace" precisely and clearly, or you can sing it and pretend that you're an R&B star and add lots of riffs. You can also add a lot of twang and forward resonance and make it sound like a country song. Pretending that the song is from a specific style encourages you to use sounds that you typically hear in that type of song. Understanding what makes a song sound pop or country allows you then to use those elements in the song you choose to perform.

Accompanist

When you decide how you want to sing your song, mark your music with the directions so the accompanist knows how to follow you. You can highlight the tempo and dynamic markings to make sure that your accompanist sees them; if none are written in, write them within the piano part. You often see tempo markings above the vocal line. To make sure that your accompanist sees them, go ahead and write them in the space between the two sets of five lines down in the piano part. If you want to change the style of singing, you need to change what the accompanist plays. Some accompanists are great at this, and you can just ask them to play a piece in the style of a country song even if that's not what's written on the page. The accompanist simply changes the way the chords are played and perhaps changes the rhythm on the page to match your vocal changes. Accompanists who don't play a lot of contemporary material may be really good at changing the tempo and dynamics, but not so good at making up an accompaniment that sounds like a pop song.

Don't assume that an accompanist can change the accompaniment on the fly. If you want to change a familiar song at an audition to sound very different than how it's normally played and sung, ask in advance.

Chapter 18

Acting the Song

1f you think about the performances you've seen on television or live in a theater, you likely remember the choreography, the great scenery, or a singer jamming to a tune before a panel of judges and a huge crowd — all the pizzazz. What if you have to stand onstage and sing a song by yourself with only the piano for company? You've come to the right chapter for some ideas on making your solo routine a stellar performance.

Your biggest job as a singer is to say something when you sing. Standing up and singing memorized words is just the beginning. Apply your acting skills to a song for a powerful performance. Give your audience a reason to look at you and listen to your performance.

Seeing the Song As a Story

Every well-written song takes the listener on a journey that uses text and music to tell a story. In this section, you find out how to work with the text of your song to understand it as a story, how to work with your voice to portray that text with emotion, and how to get the music and text to work together.

Chatting it up before you sing

Well-written songs offer you an opportunity to create a partnership with the words and music. Working the text as a speech or monologue, you may find that the song doesn't mean what you originally thought it did. Just as when reading a poem for the first time, you may not initially absorb all the meanings.

The second time around, several new things may jump out at you. The more you read the text, the more you can enhance the relationship between your singing and the words coming out of your mouth.

Don't fall into the trap of thinking that just singing the song well is good enough. It isn't. Singing well is a wonderful start, but you want to take it a step farther. Saying words out loud forces you to decide what the words mean. For example, you can emphasize the words "I had a cat" in three different ways:

- ✔ If you emphasize *I,* you're saying that you — and probably you alone — had a cat.

- ✔ If you emphasize *had* you may mean that the cat is no longer with you.

- ✔ Emphasizing the word *cat* may mean that you had a cat instead of a dog.

Playing with the various words makes you think about what you're trying to say and how best to say it. As you speak through the text of your song, make specific choices about what you think the text means, as you did when you said, "I had a cat." Your specific choices give listeners an opportunity to really focus on your story so they hear the words, not just the glorious sounds of your voice.

Emphasizing repeated words is just as important. When your song repeats certain lyrics, you want to say them differently, as if each time they have a new meaning. Think of a line from your song and repeat it several times. Most likely, you emphasized it differently each time to try to get your point across. When you repeat the lyrics, you have another chance to get your audience to understand you.

When you begin to work your text as a monologue or add expression to your singing, you may find that your eyebrows tend to go up. If so, put a piece of clear tape on your forehead to convince them to go back down. Place the tape vertically on your forehead so you can feel it each time your eyebrows flex. With practice, you can find a way to express your thoughts without tightening anything on your face.

Musical responses

In songs, the music has something to say about the character and the text. The music is a vehicle for the voice to tell the story. As you listen to your song (the piano part recorded by your pianist or a recording of you singing the song), think about what the music has to say about the story. Often the setting of the text with the music enhances the delivery of the text. In the song "Wouldn't It Be Loverly," from *My Fair Lady,* Eliza Doolittle's text moves at the same pace as a person speaking the text. By setting the text at a normal speaking pace, the music helps you sound as if you're talking and telling a story with music. In the song "Ya Got Trouble," from *The Music Man,* you know just by hearing the sound of the accompaniment that Harold Hill isn't going to sing about what a beautiful morning it is. The short, detached sounds from the accompaniment tell you that trouble is brewing. Some songs include times when the singer gets to rest. During these times, the music is talking and you want to respond to the music and your upcoming text. Read on for suggestions on what to do during an interlude.

Accounting for interludes

If the song has an *interlude,* a passage in the music when you're not singing, you need to figure out how to handle that period of time. Interludes can be perplexing. What in the world do you do to kill that time? You think specific thoughts that support and continue the plot during musical interludes of a song. Subtext can take you from the musical introduction (prelude) right to the song's first line. An example of subtext in a song could be what the girl is thinking during the prelude (introduction music) of *Love Story,* recorded by Taylor Swift. In the prelude, she's thinking about the boy and what she'll say to him. Maybe she's finally gotten up enough nerve to tell him that she likes him and she's thinking about the best way to tell him. Or he may be packing his things because he's really mad at her and she's thinking (subtext) during the prelude about what she can say to get him to forgive her and stay.

The interlude may be really simple, but you still want to hear the music and let it be part of your story. Think of the piano as your scene partner. Even if you're onstage alone singing a song, the piano is offering you some feedback within the structure of the music. You don't even have to read music to figure it out. You just need to listen to the music and decide how it's helping to tell the story.

Exploring Character

You want to make your performance well rounded and interesting to the audience, so you need to do some detective work on your song. Take a close look into the character singing the song. Every song has a character and a story to tell. Sometimes the character is just like you and sometimes it's someone very different.

Getting into character means temporarily inhabiting the life and circumstances of a character for a story. In this case, the story is presented in the lyrics of the song. If the lyrics are from an opera or musical, your song and your character have an entire life for you to explore. Songs from the radio usually aren't from a show, so you get to decide the circumstances.

If you just can't find the answers to some of the questions about the character singing the song, make a good guess based on the other details you've read in the script, or create a story or scenario that supports the words of the song. Making up the missing details of your character's life helps you create a complete picture of exactly who this person is. As long as your scenario leads you to say and sing the words on the page, it can work. If your scenario is so far fetched that it distracts you and you're too busy to sing, make it a little less complicated for now. Simple is good.

Characterizing your character

Answering fundamental questions about the character singing your song leads you to some specific details about how to portray that character when you're alone onstage.

You want to uncover the facts given in the lyrics. Some basic questions to answer include these:

- ✔ **What is the character's name?** The character in a radio song is you.

- ✔ **How old is the character?** Your character's age and physical condition play into how you interpret the song. Young characters move differently than older characters.

- ✔ **What is the character's occupation or station in life?** Knowing that your character is the local sheriff means that he dresses, carries himself, and behaves differently than the town drunk who lives in the alley behind the gas station. The drunk may slur his words, but the sheriff may be well spoken.

- ✔ **What does the character look like?** Knowing the character's occupation gives you your first clues to how the character looks and carries himself. The town drunk probably is disheveled, with wrinkled clothes and a red face from too much alcohol. The rest of the details you can glean from the text. If you're in a theater production, often the other characters in the show say things about your character, and you can use this information to help you further decide what your character may look like.

- ✔ **Who are you singing to?** If your song is from a musical or opera, you usually know who you're singing the song to. With songs on the radio, you generally get to decide who you're singing to — even if that person isn't in the room. You simply imagine that the person is in the room and pretend that you see their reaction. All those conversations that you have with people who aren't in the room — such as when you argue with your boss while you're brushing your teeth — use the same kind of visualization you do while you sing your song. You pretend that your boss reacts and you reply. Same goes for your song: Choose someone to sing to and decide how that person reacts to what you say.

✔ **What do you want from the person you're singing to?** Do you want him to leave you alone and move out of the apartment? Or do you want him to forgive you for something you said or did?

✔ **How does your character change during the course of the song, and what stage is the character in during this song?** Eliza Doolittle changes drastically during the course of *My Fair Lady.* By knowing the story, you know what stage of character development she's in when you sing her song. If your song isn't from a show, do your detective work to determine the facts from the lyrics, and then choose what you think should happen during the course of your song. Keep your scenario simple.

✔ **Where does this song take place?** Knowing where the story takes place can also change how you sing a song. If the setting of your song is the middle of a hot summer afternoon, that's very different than singing a song as you watch a blizzard outside your window. Marc Cohn sang "Walking in Memphis," which gives a clear picture of where the song is taking place. Even if it's not spelled out in black and white, make a choice about where the song is set and picture that place in your mind.

Knowing your character's background gets you to dig for the basic information available about your character. Allow yourself some time to digest the lyrics as you're working on the song. See the big picture first. Summarize the details and then move on to the smaller details. You want to know about both the inner and outer lives of the character.

If you know this basic information about your character, you know whether this person is similar to you or the exact opposite. Personally, I love playing characters who are opposite from my own personality. What better way to live a secret life?

Discovering your character's motivation

Singing is a way of expressing huge, heightened emotions. A song conveys feelings so big that the character can't just say it; he has to sing about it. Just in case you don't rush into song every few minutes in your everyday life, keep reading to discover how you can get to that huge, heightened sense of awareness that makes you just want to burst out singing.

Before singing a song, you want to know a few things. You want to know what happened just before this song to motivate your character to sing and say the words. Why does your character sing, and how does your character intend to overcome any obstacles? In this section, you uncover the answers in some familiar songs so you can fill in the blanks about your own song. Some songs aren't from a musical or opera. For these songs, you need to do enough work with the text that your imagination leads you to the right answers.

Some event usually motivates the character to sing a song. Maybe the character has a problem to overcome, is in a predicament he wants to change, or wants to help someone. The character needs some sort of predicament, good or bad, to sing. The obstacles the character encounters also are pretty important. The predicament or obstacle can be unrequited love, happiness so intense you have to tell the world, or a bad relationship that you don't know how to end. Aunt Eller in *Oklahoma!* sings "The Farmer and the Cowman Should be Friends" because she wants the men to stop fighting and get along. In the movie *The Wizard of Oz,* the Lion is motivated to sing "If I Were The King of the Forest" because he wants courage and he's tired of being afraid. Another song with a specific motivation is "Return to Sender," which you may have heard Elvis Presley sing. He's motivated to sing the song because his letters keep coming back, even though he's said he's sorry, and it's breaking his heart.

Planning actions to get something done

You want to plan an action that helps your character get what he wants. An action sounds like something that you have to leap around the stage to accomplish, but it's not. You can stand still and have a plan of action. After you decide why you're singing the song, you create a plan to get what you want and overcome the obstacle. An example of an *aria* (a song from an opera) that illustrates a specific action comes from the opera *Carmen.* Carmen is arrested, and Don José is supposed to take her to prison. She sings the aria "Seguidilla" to entice Don José into letting her go. Her plan of action is to get him to release her, and she gets her way because she seduces him with her body and voice.

Getting Physical

Most singers feel stiff if they just stand still and sing a song. Knowing how to move, where to move, and what to move when you sing keeps you looking good as you sing. When singing a song, your choices are to stand still or move around the stage. You find some advice on how much to move in the "Movin' and groovin' with your song" section, later in this chapter, and you get help with gesturing as you're singing in the "Gesturing appropriately" section, coming up later in this chapter. Because focusing your eyes is important for your song, you find out just ahead who to look at while you're performing — and why you shouldn't close your eyes while you sing.

Figuring out where to focus

When singing a song, you can sometimes look in one spot and sometimes look around. Knowing the story of your song helps you understand the type of song you're singing, and this understanding tells you where to focus your eyes. If you're talking to just one person, you may focus on the back wall or a place out in front of you. An example of a song in which you may talk to just one person is "I Can't Make You Love Me," by Mike Reid and Allen Shamblin. If that person isn't in the room, but you're daydreaming of him, you may gaze out into the distance longingly. An example of this is Elton John singing for Princess Diana's funeral. She wasn't present, but you knew that he was singing to her. Your eyes may move around when you're talking to a group of people, but they don't move like you're watching a tennis match. In the opera *Così fan tutte,* Guglielmo talks to all the women in the audience when he sings, *"Donne mie, la fate a tanti,"* which translates, "I would like a word with all you lovely women."

Notice other people as they're telling a story: Their eyes automatically look around in different ways. When you're trying to remember something, you may look up at the ceiling. This is a common reflex when you're trying to dig something out of your memory bank. When you're watching one person, you may hold your gaze on that person and not look away. If you start to think about what you're saying, you may look away from your audience as you think. These are all natural and normal movements of your eyes. When singing a song, you can also have this same natural movement of your eyes moving away from the person you're addressing and then back.

Closing your eyes isn't an option when you want to act and sing. In everyday conversations with other people, you keep your eyes open. You don't have a conversation with someone and close your eyes unless you're lying on the couch talking to someone across the room. Singing a song involves having a conversation with someone and telling a story. You want your eyes open to talk to your audience. Closing your eyes cuts off your biggest means of communicating with your audience. They're left out because, by closing your eyes, you're communicating only with yourself. Give your audience a reason to look at you and watch you when you sing.

If you get distracted looking someone in the eye as you're singing, try looking at their hairline instead. Try it sometime on some friends and ask them if they can tell whether you're looking them in the eye. More often than not, they probably have no idea. Ask your friend to do the same to you so you can see what you look like. Try this until you're comfortable singing your song and maintaining your focus on your task.

Gesturing appropriately

The big question beginning singers ask is what to do with their hands. Well, what do you do with your hands as you speak? If your hands normally move when you speak, you may feel stiff if they remain frozen at your side during your song. Work the song as a monologue to discover what's happening and how the character may react to the actions in the story. Basically, you gesture when you react. For example, think about how you'd move in reaction to "Whoa! Don't bring that spider any closer to me!" Or how would your hands gesture if you were saying, "I wanted to buy that doll, but the woman snatched it out of my hand" or "Here I am!" or "When are you going to clean up this incredibly messy room?" If you recognize the same kind of opportunities in a song, you feel more like yourself gesturing with your hands than trying to plan something interesting to do during your song.

You may have noticed that when you gestured and said the phrases, your arms moved to gesture and then dropped. That motion is too abrupt when singing. You want to gesture and then release the gesture and move your arms and hands back down. On the other hand, sometimes people go too far in gesturing by holding the gesture for a long time. You may look frozen as if you aren't sure how to put your hands down.

The following exercise gets your hands in the right place for gesturing:

1. **Put your hands by your side.**

2. **With your thumbs leading the way, move your hands up toward each other and then out in a big arc, with your elbows away from your body and your palms up and open.**

3. **Draw the Chanel logo — two back-to-back Cs,)(— in the air.**

   Start with your hands at your side and trace your hands from the bottom right hand of each *C* until your hands are out to the side of your body, with your hands about as high as your shoulders. To make the gesture look natural, you want distance between your elbows and the sides of your body.

Gestures can vary widely, but this is the most basic shape of a gesture. As you practice this movement, you'll be able to do it faster and vary it slightly by using just one arm or by moving your arms higher for those times you need a big emphasis for your text.

Avoid these gesturing pitfalls:

- **Pantomiming:** Pantomimic gestures only mime the text. For example, if you plan specific movements without thinking about why they help your story, such as lifting your hand to the sky when you say the words "Moon and stars," or placing your hand on your chest when you say "heart," you're not doing your job as an actor. What roles do those two elements play in your story? Your audience knows exactly where to find the moon and stars — give them something more. Pantomime may work if you're creating a comic character, and pantomime is one way to play the character. However, serious songs work best when the gestures come from what you're saying and thinking about the song, not from pantomime.

- **Choreographed moves:** If your song is fun and spunky, allow your joy of singing the song to reflect through your story, not through choreography. You don't need to plan any movements before you do your work on the text of your song. You want the gesture to feel organic, as if you're experiencing it for the first time every time you sing the song. If you've chosen a dance number for your song, you can assume that some movement is in order. Singing while dancing requires a great deal of stamina. Plan where to breathe in the song so you can practice your breath control.

Translating a song in a foreign language

Singing in another language is common in classical music. But singing a song in another language doesn't let you off the hook with your responsibilities as an actor. You want to know exactly what's happening in each phrase so you can deliver each word with conviction.

- **Create a word-for-word translation.** The first step is to look up each word so you know exactly what you're saying. It's tough to find the operative word in the line if you aren't sure what half of the words mean. When you find the definition for each word, create a paraphrased version of the text in English. If the word-for-word translation turns out to be, "To you with love I only," you can paraphrase to "I love only you," which makes perfect sense.

- **Compare the word-for-word translation with a paraphrased version of the text.** You may find the paraphrased version on the copy of your song underneath the foreign-language text. Remember that you can't really commit to the paraphrase until you know which word means what in the original language. Sometimes the poetic

translation underneath the original text has little to do with the original meaning of the poem. Always do your own translation as well, just to check.

- **Practice speaking the word-for-word translation in English, the paraphrase in English, and the text in the foreign language.** After you do all your homework, you want to work the text as a monologue, both in English and in the foreign language. The operative words in the English language may not be in the same order as in the foreign language. Strive to be a great actor and singer, regardless of the language or style of music.

Some of the newer books being published for classical songs or songs from operas, called *arias,* include word-for-word translations and paraphrases of the text. If you want to sink your teeth into the language, get a good dictionary with a pronunciation guide as well as the definitions of the words. If you buy the dictionary with the pronunciation guide, you save yourself so much time looking up the diction rules. You can also consult numerous Web sites for translating text.

Movin' and groovin' with your song

When you sing for an audience, you want the listener to both see and hear you connect your story and singing. Whatever movements you make around a stage or around the room need to enhance your singing and the story. Being able to move and sing is important, yet starting small is best. Consider these tips on coordinating movement with music:

- ✔ At home, practice singing while doing simple tasks, just to practice doing two things at once.

- ✔ When you're comfortable moving and singing, speak through your song lyrics and notice what gestures you make. Knowing how you gesture when you speak helps you figure out how to move when you're singing.

- ✔ Some songs don't require much movement. Err on the busy side at first when you're practicing, and then pare the movements until you're sure that you're moving in response to what you're saying. Just moving for its own sake when you're singing doesn't enhance your song. For example, classical songs don't require much movement or many gestures.

If singing is new to you, adding some sort of movement may be too much for you right now. Take it one step at a time when you're figuring out how to perform your new technique with a new song.

Chapter 19

Confronting Your Fear of Performing

In This Chapter

▶ Identifying the root of the anxiety

▶ Tackling the anxiety by preparing

▶ Evaluating your progress at each performance

*P*erformance anxiety is a big problem among performers of all kinds and at all levels of experience. Finding ways of dealing with anxiety and turning nerves and adrenaline into positive forces in your performance are just as important as great technique. For the times when those butterflies in your stomach get out of hand, this chapter offers some dependable methods of working through your anxiety.

Facing the Symptoms

Knowing what you're afraid of is half the battle. After you pinpoint the source of your fear, you can take charge of it.

These fears are the most common fears:

- ✔ Cracking during the performance and not being able to hit the high note
- ✔ Looking stupid in front of friends
- ✔ Forgetting the words to the song
- ✔ Fearing success or failure, rejection, or the unknown

Naming the fear enables you to go after the problem and beat it. Throughout this chapter, you can read about the common concerns and determine what's scaring you. After you find the source, move forward and find a solution to eliminate the whole problem, not just the symptom.

Running in place simulates adrenaline

A rush of adrenaline brings about a racing heart. You can duplicate that feeling by running in place until you're out of breath . . . and then singing your song. Being out of breath while you practice helps you get used to singing phrases when you desperately want to just exhale and not sing. Breathlessness is similar to what happens when anxiety strikes during a performance. Every time you take the breath, you can feel it falling into your body. As it falls into your body, realize that you can sing even when your heart is pounding. It's just not easy.

You may find comforting the knowledge that thousands of other singers face the same icky anxiety you feel right before a performance. The symptoms include butterflies in the stomach, shaky knees, dry mouth (sometimes called cottonmouth), a sudden urge to cry or run away, trembling hands, a racing heart rate, nausea, cold hands but sweaty underarms, and the urge to pee no matter how many times you visit the bathroom. Did you find any of your symptoms on that list? I certainly see mine.

News flash: Adrenaline isn't the enemy! In all honesty, you want a little adrenaline to boost your performance.

Assuming that you must be calm before a performance sets you up for pangs of anxiety when you don't turn out to be as cool as a cucumber. Expecting to be nervous and jittery, on the other hand, can enable you to sing through your anxiety. In fact, you can use the fight-or-flight excitement of adrenaline coursing through your body to enhance your performance. In reframing your thoughts about the performance, you change from fight-or-flight adrenaline to a rush of excitement that can help you seize an opportunity.

Alleviating Anxiety through Preparation

With your symptoms out in the open, you can talk about how to relieve your anxiety. Make a choice to change your thoughts about your performance. If you continually dread the symptoms that you know are going to arise, you won't get past the first paragraph without thinking that this tactic won't work. So remind yourself that you're anxious because you fear *something;* the symptoms don't just randomly appear.

Practicing well

The biggest key to alleviating anxiety is preparation. *Preparing* isn't the same as *overpracticing* or aiming for perfection. Overpracticing is practicing so much that you lose sight of the joy of singing and focus only on singing perfectly. Aiming for perfection takes the fun out of singing because everything becomes a contest, if only with yourself.

The following pointers can help get you prepared for performing.

- **Stay positive and motivated as you practice.** Figure out a way to motivate yourself. What kind of reward do you need to get yourself to practice regularly? People who don't like being alone often don't like to practice. You must recognize that and then be disciplined to do your work. Your positive thinking during your practice sessions carries over into your performance.

- **Set goals for each practice session.** The first practice session goal may be to successfully sing through the song without words to find consistent breath flow (see Chapter 4). The second practice session goal may be to keep that same easy flow of breath as you sing the words. Trying to tackle too many goals at once causes frustration.

- **Practice at the level you intend to perform.** You have to practice all the details of your song separately, and then gradually put them all together until you consistently create the sounds that you want to create in your performance.

- **Set a deadline for memorizing the song.** Your long-term memory needs to have locked in the melody and words of the song. If you attempt to memorize the song the night before the performance, you may be overwhelmed trying to deal with the excitement of performing and the details of remembering the words at the same time.

  I recommend having the song memorized at least one week before a performance. You then have seven days to work on the song without looking at the music. If you're singing a group of songs, you may want to have them memorized earlier so you have time to work with the accompanist and work on your acting objectives (see Chapter 18) as you use your singing technique.

- **Speak quickly through your text to help you remember the words.** Forgetting the words of a song that you've memorized usually happens because your concentration momentarily slips. For example, you may start thinking about being happy that the high note sounded good and, suddenly, as you're getting back to business, you have no idea where you are in the song. Practicing your concentration and speaking quickly through the text on a regular basis helps you commit the text to your long-term memory, not just your short-term thoughts. After you memorize the text of your song, speak the words aloud quickly without pausing for punctuation.

Playing to your strengths

Doing things that you know you're good at builds confidence and relieves anxiety. Setting yourself up for success by playing to your strengths makes even more sense when you're nervous about performing.

Use the following tips to put yourself in a winning frame of mind:

- ✔ **Choose pieces that enhance your strengths.** Singing one song in a performance means that you have an opportunity to find a piece that really shows your areas of expertise. When you need to choose ten minutes of music, the task naturally gets harder, but finding the appropriate material is part of the preparation. Chapter 16 deals with choosing music.

- ✔ **Focus on your strengths.** Singing songs that require agility is a great goal when you feel confident with that material. If not, make the performance showcase your fabulous tone, breath control, or any other aspect that you feel confident sharing.

Managing your thoughts

Performers who don't experience performance anxiety may tell you to just get over it and stop being afraid. I like to call those people adrenaline junkies. They love that rush of adrenaline just before the performance. But trying to stop being afraid may only frustrate you. You have to deal with your anxiety, which is different from adrenaline. Anxiety adds a sickening sensation on top of the adrenaline. You don't want to stop the adrenaline — you want to eliminate the underlying fear that leads to anxiety about performing.

Anxiety brings negative thoughts into your head. Negative thoughts may try to convince you that you're going to forget the words even though you know the song well. Just hearing so much busy talking inside your head can ruin your concentration and make you forget the words.

Sometimes you can use negative practice to find the extremes of your symptoms. Try making the symptoms worse the next time you practice — for instance, visualize or imagine a critical audience. You may experience some symptoms of anxiety. Notice what those symptoms are and how you feel about the audience. As you feel that sense of dread, sing through your music. Visualize yourself being able to complete your task, regardless of how grumpy your imaginary audience looks.

Making a list of the negative thoughts that frequently pop into your mind is a way to manage your thoughts. Facing those thoughts helps you recognize that they aren't helpful and can prompt a switch to positive thoughts instead. Making a list of affirmations to counter your negative thoughts also can help you retrain your mind to focus on the positive. Affirmations include saying things such as, "My singing is improving each day" and "I'm confident that my breath control gets better with each practice session."

You can create a performance cue that summarizes your goal and helps you focus on the positive. For example, your performance cue can be "Release and breathe" (release tension when you open the muscles in the body to inhale) or "Drop and open" (release all the way down into your feet as you inhale and open the back space for the next phrase). Keep the cue positive — something to do instead of what *not* to do. Instead of saying "Don't mess up," you can use "Stay focused" as a positive cue that helps you remember to stay in the moment.

Getting up the nerve

Your thoughts may turn to the audience whenever you become concerned about what they think of you and your singing. You can't get rid of the audience; after all, an audience is a necessity for your performance. You can, however, pretend that the members of the audience aren't really in the audience. You don't have to sing directly to the audience or look them in the eyes. You can look over their heads so you don't have to worry about reading the expression on their faces when you look them right in the eyes.

Doing your job as you sing means that you must tell a story. Insecurity can lead you to believe that everyone is looking at you harshly. Reframing your thoughts so that you accept the audience and let go of the hostile image you may have of the audience can go a long way toward overcoming your doubts. You've probably heard this suggestion for overcoming stage fright: Imagine that all the people in the audience are sitting in their underwear. You can also remind yourself that the audience chose to attend your performance, and they want to hear you sing well.

Building performance focus

Have you ever been so focused on a task that you lost track of time or were startled when someone came up behind you? You want this same kind of focus as you perform. Focus totally on your task at hand, leaving the rest of the stuff for later.

To help you practice concentrating, try these suggestions:

✔ **Stage some distractions.** Practice in front of an audience of friends and ask them to randomly whisper, rustle paper, drop a book, or stand up and walk around while you're singing. The first few times, you may lose your composure, but just laugh it off and keep trying until you can hold your concentration and ignore the distractions.

✔ **Practice concentration.** Set a timer for five minutes and practice focusing totally on your singing for those five minutes. Five minutes may seem like a short amount of time — until you have to fill it with only one task. You may find your mind wandering and thinking about something else. That's okay. Set the timer and try again.

Working up to concentrating for the full five minutes may take a few days. You can also practice focusing and then intentionally letting your mind wander so you can tell the difference.

✔ **Leave distractions at the door.** That fight you had earlier in the day, the report that's due tomorrow, your upcoming vacation — any number of everyday concerns may occupy your mind. Create a ceremony that enables you to leave those distractions at the door.

For example, you may want to put a basket outside your practice room door and mentally dump all your worries and frustrations into it before you enter the room. You can also write a to-do list before your session so you know exactly what you need to think about right after you practice. Acknowledge that you still have to resolve those issues in your mind, and then move to the current task at hand.

Cracking isn't the end of the world

Cracking happens when the singing muscles stop working properly just long enough for the sound to stop. Maintaining a steady flow of air, especially on high notes, helps prevent the crack. Sometimes singers crack when they're suffering from severe allergy problems or other ailments that make their voices feel different. Young singers may crack as they figure out how to sing higher notes. Young men may experience some cracking during puberty and afterward as they discover how to sing higher notes without too much pressure in the throat.

Giving yourself permission to experience the crack enables your body to release some of the tension associated with the fear. Ninety-nine percent of the time, whenever I give my students permission to crack, or ask them to please let the note crack just to know what it feels like, they don't crack. Give yourself permission to not be perfect. It's impossible to be perfect. If you average the one note that isn't so perfect with the other hundred notes in the song, you have pretty slim odds for cracking.

And if you do crack on a high note, it isn't the end of the world. I've seen singers crack, and members of the audience didn't boo, because they understood that it was just part of the growing experience for that singer. The first time I saw a professional crack in a concert, I was secretly thrilled — not because the singer cracked, but because he kept going, with the understanding that his voice wasn't working properly at that one moment in time. The rest of the notes in the concert were glorious, but the cracked one gave me hope.

The fear of cracking may disappear after you sing the same phrase several times without any problem. Make a list of all the things you have to do when you sing (your practice to-do list from Chapter 10) and keep practicing them until you can do them all at the same time. You may have to practice doing two skills at once before you try to do four. Practicing these skills helps prevent cracking: keeping a steady flow of air moving as you sing (see Chapter 4), opening your throat (see Chapter 6), and knowing your capabilities by understanding what your voice can do in each area, such as your head voice (see Chapter 11). Enabling yourself to do several things at one time takes courage and determination. Most people are capable of multitasking, and so are you. You can drive your car, change the station on the radio, and have a conversation with the person in the passenger's seat all at the same time. You can certainly apply this same process to singing.

You may find that acting helps you sing the high note without cracking. You may get so caught up with your story in the heat of the moment that you go to sing the high note and the breath just moves for you. How cool is that?

One of my colleagues gave me two pieces of great advice a few years ago: "Never let anyone live in your head rent free" and "Have conversations only with people who are in the room." Table any conversations in your head with people who aren't in the room with you. What great advice!

Performing to Build Confidence

Even with all the tips I offer, you must perform to get over performance anxiety. You must put yourself in the hot seat on a regular basis to find your groove. Basketball players practice their shots so their bodies remember those sensations in the heat of the moment. You, too, must put your skills to the test in the heat of the moment. You know you're ready to take it public when:

- ✔ You have a burning desire to move past the anxiety.
- ✔ Your technical skills are polished enough that you can depend on them.
- ✔ You find a song that complements your current abilities.

Find a small gig to get you started. By *gig*, I mean anywhere you can sing. Sing for one friend, then for your family, and then for a small gathering, such as at a nursing home. Sing in the church choir with the group, and then sing a solo for a Sunday school class before singing it for the entire congregation. Or sing with the community chorus: Sing with the chorus, then sing small solos, and then shoot for the solo in front of the community.

Devising a game plan

For every performance, make a plan of action for success. Assuming that you're going to succeed means that you will. Assuming that you're going to fail is the same as giving in to those voices in your head.

Reframe those stupid things people have said to you in the past about your performing abilities. Being critical is human nature, but remember that it's only one person's opinion. If I'd listened to things people said to me, I'd never have written this book or dared to be a singer in New York.

Try these tips to get your game plan in place:

✔ **Make a specific timeline to get yourself ready to sing at the time of your performance.** See Chapter 10 for more on creating a practice routine. After you develop your practice routine, you'll know how long it takes for your voice to be ready to sing at your best. You can plan your warm-up time for the day of your performance to get ready. Consider these suggestions:

- Take time to vocalize or warm up the notes you'll sing in the performance.

- Vocalize long enough for your voice to be singing at your peak when you walk on the stage.

- On the performance day, sing through your song enough times that you feel confident, but not so many times that your voice feels tired.

✔ **Invite someone who helps boost your confidence.** Do you know someone who can encourage you as you walk out for the performance? Discuss your fears with this friend or confidant and then discuss your feelings after the performance. You may find that your perception of that awful note isn't what your friend heard. Having a support system with you helps you quiet negative thoughts that may creep into your head.

✔ **Look at each performance as an opportunity to succeed.** You have to expect success before you can achieve it. Success doesn't just happen, but you can make it happen.

✔ **Practice what you intend to do.** If you plan to take a moment and take a breath before you begin to sing your song, practice it that way. Taking that moment to quiet your mind and settle your racing heart is worth it. By practicing and visualizing your success, you can more easily make it happen. You can also practice walking across the stage, singing your song, and then bowing. You may have to practice this in your living room, but you want to practice what you're going to experience in the performance. (See Chapter 24 for more tips on performing well.)

✔ **Chart your improvement.** Make a list of what you want to accomplish, and, with each performance, shoot to accomplish one more task on the list.

For example, the first task may be remembering all the words. By practicing with distractions at home, you boost your ability to concentrate. When you remember all the words at your first performance, you may want to try remembering the words and breathing consistently at the second performance. Just getting the breath in your body and then using it helps with many other technical problems. Give yourself a gold star when you achieve each goal.

Before singing your song in public, try it in front of some friends. If you give smaller performances a few times before your big one, the song may seem familiar and not so scary.

Evaluating your performance

Progress happens because of each step you take. After every performance, look at how you did and how you felt, using the lists in the following sections. Because everything in your life affects your singing, decide what steps worked well for you and modify the ones that didn't.

Looking at preparation and performance issues

Check the technical aspects of your performance to discover what you can improve upon. Look at what did and didn't work well, and make adjustments for next time. Ask these questions after your performance:

✔ Did you rehearse enough with the accompanist?

✔ Did you work the song enough from memory?

✔ What did you do well during the performance?

✔ Did you get enough sleep the night before or in the days before the performance?

✔ Was your warm-up long enough, high enough, and early or late enough in the day?

✔ Were you focused on the moment (or on the audience's reaction to your singing)?

✔ Did the steps in your pre-performance routine work well?

✔ Did you leave enough time for dressing?

✔ Did you take time to visualize the performance in your mind?

Be fair when charting your progress. Seeing gradual improvement in your quest to manage adrenaline and fear is important. Several months may pass before you feel comfortable singing in public, so give yourself some time. After each performance, list what you did well. When you accomplish more than what's on your list, recognizing that accomplishment is important. Taking consistent steps toward your goal is the key.

Be brave. Take a risk. You won't know until you dare to try.

Checking your anxieties

To ease your anxiety, answer the following questions to help you remember how you felt.

- ✔ **How did you feel right before the performance?** If this performance is the first one you're evaluating, the answer to this question may be, "I felt unprepared, terrified, or nauseous." Recognizing these symptoms may help you realize that they aren't debilitating and may ease up over time.

- ✔ **What were your symptoms of anxiety, if any?** The symptoms may include sweating, a racing heart, and the urge to run away. By tracking the symptom, you can see that it lessens with each performance or that you just make the choice not to run away, because you enjoy the performance after you get to the stage.

- ✔ **What was your level of anxiety at the beginning of the performance? In the middle of the performance? At the end of the performance? After the performance?** Many singers say their anxiety is worse just before the performance but that it goes away as they begin singing. If the anxiety hits in the middle of the performance, you were probably anticipating the high note and worrying about how to sing it. Continuing to work on your technique allows you to gain more confidence in your technique, to alleviate the stress over that part of your voice. Stress after the performance may mean that you're worried about what people may say to you after the performance.

Asking these questions helps you see your progress over the course of a few weeks or months.

Chapter 20

Auditioning a Song

. . . .

In This Chapter

▶ Getting the lowdown on auditions

▶ Picking a winning song

▶ Preparing for the big day and more

▶ Finding out who and what to expect

. . . .

*W*ant to audition for the local theater or opera company? A Broadway show? Reality TV? A rock band? Before planning your debut, you need to know how to prepare for an audition. In this chapter, you explore how to choose and prepare an appropriate song for the audition. You also find out about what to expect at an audition so that you're prepared to knock their socks off!

Auditioning is a skill that you can develop. For auditions, you want to make sure that your singing technique is in tip-top shape for the style of music you want to sing. Check out Chapter 14 for training for different styles of singing. This chapter outlines what you need to know when you're ready to audition for a performance.

You may also want to get some advice from someone who understands the audition process, such as a voice teacher, acting teacher, or coach. This person can help you choose your song, hone some basic skills that will help you present yourself at the audition, and decide whether your material is good for your voice.

Tailoring Your Audition for Any Venue and Any Style of Music

Different styles of music have specific guidelines for auditioning. No matter what style you sing, here are the big things you want to keep in mind for any audition:

- ✔ **You want a great song to showcase your talent.** Sometimes you're told what to sing at an audition and sometimes you choose. Either way, you want the song to showcase you and your talent. The people you're auditioning for are meeting you through your song. What kind of song you choose says a lot about you.

- ✔ **You need to prove that you're an entertainer.** If you're shy, you need to step out of your shell at an audition to be a soloist. If you're auditioning, you're saying that you want to be in front of an audience and entertain people. The person hiring you needs to know that you can sell your song. Think about the successful performers you've seen. They show spunk and personality and really put themselves into their song.

The following sections include basic guidelines for auditions for different styles of music.

At the opera

In the operatic world, knowing your specific voice type or voice category, which is also called a *fach* (pronounced "fahk"), and sticking to it is important. See Chapter 2 for more details about the different types of voices and voice categories. Listing only *arias* (songs from an opera) within a specific vocal category on your audition form or resume is a good idea.

By listing arias from several different categories, you give the impression that you haven't yet determined your voice type — or, worse, that you don't know what you're doing.

Skills that you have to demonstrate at the opera audition include the following:

- ✔ Solid musicianship
- ✔ An ability to present the music exactly as it is written on the page
- ✔ Versatility in several languages
- ✔ Acting ability

Opera companies are looking for singers who sing well, look the part, and can also act. The opera world includes a lot of competition, and companies can be choosy.

Onstage at the theater

In musical theater, you need to switch your style of singing with ease. Right after you sing your lovely head voice selection, such as "I Could Have Danced All Night" from *My Fair Lady,* you may be asked for your belt song (an example of a belt song is "Tomorrow" from *Annie*) or pop-rock song (such as "Take Me or Leave Me" from *Rent*). Bouncing back and forth between the styles is expected, and you have to practice all three until they're comfy. You may find some musical theater performers who aren't belters, but you're better off knowing how to do all three.

At the musical theater audition, you're expected to use great acting skills to portray the story and take the listener on a journey in a variety of songs ranging from standards to pop-rock songs. The journey may last only 16 bars, but you have to take the audience for a ride, no matter how short the trip. You also want to dance well, or at least move really well. Sometimes auditions are held for nondancers, but most of the time you have to dance or move well to get into the musical.

Research performers who have previously played the role you're auditioning for to see whether your look is similar. After you make it through the doors, you may be *typed.* Typing at a musical theater audition doesn't mean that your fingertips fly across a keyboard. *Typing* refers to whether you're the right *type* for the role. The *casting panel* (usually made up of the casting director, director, musical director, and choreographer) look at you to determine whether you're physically right for the role. If you physically fit what they're looking for, you get to stay at the audition and sing and dance.

In the club

If you're a jazz, country, pop-rock, or R&B singer, you may want to audition for gigs in clubs. If you have a chance to audition for a local bar or nightclub (or a similar venue), your audition works much differently than an audition for opera or theater. In those genres, the show usually is already written; you're auditioning for a specific part. When you audition to play in a club, you make up the show!

You may write the music or perform groups of songs that have a particular theme to keep an audience clapping and singing along. Skills that you have to show off include great storytelling while singing and showmanship. You need a spark in your performance so that people want to watch you. For this kind of audition, you want to have a group of songs ready to show that you can hold the audience's attention for at least a half-hour set. You may sing only one song at the audition, but you want to have more options ready.

During an audition for a band, the singer sings some songs along with the band members so they can get a sense of how the singer's voice sounds and how well that singer blends with the group. You need a good ear to hold your melody and blend with the instruments, and you need to be confident when you sing so the band follows you. Vocally, you need to purposely make varied sounds, from clear tones to breathy and wispy tones, to portray the text of the song.

Club singers often perform in dark, smoky clubs and need to keep their body and voice healthy.

If you're not auditioning with a band, find songs that work well with piano and don't require a back-up band to sound good. Or bring your own tracks. When you perform pop-rock or R&B, you may have to dance and sing at the same time. Showmanship counts a great deal in this business, but the showmanship should enhance great singing technique.

On television

Auditioning for television is thrilling, but it may feel like a different world if you've performed only in small theaters or the church choir. Here are some basic guidelines for auditioning your song for a televised performance:

- ✔ **Self-confidence is a must.** Being confident means letting go of your shyness but not being cocky. You want to be mentally prepared so you can handle the stress of a high-pressure audition. Self-confidence makes your audience feel at ease because they don't have to worry about you — they can enjoy your performance. Being cocky may turn them off because it may look like you're too good for them. You want to show a spark of star power without being arrogant.

- ✔ **Choose material that highlights your strength and is appropriate for the audition.** You have to determine your strength and which song will show off your assets. If you aren't sure about the material, hire a reputable coach to give you feedback.

- ✔ **The camera is your friend.** If someone asks you to *slate,* he wants you to announce your name and your song to the camera. The camera picks up every little detail, so practice in front of a camera prior to the audition. A small hand-held camcorder is fine. Record yourself practicing your audition. Pay attention to your body language; do you appear confident? Ask someone who has done television auditions to give you feedback.

- ✔ **Your outfit really matters.** Wearing something that shows your body at its best is key for a television audition. The outfit should show your style and represent your personality.

Choosing Audition Songs to Highlight Your Strengths

Choosing songs to practice is different than choosing songs for an audition. You want to practice songs that expand and challenge your vocal technique. But songs for the audition need to highlight your strengths and accomplishments from all those hours of practice. When you audition, you need a variety of stories and acting choices, as well as multiple vocal colors and good range. You also need to research the audition so you know who and what you're auditioning. You can then highlight your strengths appropriately. The following sections explain in more detail.

The hardest part of auditioning is choosing the songs to sing. Choosing songs that are perfect for you and that show off your talents is an art. This artful skill takes time to develop, so keep looking at songs to continue expanding your book of audition songs.

If you can, find out what kind of song is appropriate for your audition. If you're auditioning for musical theater in a big city, for example, the ad for the audition may tell you what kind of song to prepare. Sometimes the ad tells you to sing something from the show you're auditioning for; sometimes it tells you *not* to sing something from the show. You want to choose a song that's similar to the show you're auditioning for *and* similar to the character you want to play. Having a variety of song choices ready gives you a chance to choose something on the spot when you're asked for a contrasting song.

Showing versatility

Yes, variety is the spice of life, and your choice of songs should offer variety. A little variety gives you an opportunity to show off a well-balanced set of skills. Song number one can be a song that shows off glorious high notes, and song number two may have a sassy belt that shows off your ability to change gears quickly.

Find songs that show off your strengths as a singer, and try to find variety within each song. The biggest pitfall to avoid is choosing only songs that develop the same kind of character (or same personality) and showcase the same kind of vocal sound. If you show only one side of you, the auditioner can't see that you're a skilled performer who can sing different kinds of songs and can add variety and spice throughout the show.

The following list offers ways to show versatility at specific types of auditions:

- ✔ **Opera:** When you know your voice type and fach, choose a variety of arias based on language and characters that you think fit you and your voice. (If you don't know your voice type, fach, or aria, check out the earlier section, "At the opera.") The most common languages the opera company expects you to know or to sing well in are French, German, Italian, and English. Get some help from your coach on polishing your languages so that you sound like you actually speak the language, even if you don't.

- ✔ **Musical theater:** At many musical theater auditions, you may be asked to sing a pop song, but to show a variety of song styles, you want to have early musical theater songs (not just the shows that have been written in the last ten years), later songs, and pop-rock songs, too. Often singers confine themselves to singing contemporary songs, but to show versatility, they choose one ballad and one up-tempo song from the top three broad categories: musical theater songs written before 1960, musical theater songs written after 1960, and pop-rock songs. If you have one song from each of these three periods, continue to branch out and add more contrasting songs to your repertoire that highlight your voice and acting skills.

- ✔ **Radio songs:** If you're auditioning with a song from the radio in pop-rock, country, or R&B, you want to show the versatility of your voice. Choose a song that shows off your vocal skills. You have to show that you can belt the high notes and make it sound like it's easy, use the right kind of sound for the style, and prove that you can entertain an audience. The sound for a rock song isn't the same as the sound for an aria — see Chapter 13 for help with your belt and Chapters 11 and 12 for help with the registers of your voice.

Some auditions require that you sing *a capella* (without accompaniment). Choose a song that sounds good without accompaniment and one that you can confidently sing without backup. Record your practice sessions so that you're aware of how your voice sounds on your song and how well it works when you're singing alone.

Connecting with the lyrics

You can't choose a song just because you sing it well. If you just sing it well, you can sell a recording instead of asking an audience to watch you sing it. When you find a song that you sing really well, you need to figure out how to make it work for you as an actor. Keep these tips in mind:

✔ Don't sing a song if you don't like the words. Make sure that you can relate to the story. Take the time to really home in on a great story that supports the song and gives you a reason to sing it. Check out Chapter 18 for some help on telling a story while singing.

✔ Choose age-appropriate stories. A 15-year-old girl could choose an age-appropriate story about growing up and liking boys but shouldn't be singing about struggling to pay the mortgage.

✔ The stories in the songs should vary to show different aspects of your personality and acting abilities. After you find that wonderful ballad about your long-lost love, find a funny song that shows off your comic timing, or another song that contrasts with the love song. The two songs should vary in tempo to create even more contrast. But don't get off the bus yet. Stay on and keep searching for a song that shows off fire and determination.

Avoiding the wrong audition song

It's the wrong audition song if one of these conditions applies:

✔ You don't like the song.

✔ It's out of your league as a singer or musician. For example, the song is out of your range, most notes sit too high, or it's too difficult musically.

✔ The song needs a band to make it work. You're likely to have only a pianist backing you up at most auditions, so stick to songs that work with this type of accompaniment. If you'll have a band at your audition, make sure that you know what key you want your song in and bring lead sheets.

✔ The song makes the listener think of the famous person who made the song a hit. You want the listener to hear you and focus attention on you. It's hard to find great songs that no one famous has performed, but be aware of this point as you're choosing your song. If you remember that famous performance, chances are good that someone else will too. The reality-show contestants who sing the famous song really well are the ones who figured out how to make the song their own.

✔ You couldn't sing the song on your worst day. If you constantly have to be aware of your singing technique when you sing it, choose something else.

✔ Making a 30-second cut is impossible.

✔ You can't get through the song without crying.

✔ Every accompanist you've worked with has trouble sight reading it.

✔ **The song is really negative.** Because singers should choose songs that represent their personality and their skills, a negative song may make you look negative. Most people prefer to work with someone positive.

✔ **The song is *overdone*.** The eternal question is "What's overdone?" Each year, the answer to this question can change. Assume that if it's a song that everyone knows and loves to sing, it's probably done quite a bit. If you have a copy of the song in a popular music book, so do several thousand other people. If you see the show listed in the trade paper *Backstage* or *Classical Singer* all the time, your song is probably super popular. You don't have to find obscure songs, but if ten other people sang your favorite song at the last audition, it may be overdone.

Preparing the Music

Preparing music for auditions is a tricky game. Notebook preparation is a big part of your audition success. If your music is easy to read and the accompanist plays it well, your audition will run smoothly. It's common in all types of auditions to have a notebook with songs. For opera and musical theater, you'll have copies of songs or arias. Other genres, such as pop-rock, R&B, or jazz, require that you either have a copy of the music or create a *lead sheet* — a sheet with the melody, chord progressions, and lyrics written out for the accompanist. Your coach can help you prepare this notebook for your auditions, or you can hire your coach to come to the audition with you. Occasionally you'll be asked to bring a recording instead of sheet music.

The biggest rule of notebook preparation is that whatever is in your notebook or in your bag is fair game at the audition. The audition panel will most likely ask you what you want to sing first. If you sing your favorite song and they ask to hear something else, be sure that your notebook of audition songs doesn't include a song you haven't rehearsed. You'll be giving your notebook to the audition pianist to play from, and he may flip through your notebook and suggest one of those unprepared songs as you're handing out your resume or talking to the other people in the room. You don't want to have to say that it's not ready. Keep all your songs that are ready in one notebook and the songs that are works in progress in another. To prepare your songs for your audition notebook, follow these guidelines:

✔ **Punch holes in the music and insert the pages into a three-ring notebook.** Put the sheets back to back, just like they appear in a book, and punch the holes or copy the music double-sided. When turning the page, the accompanist should see two new pages of music, just like a book. Tape (don't staple!) the sheets together on the top and bottom-right corners if your pages aren't double-sided.

Another option is to photocopy the song and slip the pages back to back into nonglare sheet protectors. You can purchase these at most office supply stores. Be sure to purchase the nonglare protectors so the lights in the room don't create a glare off the music.

Some pianists refuse to play music in nonglare sheet protectors or in a notebook, and some love it. If nonglare sheet protectors aren't an option, copy the music and tape the pages to file folders (or something that stands up easily and won't blow over), or tape the pages together so they're connected and the pianist can spread out the music on the music rack. You want the pages to be connected with tape because a breeze in the room will blow away single sheets.

✔ **Original scores written by hand are hard to read.** When the earlier musical theater shows were written, the composer wrote out the music by hand. Older copies of original scores done by hand are hard to read. If you have to err on the safe side, find a copy of the music that's a little easier to read.

✔ **Know when to bring a copy of the song or a lead sheet.** Bring a full copy of the song, not a copy from a fake book or lead sheet for opera and musical theater auditions. Books that offer a thousand songs in one book are usually fake books. A *fake book* has only the words, the chord symbols, and the melody line; the accompaniment part isn't shown. For auditions other than opera and musical theater, bring your lead sheet. You can copy your lead sheet from a fake book or you can ask your coach to help you prepare yours if you want the arrangement of the song to vary from your fake book.

Choosing the key

I highly recommend that you try to find the song in the key that you want to sing it in. If you sing a song that's in the wrong key, you may end up sounding more like Kermit the Frog than Kelly Clarkson or Renée Fleming on those high notes. See Chapter 16 for Web sites that allow you to find out what key sheet music is in or choose the key you want before you buy it. Opera arias are seldom transposed. You may find art songs in different keys in the music store, but the arias are usually sung as written on the page. Keep reading for help if you plan to sing something other than arias at your audition.

You can't assume that your audition accompanist can or will transpose by sight (put the song in a higher or lower key while playing). Purchase the song in the key you want to sing it in, or have someone transpose it for you before the audition. An accompanist may refuse to transpose at sight if the song is just too difficult, and it's her choice. You don't want her to transpose something at your audition if she thinks she may mess it up. You need the piano to sound really good as you sing.

Still, if you finally find a wonderful song that's *almost* perfect for you — maybe the notes are a tad too low or too high — you can get it transposed. When a song is *transposed,* someone — you or someone you hire — puts the song in a key other than the one it was originally written in so the melody sounds higher or lower.

If you transpose your song (or have someone else do it), keep these points in mind:

- ✔ **You may want the beginning of the song much higher, but that means that the tricky middle section also gets higher.** It's one thing to have some really cool high notes, yet it's quite another to sing those cool high notes over and over when you raise the key. Look at the range and *tessitura* (where most of the notes sit in the song) to determine how much higher or lower to change the key. Practice the song in the new key, whether higher or lower, to make sure that you can manage all the notes in the new key.

- ✔ **Hiring someone to transpose an entire song is expensive.** In transposing, the person has to copy the music (by hand or by using a computer program) into another key, which can be time consuming and costly. You can expect to pay way more to have a song transposed than it would cost you to purchase one in the right key for you. A song in sheet music that costs you less than $10 may cost well over $50 to transpose. If you know a little bit about music, you may find software such as *Finale* helpful in transposing your song.

- ✔ **Make sure that you have an accompanist read the transposed copy of your music before the audition.** Don't assume that the person who transposed it didn't make any mistakes. It won't take long for someone to play through it, and then you know exactly how it sounds in the new key and whether this key really does fit your voice.

Making the cut

In the beginning of your audition quest, you may not have the opportunity to sing your entire song. For each song that you plan to sing at your audition, choose 16 bars or 8 bars (called a cut) in advance and prepare this selection. (Still, knowing the entire song is best, just in case you're asked to sing it. Opera companies and many local community auditions, for example, may allow you to sing the whole song. That opportunity is great for you, but even in these situations, be prepared with a cut, in case they start to run late.)

A *bar* or *measure* is what's between the bar lines. Notice the vertical line going down through the five lines on the musical staff. That's a bar line. In between two bar lines is a *measure* (which is also known as a *bar*).

When you cut the song, you can count out the measures or assume that you have about 30 seconds to sing. That's a short amount of time, so make the most of it. When deciding on the 16 bars, keep these points in mind:

- ✔ The 16 bars (or 16 measures) need a sense of completion. The cut must make sense lyrically, and the music must have a sense of completion. Successful cuts are often the last 16 bars or go from the middle of the song (called the bridge) to the end.

- ✔ The biggest mistake is assuming that you can start at the beginning and just go until the end. You're going to be cut off, and that cutoff may happen right before the best part of the song.

- ✔ In the heat of the moment, choosing which section to sing is difficult. Making the decision before the audition gives you time to think about the cut, practice the cut to make sure that you really get to say something, practice hearing the note, and then start on that phrase.

- ✔ Choose a section that really shows off your vocal range and your acting abilities.

Marking the music

As you rehearse and prepare your music, highlight whatever an accompanist may find tricky in the song. If you're taking it to a pianist to play it for you, ask her to mark it. Assuming that you're on your own and feel confident that you can mark your music yourself, use a highlighter and highlight the following:

- ✔ **Directional symbols,** such as a repeat sign, a *DS al Coda,* or a double bar. (See *Music Theory For Dummies,* by Michael Pilhofer and Holly Day [Wiley], for an explanation of these markings.) Highlight them so that the accompanist can see them ahead of time. You can also point out the marking so that she knows how to map out the page turns.

- ✔ **Tempo changes** that are important and that may not be well marked in the music. You can provide your starting tempo, but mark any changes so that the accompanist can easily follow along.

- ✔ **Places where you ad-lib what's on the page.** If you're singing a section very freely, mark it so that the accompanist can follow you, or create chords to support you while you ad-lib or riff.

Keeping track of your auditions

In addition to your collection of songs for audition purposes, keep a journal or notebook of auditions. You can keep a record of what you sang, who was at the audition, where the audition was held, who helped you get the audition, what kind of audition it was, whether you got a callback or a job offer, any comments that were made during the interview, and the names of the people you met. It's surprising how fast you can forget these details. When you go back to sing for the same company at a later date, you want to refresh yourself on what changes they asked you to make to your song, to see whether you're easy to direct; who was there so you can say hello; which songs they liked or didn't like so you can choose something else, if necessary; and any other information that may improve this audition.

Rehearsing with an accompanist

Hearing a pianist play your song or aria before you take it to an audition is important. If you don't read music, this is even more important. You may erroneously assume that your song is the exact same version that you heard on the radio, so it may come as quite a shock when you hear your song for the first time at an audition and have no earthly idea what those sounds are. Remember that publishing companies usually publish songs in keys that are easy to play. If the singer on the radio sings the song in a really hard key with many *accidentals* (sharp, flat, or natural signs placed before individual notes to indicate that they're a half step higher or lower), the publishing company may change the key to make it more accessible to beginning pianists.

Singers who also play guitar may really enjoy accompanying themselves for an audition. Adrenaline may cause your hands to shake, so practice in front of an audience before the audition to work out the nerves. When you audition or practice with a guitar, you want to maintain your alignment, coordinate your breath just as you do with the exercises in Chapter 4, and look at your audience. You can look at your guitar, but look up frequently so that the audience can see your eyes and connect with you.

By having a pianist read your music for you before an audition, you get an opportunity to check the key to make sure that it's exactly in the range where you want to sing. The following sections explain what an accompanist can do for you.

Taking the lead

Your voice teacher may have been playing the song for you, and you may be comfortable with that version. When you take it to someone else to read it for you, you have to be much more specific when you lead.

A good pianist waits to hear the consonant on the downbeat before playing the chord. If you wait to hear the chord from the pianist, you may be waiting a long time. You may get an audition pianist who wants to lead you, but that usually happens because you're not leading or the accompanist feels like you're in trouble. Sometimes the pianist speeds up if you're struggling to maintain the longer phrases because he assumes that you won't struggle so much with maintaining airflow. You have to be confident enough to lead and know that, when you lead, the accompanist will follow.

The speed with which you take your first breath also indicates your tempo. If you take a quick breath, the accompanist assumes that the song is going to move out. If your breath is slow and deliberate, he can assume that the piece is going to move slowly.

Getting help with musical notation

The pianist can check the cuts you made or new directional markings that you inserted. If he has trouble following the markings, ask him how to write it out to make it clear to someone who's never seen the song.

If you've changed the key and put new chord symbols over the line to indicate the new sequence of chords, make sure that the pianist checks these for you. One tiny error can lead you to the wrong high note at the end.

You may also want to ask the pianist to help you mark the song to make your needs clear. If you want to slow down at the end or get louder in one section, ask him to help you mark the piece so that any accompanist can read ahead and see those changes coming. If your tempo is really important, you may want to ask the pianist to write in a metronome marking to indicate exactly the speed at which you want to sing. (See Chapter 10 for more on metronomes.) The audition pianist won't have a metronome on the piano, but she can see the marking and estimate your desired tempo.

Bringing a recording

Providing your own recording to sing along with at the audition gives you a chance to rehearse and get familiar with the accompaniment. You want to ask what to bring to the audition. Some audition rooms have a CD player; some have a hookup for your iPod. Make sure that your CD is a good-quality recording to sing along with. Whether you use *GarageBand* or hire an accompanist to record it, use a good-quality recording system so that the sounds on your CD make a good impression at the audition.

Nailing the Audition

To nail your audition, you want to be prepared. Your audition may draw a lot of competition; being really prepared increases your chances of getting the gig. The following sections offer some preparation tips.

Doing your prep work

Knowing your style, choosing your song, and preparing your music are the most important steps you take in preparing for your audition. But you don't want to let the small things fall through the cracks, either! Depending on your selected genre of music or the size of your city, you may not have to do all these things. In bigger cities with more competition (particularly in the musical theater genre), you want to make sure that you do everything you can to be prepared.

- **Know the scene.** If you're auditioning for musical theater, read the trade paper *Backstage* for at least one year. For opera, do the same with *Classical Singer*. You want some time to get used to the audition listings and to prepare your *audition book* (a notebook that has photocopies of all the songs you're prepared to sing for auditions) for any type of show. As you're preparing, set some goals — both short term and long term — so you have a plan of action. For other styles of music, you can find auditions listed online at sites such as www.backpage.com or you can hire a coach who can help you set goals and find local auditions.

- **Get your resume and headshot ready.** A resume and headshot are like a calling card for the entertainment industry. If they like you, they will keep your resume to contact you. When you put together your resume, list your important credits and assume that someone will spend only about 30 seconds looking at it. If you list every single thing you've done, the audition panel may miss the credits you really want them to see. You also want your resume to be only one page. Don't fib or stretch the truth on special skills. Be specific when listing your voice type for classical auditions; adding information about belting is important for musical theater auditions (mezzo belter, soprano with high belt, baritenor, and so on). You want to list your range along with your voice type on your resume. They want to know your performance range, the notes you're confident singing in performance.

At most auditions, singers bring a photograph called a *headshot*. This headshot is usually an 8-x-10-inch, color photograph of just the head or upper body. The photo also usually has the singer's name printed on the bottom in the border. Your photo needs to look like you at the audition. Staple the headshot and resume together, with the smooth side of the staple facing the resume side, or use double-sided tape to attach them.

If you're not sure whether you should take a resume and headshot to your audition, you can ask. (If you're auditioning for musical theater, call the theater office or the contact person listed in the audition ad.) But assume that the answer will be "yes"; it's better to have it ready, just in case.

- ✔ **Pick up audition skills** from classes or advice from teachers.

- ✔ **Practice the way you'll audition.** If you know you'll use a microphone at the audition, practice with one. At the audition without a microphone, you'll have to show that you can project your voice. Work on creating a resonant sound to project at the audition. Chapter 11 contains information about projecting sound in the specific areas of your range and Chapter 24 has some tips on singing with a microphone.

- ✔ **Prepare your speaking voice** for the *sides* (material from the show that you're asked to sight read or prepare for the callback). See Chapter 13 for help with your speaking voice.

Dressing in the right outfit

At your audition, remember that other people are looking at you from the minute you walk in the door — not just when you sing. You want to show off your body and look great in your outfit. If you're auditioning for a musical or a production with a specific character, think about what the character you're auditioning for looks like. You want to suggest the character but not dress exactly like the character. For an opera audition, you want to look classy. Wearing jeans and your cool tennis shoes is fine for a pop-rock audition, but not for an opera audition. If you're not auditioning for a character role, choose an outfit that shows off your personality and highlights your figure.

Also remember that you may not be cast the first time you audition, but you still need to make a good impression. Sometimes directors ask you back to audition again to make sure that you're outstanding every time you audition, not just on a good day. Though your mother may not like it, wear the same outfit for the callback.

Knowing who will attend the audition

For every musical production from a video to a musical to a singing contest, a producer, musical director, stage manager, choreographer, director, casting director, and general manager run the show. These are theater bosses who hold the line. You may see any or all of them at your audition.

- **Producer:** Pays the money, or finds it, so the show can go on.
- **General manager:** Keeps up with how the money is spent.
- **Casting director:** Calls in the actors to audition for the parts in the show or talks with their agents.
- **Director:** Acts as the guide and traffic cop for all the actors on the stage.
- **Musical director:** Shoulders the responsibility for the quality of the music in the production. Tasks may involve everything from working on arrangements for specific numbers to playing the piano at performances. When the musical director isn't available, the rehearsal pianist is called in.
- **Choreographer:** Creates the staging or directions for who moves when and where during the show.
- **Conductor:** Waves her arms in time to the music so that the musicians in the orchestra pit and the singers onstage can follow along.
- **Stage manager:** Keeps everybody and everything in order.

Be nice to everyone at an audition. You never know who you're talking to. That person may be the director's assistant — or he may end up directing the next show you audition for.

Greeting the audition accompanist

The audition pianist can be your friend or foe, based on how you behave. Most of the time, the pianist who is at the audition is a really swell person who plays like a dream.

A few simple actions that seem harmless to you can really set off an accompanist. Allow me to share a few tips:

- Don't try to shake hands with the audition pianist, even if you think it's good manners. Shaking hands translates to squeezing someone's hands, no matter how gently. The pianist doesn't want swollen fingers after shaking hundreds of hands during a long audition day.
- Smile and address the pianist with respect when you provide your tempo or point out the road map in your song. Briefly, but very nicely, describe what you've highlighted or point out any tough spots. Your

conversation with the pianist has to be quick — be brief and to the point. Practice briefly describing your tempo and the road map of the song, and practice how you'll indicate to start.

✔ Never snap your fingers to give the accompanist the tempo. Snapping may be an easy way to describe your tempo, but many accompanists take offense to it. Instead, quietly speak a few words at the speed you want to sing.

✔ Explain how you plan to indicate that you're ready to begin. You can nod your head or look up to let the pianist know that you're ready to begin.

✔ You can hope that the audition pianist can transpose at sight, but you can't assume this skill. Feel free to ask whether she can transpose, but if she hesitates or says no, choose something else to sing.

Reading music on the page and transposing at sight are two different skills. Unless someone is used to transposing a song, it may not be her strongest skill. You may also hear more wrong notes as the pianist attempts to read it in your favorite key. Be safe, and get the song transposed and written out well in advance of your audition. Better yet, choose a song that's already in the key you can sing well. See the "Choosing the key" section, earlier in this chapter, for details on choosing a song in the right key.

✔ Thank the pianist just before you leave. You may not know the pianist personally and may assume that he's just a really cool person who only plays the piano. But the audition pianist may be the musical director. Be sure to read the suggestions on how to prepare your music for the audition so that the pianist enjoys meeting you and playing your song.

Acting at the audition

Acting while singing is a must. Your acting preparation of your song needs to be as detailed as your musical preparation. Check out Chapter 18 for information on acting while singing. You want your audience to watch you during your audition, and if you aren't acting, they have no reason to look at you.

At an audition, your choice of where to direct your eyes is similar to where you direct your eyes if you're telling a story. The only decision you have to make is whether to look at the person you're singing to. Most of the time, the answer to that question is to *not* make eye contact. However, if you have a fun song that has spunk and character, do look at your audience. Songs that address your invisible scene partner are best directed to that imaginary partner on the wall directly in front of you. Because you're pretending that you're talking to that scene partner, you want to look at him as if he's in the room with you, but not stare at him. When you have a conversation with someone, you look at that person and then look away, but you don't stare at him. You don't want to stare at the wall when you sing your song at your audition.

Knowing when to hire an agent

You need an agent when you have enough performing experience that you need to get into the bigger, more prominent auditions. An agent helps you get performing jobs, but the agent doesn't do all the work. The agent can only get you the audition. You have to be good enough to land the gig. An agent usually takes 10 percent of your performance income, whether he gets you the gig or not. If you think you may be interested in an agent, start reading the articles in the trade papers *Backstage* or *Classical Singer* about agents and managers to see whether you're ready for that kind of business relationship. For more detailed information about agents, managers, freelancing, auditions, and contracts, pick up a copy of *Breaking into Acting For Dummies,* by Larry Garrison and Wallace Wang (Wiley).

Assuming that the casting director for whom you're auditioning is sitting near the middle of one wall in the audition room, focus your eyes a few feet on either side of him (or them, if there's more than one person). Most acting teachers tell you to keep your eyes centered in one spot on the wall so that you don't have any odd body angles in an audition. That's good advice in the beginning of your training. As you get more accustomed to different kinds of focus and multitasking, you can widen your focus.

Preparing mentally

Being mentally prepared for an audition means doing your preparation work (practicing, preparing your headshot and resume, researching the audition, and so on) and visualizing yourself successful at the audition. You want to mentally prepare for success because with success comes the responsibility of performing well under pressure. Mentally preparing is as important as preparing your singing voice. Check out Chapter 19 to help with performance anxiety.

Part V
The Part of Tens

The 5th Wave   By Rich Tennant

"Well, that's the last time we hire a high soprano to sing at the glassblower's convention."

In this part . . .

Famous performers don't always have great technique, but in this part, I show you ten singers who do. Check it out to see whether I included the singers you like. In this part, I also answer ten of the most frequently asked questions about singing — you know, those questions that you want to ask but you're not sure who has the answers. If you're concerned about vocal health (and you should be!), this part also gives you ten tips for maintaining yours. This part finishes with ten great performing tips. Explore the suggestions to make your performance fabulous.

Chapter 21

Ten Performers with Good Technique

Which singers have good technique? Some great performers have great vocal technique, and some great performers are still working on theirs. Check out this list of ten singers to see whether I list your favorite. You find pop-rock, country, musical theater, and classical music performers on this list.

Although I limit the number of singers with great vocal technique to ten, you can be sure that the true number of wonderful singers with great technique is much higher. The eclectic nature of this list just goes to show that good technique crosses the lines of style, gender, age, race, and song.

Kristin Chenoweth

Tiny little Kristin Chenoweth packs quite a punch with her voice. Her solid training allows her to move back and forth from *legit sounds* (head voice–dominated sounds similar to classical singing) to belt. As a high soprano, she demonstrates her versatility in songs such as "14G," where her head voice and her high belt are equally polished. Her signature roles include Sally in *You're a Good Man, Charlie Brown;* she also originated the role of Glinda in *Wicked.* Find out more about her career at www.kristin-chenoweth.com.

Linda Eder

Linda Eder's career has spanned both the pop world and Broadway. Her early recordings provide a window into her career as a strong, confident soprano, singing well above the staff in songs such as *Vole Mon Age.* Her big break on Broadway was Lucy in *Jekyll & Hyde.* My favorite recording of hers is "Bridge Over Troubled Water," where she shows off her amazing vocal flexibility and command of her instrument. Find out more about her at www.lindaeder.com.

Renée Fleming

American soprano Renée Fleming wows the audience with her sumptuous tone, flexibility, and exquisite dynamic precision. She started out as a jazz singer and blossomed into a world-class opera singer. Renée is one of those singers who can skillfully vary her tone to match the emotional journey of her character. Her signature roles include the title roles of *Rusalka, Manon, Thaïs,* and *Arabella.* Find more about her at www.reneefleming.com.

Faith Hill

Mississippi-born Faith Hill made a huge splash as a pop and country singer. She crosses over into both styles and shows off her sassy high belt as well as a steady vibrato. Her signature songs show the variety of sounds she makes with her voice. "Cry" shows her high belt, "It Matters to Me" highlights her mixed belt and even vibrato, "Take Me As I Am" demonstrates her chatty belt, and "The Way You Love Me" shows off her mix belt. Mega hits that top the pop and country charts include "Breathe" and "This Kiss." Find out more about Faith at www.faithhill.com.

Michael Jackson

Michael Jackson (1958–2009) is considered the King of Pop. Michael's career spanned his entire life: He started performing as a child onstage with his brothers in the Jackson 5 and then moved on to a solo career. Michael's troubles may have overwhelmed his personal life at times, but his amazing voice was always there. His recordings as a young boy demonstrate an amazing falsetto and mix. He continued to develop his mix and belt and proved himself to be a versatile vocal chameleon on albums such as *Thriller* (which claims the best video of all time and best-selling album of all time). Find out more about Michael at www.michaeljackson.com.

Toby Keith

Toby Keith's songs range from comic songs with fun musical turns to smooth ballads that show off his confidence in sustaining long phrases. His tone varies from chatty to warm and rich. Toby easily varies his tone in his songs to demonstrate his solid storytelling skills. Signature songs include his early recordings of great country stories, such as "Should've Been a Cowboy"; the comic song "Who's Your Daddy?"; the sarcastic song "How Do You Like Me Now?!"; and ballads such as "You Shouldn't Kiss Me Like This" and "When Love Fades." Find out more about Toby at www.tobykeith.com.

Beyoncé Knowles

Beyoncé Knowles may sing R&B, but her technique is solid enough that she can sing other styles with ease. Her performance in *Dream Girls* allowed us to see her vocally morph from a head voice–dominated mix into a full, sassy belt. Her showmanship only enhances her broad skills; she's not hiding behind the mic. Beyoncé's signature songs include "Sweet Dreams" (hear her alternating registers with ease); "Get Me Bodied" (chatty belt); "The Closer I Get to You," with Luther Vandross; and "Halo." Find more about this mega-star at www.beyonceonline.com.

Elvis Presley

Elvis Presley (1935–1977), the King of Rock and Roll and my favorite male singer, brought simple songs dancing off the page. His voice moved easily from high to low. Throughout his movie and singing career, he enjoyed huge success as a sexy singer. His career spanned 33 movies and resulted in 140 albums and singles, and his music crossed the lines between gospel and rock and roll with a blues feeling. Growing up in Memphis, Elvis was surrounded by famous gospel and blues singers who made a lasting impression on the young singer. Signature songs include "Love Me Tender," "Jailhouse Rock," "Blue Christmas," and "Viva Las Vegas." To find out more about Elvis, go online to www.elvis.com or check out *Elvis For Dummies*, by Susan Doll, PhD (Wiley).

Anthony Warlow

Australian Anthony Warlow has the full, rich tone of a leading man and the ability to create huge variations of tone to portray the text. His roles and recordings show off his wide range and versatility. Within his recordings, you can hear him move from falsetto into a mix and then even farther into chest voice. Signature roles include the Phantom in *The Phantom of the Opera*, Papageno in *The Magic Flute,* and KoKo in *The Mikado.* Use your favorite search engine to find out more about him or listen to his videos online.

Stevie Wonder

Stevie Wonder made a name for himself and his high tessitura because of his solid musicianship and ability to pour his soul into his songs. He showed off his belt throughout signature songs such as "Isn't She Lovely" and "I Wish," and showcased his falsetto and mix in "As" and "You Are the Sunshine of My Life." Some of his great hits include "My Cherie Amour," "Signed, Sealed, Delivered, I'm Yours," and "I Just Called to Say I Love You." Find out more about this marvelous musician at www.steviewonder.net.

Chapter 22

Ten Frequently Asked Questions about Singing

*I*f you don't know the answer to a question, then it's not a stupid question. Most new singers ask the same questions, so I've compiled the answers to ten frequently asked questions about singing. Read through the following questions and their answers to help with your singing. The answers may inspire you to ask your voice teacher other questions that aren't covered in this chapter.

Is Belting Bad?

Belting isn't bad for you if you do it right, and sopranos can certainly belt. In fact, sopranos often have an easier time with belting than mezzos. Belting *is* bad for you if you use a heavy chest voice to create the belt sound. Check out Chapter 13 for information about working with your speaking voice and creating a healthy belt sound. You can also hear a singer on the CD demonstrate healthy belting.

What Should I Do If My Voice Feels Off?

Plenty of factors can cause your voice to sound less than its best. Consider three possibilities:

✔ Thinking too much about how you sound as you sing may make you nervous, and then your voice may not sound your best. Check out Chapter 19 for some help with performance anxiety, or see Chapter 18 for help with acting and singing.

✔ Not getting enough sleep can cause your voice to feel sluggish and not respond as easily as it normally does. Singing too much the day before or the day of an audition also can cause your voice to get tired. See Chapter 23 for more information about maintaining a healthy voice.

Your singing muscles are like other muscles in your body. Working out is just fine, but they need a rest after the workout.

✔ Emotions affect your singing voice. Crying can make your vocal cords swell and feel puffy, too. Wait until after your performance to watch that sad movie.

If your voice is husky, breathy, strident, muffled, hooty, or *off* in any other way, first read about *onset of tone* in Chapter 6. If after working on onset of tone your voice still isn't clear, take some time to read about healthy speaking habits in Chapter 13. If you're abusing your speaking voice, you may also be making your singing voice work much harder to produce gorgeous sounds. Husky tones usually result from some sort of abuse of the singing voice or the speaking voice. Medications may cause your throat to be dry and scratchy. You can read Chapter 23 for more information about medications and their effect on the singing voice. Breathy tones usually indicate that the cords aren't closing completely and are allowing too much air to escape. Strident tones typically result from too much physical pressure or not enough balance of sound in the resonators. Try the exercises in Chapters 4 and 6 on opening the throat to feel the release of the added physical pressure. Muffled or hooty tones usually come from not making specific vowels or allowing the resonance to live too far in the back of your throat. Read Chapter 8 on vowels and the shape of vowels, and then read Chapters 5 and 6 for some help with tone.

How are an Accompanist, a Coach, and a Voice Teacher Different?

Three specialists can help you prepare your song or help you with singing technique. They have different skills and strengths; read on to figure out which one is right for you:

✔ A *pianist* or *accompanist* is someone who plays the piano for you to practice singing but doesn't offer advice on singing technique. An accompanist usually charges less than a coach does because this role isn't as demanding. Their strength is great piano skills.

The word *accompanist* is often mispronounced. The correct pronunciation is uh-*kum*-puh-nist — there's no "knee" in the word.

- ✔ A *coach* is someone who plays the piano well and can give you tips on your singing. During a work session with a coach, you may practice hearing the piano cue for your entrances in your song, work on the pronunciation of words, get tips on how to sing with the correct style, and find good places to breathe within the text. A coach helps with some basic tips on technique and supports the work of your voice teacher.

- ✔ A *voice teacher* is a technique specialist. Although the coach may have knowledge of technique, the voice teacher is the expert. The voice teacher may not play the piano so well but makes up for it in knowledge and advice on your technique. In your voice lesson, you can expect to work at least half of the session on technique and the other half applying that technique to repertoire. For more information about finding a voice teacher and what to expect in lessons, check out Chapter 15.

If My Voice Is Scratchy, Do I Have Nodes?

Your voice has to take quite a bit of abuse for you to get *nodes* (small calluses that form on the vocal cords). For example, you can't get nodes from yelling for your favorite team for only one day. Your cords may swell or feel uncomfortable the next day, but you have to abuse your voice for a longer period to develop nodes. (See Chapter 23 for information on vocal abuse.) Just remember, if you don't rub the cords the wrong way, you won't have this problem. If the scratchy sounds continue, try vocalizing high in your range. Nodes usually affect the higher part of your voice. If the sound is husky only in the middle part of your voice, you probably have another kind of swelling. Check out Chapter 23 for more information on vocal health, and see Chapter 13 for help with your speaking voice.

Do I Have to Be Big to Have a Big Voice?

Your voice size isn't related to your waistline. If it were, all great singers would be big and every large person would be a great singer. Actually, having extra weight around the middle makes it harder to move your body to breathe. If you're used to that movement, it's not a problem. The size of your throat and head make a bigger difference in your voice than your girth. A wide neck means your vocal cords are longer than someone with a narrow neck. A narrow neck means shorter vocal cords; singers with narrow necks are often the higher voice types. A larger head means more space for the sound to bounce around. One size isn't better than another, but they make for exciting differences between voices.

What's the Best Singing Method?

The best singing method is the one that works best for you. You can find singers and teachers who are quick to recommend their method, claiming, "It's the best." But as long as the method introduces you to breath and breath management, tone and resonance, articulation that allows you to be understood without causing tension, and the general principles of good singing, then it's a good method. My method of teaching is a combination of all the teachers I've studied with.

You may hear singers talking about the *bel canto* method of singing. *Bel canto* literally means "beautiful singing" in Italian and implies the use of smooth, open tones. This method of singing and teaching began early in the 18th century. Today *bel canto* implies beautiful singing in a more classical style.

Do 1 Have to Speak Italian to Sing Well?

Speaking Italian never hurt anyone and can only enhance your singing. Italians have been singing beautifully for many years and those singers are great role models. However, Italians aren't the only people making beautiful sounds in the concert halls. Singers of every nationality can sing well. Enjoy your native tongue, whatever it is, and sing your little heart out. Teachers often recommend Italian songs because they have a long history of teaching singing using Italian art songs and the Italian language contains fewer vowel sounds, making it easy to learn precise vowel production.

Can 1 Have a Few Drinks Before the Performance to Calm My Nerves?

Drinking alcohol and singing isn't a great combination. You can read in Chapter 23 about how alcohol dehydrates you. Alcohol also slows your reactions, and you want a clear head for singing and performing. When you mix singing and drinking, the small muscles in the throat may get too relaxed, causing you to lose coordination when you try to multitask during the performance.

Chapter 19 has some tips for dealing with performance anxiety. You may find those tips so helpful that you grow to love adrenaline (nerves) and look forward to your performance.

Why Can't I Eat Ice Cream Before I Sing?

Ice cream causes phlegm and mucus to build up. That mucus is thick and makes you want to clear your throat. Unless dairy products don't bother you, I recommend avoiding ice cream and any other dairy products before singing. Make the mad dash to the ice cream store after practicing.

What should you eat or drink? Water is a safe bet. Some singers say they don't like cold water right before they sing. You can experiment with it to see whether it makes your voice feel different.

Other singers may tell you to drink water with lemon or fruit juice to clean out your throat. It won't do any harm if you want to try it, but I don't find it beneficial. In fact, lemon is a diuretic, so it may dry out your throat.

Experiment with any food or drinks before the day of a performance so that you know exactly how your throat feels afterward. Eating a couple of hours before a performance also gives your body a chance to digest the food and gives you some energy for the performance. Some people like to sing on a full stomach, but you need to experiment singing right after eating to know whether it affects you. On the day of a performance, eat familiar foods; you don't want any surprise digestive problems during the show.

How Long Will It Take Me to Learn to Sing?

Great question — and I have no blanket answer to give you. If you know nothing about singing and the information in the book is all new to you, you'll start to hear improvement after a few weeks of consistent practice. You may not be ready for your debut at the Grammy Awards, but you'll hear improvement in your tone and your ability to transition between registers of your voice. (See Chapter 11 for more information on vocal registers.)

Moving from a basic level to an intermediate level of singing takes about six months to a year of consistent practice. As with other sports, the consistent repetition develops muscle memory. Basketball players execute drills every practice. They run laps to build stamina and practice all kinds of coordination drills. Your singing practice session needs to include drills and exercises (the kind of exercises you see throughout the book) to develop your skill and coordination. Most beginners can expect about 50 percent of their technique to stay with them under pressure. You want to work on your technique until it's solid so that your percentage of skill under pressure reaches a higher level. Intermediate-level singers may achieve about 75 percent of their potential during a performance.

Advanced singing takes years to develop — but that fact shouldn't discourage you. Great athletes continue to practice and develop their skills long into their careers. The more you practice, the more advanced level of exercises you can add to your routine.

Chapter 23

Ten Tips for Maintaining Vocal Health

*L*ong-term *vocal abuse* — any activity that causes strain on your voice — can change the quality of your singing. And your voice may not always be able to repair itself. Although most singers can minimize long-term problems with vocal rest, you need to avoid continued vocal abuse. Make your vocal health a priority now.

Regardless of whether you sing in your church choir or tour endlessly, maintaining healthy habits is essential to maintaining your vocal health.

Identifying Everyday Abuses

The following list is by no means all-inclusive. You may find other factors that greatly affect your vocal health over a period of time. Be sure to recognize problems and keep them at bay before a big performance. In particular, keep these common everyday factors in mind:

- ✔ **Alcohol:** Alcohol dilates blood vessels in your body, which isn't good for your vocal cords if you plan to sing. When the blood vessels dilate, the blood thins and comes to the surface, which makes you more susceptible to a hemorrhage on your vocal cords. Limit your alcohol, and avoid it on days when you have to practice or perform. Drink plenty of water on days when you do choose to drink, because alcohol dehydrates you and stays in your system up to three days.

- ✔ **Cigarette smoke:** The smoke often causes inflammation of the tissues in the throat, which makes singing more difficult. Avoid smoking and secondhand smoke at all times, because long-term use or association can permanently damage your vocal cords. You especially want to avoid smoke for several days before a lesson or performance.

✔ **Food:** Certain foods can irritate your voice. Dairy products often cause mucus to build up, which makes you clear your throat frequently. Pay attention to how your body reacts to certain foods so you know what to avoid the day before or day of a big concert or performance.

✔ **Medications:** Many medications dry out your throat. If you need to take the medications, compensate by drinking more water so you don't get dry when you sing. Talk to your doctor to see whether you can avoid medications (or change the timing of the dosage) on days when you have to do plenty of singing. Look for more information about medications in the "Medicating a Sore Throat" section, later in the chapter.

✔ **Pollen or dust:** Sensitivities to allergens, such as pollen or dust, may cause the vocal folds and throat to swell. Ask your doctor for suggestions to help with allergy problems. In the meantime, take some basic precautions: Clean your house regularly to prevent dust bunnies from collecting and bothering you, choose nonallergenic materials for your bed linens, use a vacuum cleaner that removes all pet hair, and avoid areas with large quantities of dust. Listen to the local weather report for the pollen count. Most areas have higher pollen counts in the early morning or early evening. If you limit outdoor activities to the middle of the day, you're less likely to encounter the highest levels of pollen.

✔ **Throat clearing:** If you're a habitual throat clearer, now is the time to break that habit and get to the root of the problem. Maybe you clear your throat excessively because mucus builds up from postnasal drip or acid reflux. Swallow instead of clearing your throat, and talk with your doctor about the cause. For many singers, throat clearing is just an unconscious habit that results from trying to clear the vocal cords for singing. Singing with a little mucus isn't going to hurt.

Incorporating Healthy Speech into Your Singing

Your speaking voice directly affects your singing. By taking good care of your voice while speaking, you ensure better health for your singing voice. (In case you missed it, Chapter 13 tells you about the speaking voice.) Try making your speaking habits more healthy with these tips:

✔ Apply your knowledge of breathing while talking — including talking on the phone. Use your body as if you were singing; pay attention to your posture and the pitch of your voice.

✔ Use full volume when you need to be heard (usually at sports events, parties, or clubs), but don't scream. You can also slightly raise the pitch of your speaking voice to help it carry over the noise and use your knowledge of resonance to project the sound.

✔ Talk at a reasonable volume; don't speak loudly all the time.

✔ Notice your articulation as you speak — avoid speaking with tension, such as jaw tension, tongue tension, or glottals.

✔ Find your optimum speaking pitch so you don't speak on a pitch that's too low for you (speaking too low usually causes a grinding sound).

✔ Practice the speaking exercises in Chapter 13 to work on your speaking habits.

Prolonged vocal abuse — including abuse of the speaking voice — can lead to *nodes* (small calluses on the vocal cords). If you catch the node early enough, vocal rest and eliminating the vocal abuse often take care of the situation. Of course, the root of the problem is just as important as the symptom. Identify what behavior caused the problem so you can prevent any reoccurrence.

Knowing When to Seek Help

Being tired after a long rehearsal or after a series of rehearsals is normal. But a problem may be brewing if your voice isn't returning to normal and you're having trouble singing. If your voice feels tired, notes that used to be clear are now fuzzy, you're experiencing a loss of range, or your voice doesn't feel normal even after a good warm-up, you may want to problem-solve for about two weeks before you head to the doctor.

First, go back to the basics. Even seasoned singers need to check in with the basics of technique:

✔ Review your breathing exercises.

✔ Practice speaking exercises to review the coordination of breathing while speaking.

✔ Check your posture.

✔ Practice in front of a mirror to see what you're doing physically.

✔ Review exercises that work on the different registers of your voice.

✔ Practice singing softly.

Going back to the basics may help you realize that you were pushing, not breathing properly, singing with tension, or abusing your speaking voice.

You also want to think through any changes that you've made in your routine. Changing detergent may cause your allergies to flare up; sleeping with your windows open may cause your voice to be dry and scratchy in the morning; drinking too much alcohol, smoking, changing your diet, or changing medications can adversely affect the voice. Any of these kinds of changes can cause temporary problems with the voice.

If reviewing the basics for a couple of weeks doesn't help and you haven't changed anything in your routine, go see a doctor. Visit a laryngologist or an ENT (ear, nose, and throat doctor) who is used to working with singers. These doctors can look down your throat with a tiny high-speed camera and watch your vocal cords in motion. They can tell you the root of the problem and how to resolve it. They can also give you advice on whether you should cancel or just take it easy during the performance. You need to cancel if it hurts to sing, you get progressively more hoarse as you sing, or you can barely make any sound.

Staying Hydrated

Your body is 50 to 65 percent water, and two important components of your singing ability — your lungs and your muscles — need water to do their job. Your lungs depend on water to keep the tissue moving easily, and muscle tissue is made up of 75 percent water. So keeping your body well hydrated helps your singing voice work better.

You can balance out your hydration with liquids other than water. Before you drink that can of soda or cup of coffee, though, realize that the sugar content in most drinks threatens your waistline and that caffeine dries you out. Caffeine also is a diuretic, which means that it makes your body get rid of water. You can't rely on that morning cup of coffee to keep your voice in good working order. Performing requires physical stamina, and a well-hydrated body keeps the body functioning at its best.

Getting Plenty of Shut-Eye

Not getting enough sleep doesn't give the tissue in your body — in your throat — time to heal. Depriving yourself of sleep only makes your voice feel sluggish. If you're sleep deprived, your voice and brain react more slowly, making it harder to sing your best. Singing longer phrases takes more effort, your voice feels heavy instead of agile when you sing the faster notes, and forgetting the next word is more likely. You may survive on just a few hours sleep at night, but is your voice also just surviving? You want your voice to *thrive*, not just survive. Try getting more sleep for a few nights and see whether that makes a difference in your singing. Even one more hour can make a big difference to your tissues. You want to recoup and regenerate during the night.

Making Sure That You're Well Nourished

You need to maintain a balanced diet. Following guidelines of basic nutrition means getting a balanced amount of whole grains, fruits and vegetables, and protein. Within this balanced diet, you find proper amounts of protein, carbohydrates, and fats. You may find that singing requires more energy, which means adding protein to your diet to enhance your body's ability to sustain you through long rehearsals.

Though it may not be your personal issue, a body that is too lean or too heavy may have trouble finding the stamina to sing and sustain the higher pitches. Make sure that you're regularly nourishing your body for stamina. Many singers wait until late in the day to eat, but your body needs something to get it started. Try to find a routine that enables you to get food in your body early in the day so you aren't snacking well into the night when your body finally feels hungry. Eat breakfast to get your body nourished right away, and don't eat a huge dinner after your evening performance. Eat a small meal before the performance, and a snack — not a huge meal — afterward. Eating a huge meal late at night will encourage acid reflux problems.

Preventing a Sore Throat or Infection

A great way to keep all those germs out of your body is to keep your hands washed and away from your face. Your mom told you to wash your hands — listen to her advice. If germs do start to attack and you feel the tickle from drainage, try one of these options:

- **Gargle with warm salt water.** Adding half a teaspoon of salt to a cup of warm water and then gargling helps kill any germs that may lodge in the back of your mouth. If you have frequent infections around your tonsils, you may find that salt water is one of your best friends. Additionally, swishing that salt water around in your mouth stops those painful little canker sores right in their tracks.

✔ **Use a neti pot.** A neti pot washes out the nasal passages with warm salt water. You can find a neti pot at your local drugstore, right next to the cold medicines. Follow the directions on the box to wash out the germs that are lingering, waiting for your immune system to give in so they can attack. You may even feel that slight tickle when the drainage begins. By flushing your nasal passages, you prevent the mucus from getting too thick and hopefully sidetrack those germs.

Medicating a Sore Throat

It's going to happen sometime, so you may as well know your options: You *are* going to catch that cold or sore throat, and you have to know how to deal with it. Use this advice for when your throat feels scratchy:

✔ **Avoid most nose sprays.** Nasal sprays that contain antihistamines or decongestants are habit forming and can cause symptoms to worsen when you stop. Use these types of sprays only in emergencies.

✔ **Drink plenty of water with your medications.** Most over-the-counter medications dry you out. As long as you're prepared for that side effect and compensate with extra fluids, you won't be shocked. Read about the lowdown on three common cold medications:

  • **Antihistamines:** These medicines stop the flood when your nose starts running. The antihistamine dries out your upper respiratory tract secretions and probably makes you sleepy to boot. Use an antihistamine to stop the flooding in your nasal passages, but know that the dryness affects your singing. Keep up with your fluids to counteract the dryness, and choose the right dosage.

  • **Cough medicine:** Most cough medicines dry out your voice. Your best bet is to find dextromethorphan with guaifenesin. The guaifenesin is a mucolytic, which brings up the mucus and keeps it flowing. Take the cough medicine, but keep drinking fluids.

  • **Decongestants:** These medicines open up your nose but dry out your throat. When you feel that stuffy nose, you reach for your decongestant, which opens the nasal passages. Keep the fluids incoming, even with decongestants.

Don't experiment with any medications right before a performance or concert. Try out medications ahead of time to know how your body reacts.

✔ **Keep some nasal saline spray handy.** As your body tries to wash out the germs (with a runny nose), you can use a nasal saline solution to help fight the infection when you're away from your neti pot (see the preceding section for more info on the neti pot). Using the spray when you're sick means you need to exercise good hygiene: Place the nozzle close enough to your nose to get in a good squirt, but not so close that the cold germs from your nose get on the nozzle. You don't want to get those cold germs back the next time you use the spray. This technique may get a little spray on your face, but you'll just feel like you dunked your face in a tiny ocean.

✔ **Steam it up with a humidifier.** The winter heater may dry out your home, so keep the humidifier running, especially at night. Rinse it out daily so that you don't end up growing a mold farm in the leftover water. The water condensation on the windows will dry, but feel free to turn off the humidifier if it looks like it's raining on the inside of the house. You may prefer to use a cool-mist humidifier. If so, be sure to use distilled water as directed by the manufacturer and wash the machine regularly to keep it clean.

✔ **Thin out your mucus.** If you suffer from postnasal drip, you probably have mucus that's too thick. You can try over-the-counter medications with guaifenesin (active ingredient in Mucinex and some cough medicines) to help move the mucus. Use the nasal saline solution or other medications from your doctor to help thin the mucus without drying out your throat.

✔ **Use acetaminophen (active ingredient in Tylenol) instead of ibuprofen (active ingredient in Advil).** Acetaminophen is the only pain medication that singers can take and still safely sing. Ibuprofen and aspirin dilate blood vessels and make you more susceptible to bursting a blood vessel. Keep in mind that your vocal folds are opening and closing 440 times per second if you're singing the A just above Middle C. The movement is even faster the higher you go in pitch. Research the pain medications you currently take and talk to your doctor about your options.

Protecting a Sore Throat

Here's a short list of what to do to protect your sore throat so it heals quickly: stop talking. You may be gregarious and love to talk even when you have a sore throat. But being quiet and allowing the voice to heal means no talking, whispering, or mouthing words. When you whisper, your vocal folds still close. Get a notepad and write out what you need to say, or just text or e-mail until your voice heals.

Keeping Your Emotional Life in Check

In case you're wondering, crying isn't the best thing for your voice. The tension and pressure from the emotional release doesn't exactly make the cords happy little campers. Even if your life is stressful and hectic, find ways to release aggression or pent-up emotions regularly so you aren't holding them inside. Many singers have walked in the door for lessons and were unable to sing because of emotional traumas hanging over their heads. Reliable friends or confidants make good outlets for those emotions. You may also use your singing as a means of expression. If you find yourself too tight and frustrated to sing, call a therapist for help so you can keep singing through the good times and the bad.

Chapter 24

Ten Tips for Performing Like a Pro

In This Chapter
▶ Picking the right accompaniment, clothes, and mic
▶ Looking 'em straight in the eye: Stage presence

Knowing how to behave when you're singing for an audience is important. Whether you're singing solo at Carnegie Hall; at a talent show in Tallahassee, Florida; with other performing artists in a local revival of *West Side Story;* at a Renaissance festival; or at a wedding ceremony, you want to make the right impact with your performance. Read these tips for some answers on the why and how of performing. I start with first things first and proceed to your last exit off the stage.

Rehearsing to Beat the Band

If you're a seasoned pro and you've been practicing on your own, you may not need to sing the music with an accompanist. However, I recommend at least one dress rehearsal and several more practice rehearsals before a performance. At the first couple of rehearsals, you can sing while reading from the music. For the last rehearsal and the dress rehearsal, sing the music from memory. Under pressure, it's shocking how quickly the words leave your short-term memory. By rehearsing the song from memory, you get even more opportunities to test your wonderful technique while using your acting skills. At the dress rehearsal, you also want to practice walking onstage before your song so you know how winded you are after climbing up the stairs for your entrance, walking around the stage, or down a long hallway.

You can rehearse alone or with an accompanist, coach, or voice teacher. (See Chapter 15 for the differences among these types of teachers.) At your rehearsal, record yourself. Listen to the recording a couple of times to get used to the sound of your voice in the different hall. If you put your recorder in the audience while you sing on the stage, your recording will sound farther away — that's the sound your audience will hear. You can also use your video recorder. If you decide to videotape the rehearsal, you need to view the tape several times to get used to watching yourself. You may want to experiment with this at home instead of trying it for the first time at the dress rehearsal. The night before is too late to change much. Record yourself earlier in the process so you can make adjustments. When you watch the video, check your alignment (Chapter 3), gestures (Chapter 18), and your entrance (described later in this chapter). You can also check out Chapter 10 for more info on why recording yourself is helpful.

Wearing the Right Ensemble

You may not have much choice in what you wear when you perform if you're singing in, say, a musical theater production. The director usually decides for you, and costumes are made to fit. But if you're a soloist at a wedding or you just got a gig as a lead singer in a local jazz band, the outfit you wear for the performance can make or break your evening. Consider whether your ensemble may distract either you or your audience. Noisy jewelry may look really cool with your new outfit, but if you can hear it when you move, leave it at home. Likewise, platform shoes may be *in,* but maybe you can't feel a forward flow of energy when you wear them. Spike heels are also tricky, because you may have a long walk across the stage or up to the choir loft.

When you practice, wear the outfit and shoes that you plan to wear for the performance. If you can't move your arms or can't breathe well while wearing a certain item, choose something else. Remember, moving your body enough to breathe is important when singing. Some items that may make it harder to breathe include snug gowns, pantyhose, cummerbunds, and bowties. If your performance attire is formal, the length of the gown or tails on the tux may require that you practice sitting down in the outfit. Gracefully moving the tails aside or adjusting your taffeta takes some practice.

Short skirts may look sexy, but if the stage is much higher than the audience is, the audience may also get a glimpse of your undies. Unless you want someone to look up that sexy skirt, save that outfit for the after-concert party. The same is true for clingy materials that may show every little blemish under bright lights and every little drop of sweat when the big moment arrives.

Take the noisy or bulky items out of your pockets before a performance, and remove watches and glasses. Wearing reading glasses in a solo concert performance isn't customary. Talk to your director about your options — a large print edition of the music is one option.

If you're performing in a concert or musical production that involves others, such as a chorale, musical drama, church choir, or local rock band, don't use perfume, cologne, or personal products that give off a fragrant odor. The smell of perfume causes some singers to have allergic reactions, such as sneezing, watery eyes, and itchy throats. Unless you're trying to sabotage the other singers, arrive fragrance free for the concert.

Finding Your Stance

When you know where to stand, practice walking into place. This may sound silly, but knowing how to walk across the stage and land in place isn't as easy as it sounds. Looking like a pro takes a bit of thought and practice. Even if you can't practice on the stage, choose a designated landing spot and practice walking across the room to find your position. You want to stop in place but also find your posture as you stop. Find your alignment (see Chapter 3), walk across the room, and maintain that posture. To land in place means to arrive at your spot facing the direction you need to be singing with your feet parallel and under your hips. With a band, you may choose to land in a more casual stance so your feet are flexible and ready to groove. Observe other seasoned performers to notice how they enter the stage and land in place ready to sing.

Singing with a Piano, Organ, or Band

Singing with an organ is different from singing with a piano. The pipes that create the sound often aren't near the organ console, whereas the sound from the piano comes out the back of the instrument. An organ may be harder to hear, depending on the stops the organist is using. After singing with an organ a few times, you get used to the difference in the sound. Just expect to listen more carefully, and you won't be surprised.

Singing with a band can also be a bit confusing the first time. If the speakers are pointed away from you — and they usually are — you may have trouble hearing yourself. Ask whether it's possible to have a speaker or a monitor turned toward you. Remember that bands often play pretty loudly, and turning the speaker toward yourself will unleash a huge wall of sound coming at you. Monitors are a great help if the volume is just right. Talk with the sound engineer if you can't hear yourself in the monitor. If a specific instrument plays your melody line, you may have to get used to picking out that sound from all the other instruments.

Singing with electronic amplification is very different from singing with a piano or single instrument. You may be tempted to push to make big sounds when your voice is amplified. Trust the feeling you normally have when you're practicing. You can use your ears, but you also need to use your sense of feeling to know whether you're pushing. You get really tired when you push and may not realize until later. The sound engineer adjusts the sound in the house — your job is to sing your best based on how it feels and let him adjust the sound for the audience.

Sometimes instrumentalists in the band add solos as they play. Ask the bandleader how you know when it's time to come back in. You can also ask one of the band members to nod to you when it's time for you to come in if the instrumentalists start adding extra measures. It's a good idea to take along your recorder to the rehearsal so you can record it. If you get only one shot at rehearsing with the band, you can always review your recording to get used to the timing.

Making Your Entrance

As you enter the stage from a doorway or wing, look at the audience and smile. You appear far more confident if you look straight at your audience as you walk across the stage. Practicing this is important. Your smile needs to look genuine even if you're nervous and don't want to be onstage. When you reach your position on the stage, pause in place to bow. Other performing venues may require you to be a bit more subdued. Singing for a church service, for example, requires a different approach than singing at a pop concert. For a church service, you may not get applause as you stand up to sing. It doesn't mean that the audience doesn't like you: Their focus is on your *message* in your performance instead of on the performance itself.

Before you make your entrance, be mentally prepared. You want your energy level to be up so you can pace your entrance just right. If you're dreading your entrance, you may walk slowly and appear petrified to sing. Even if you're nervous, make your entrance with confidence. You don't have to run, but walk at a pace that shows you're eager to perform.

Roping in Your Audience

When singing in a concert, knowing whether to acknowledge your audience or stick to your own little world is tricky. You can't always sing intimate songs in an intimate locale, but you can imagine being in an intimate locale by creating a fourth wall in your mind: Pretend to be in a room alone, with a wall in front of the audience. If your song addresses a group, make the audience part of your story within the time period of the song.

To get a feel for whether to include the audience as part of your song, watch the seasoned pros. The casual atmosphere at a pop concert is different from the more formal atmosphere of a classical performance. Know your audience and behave appropriately. When in doubt, watch the singers who perform before you. Waving to your sister may be just fine at the children's concert in the park, but it isn't okay when you're singing with the symphony in a big concert hall. When in Rome . . .

Televised performances may or may not have an audience. If you have an audience, you can communicate with them and let the cameras adjust to you. Otherwise, you have to pretend the camera is your audience. The director will tell you which camera is recording and tell you when to adjust your focus. It's tricky to sing well, tell your story, communicate with your imaginary audience, and move on cue to the next camera angle.

Ignoring That Mosquito

In a normal concert, people cough, enter late, or leave right in the middle of your song. People in the audience don't think about how it distracts the performer. When you practice at home, you may want to intentionally stage some distractions. Ask a friend to drop a book or walk into the room as you're singing, so you can practice concentrating even while they're bopping around. What may distract you at the performance?

- ✔ **Lights:** You want the light to be on your face so the audience can see you. That may seem blinding, but it also prevents you from seeing the audience, which is good. If you're nervous, pretend that no one is out there. Or visualize all the happy faces looking at you, delighted to see you. When you see the stage, mark the spot where the light is best on your face. After all, you got all dressed up for the show — you want the audience to see you. If you're too far forward or back, the light may miss you entirely and the audience won't see your face for the shadows. You also want to practice walking into the light so you can make it look natural that you're suddenly brilliantly illuminated. Otherwise, you may be looking up to find the best light as the audience is waiting for you to sing. Ask a friend to come to the rehearsal to check the lighting for you.

- ✔ **Flashing photos:** You can ask your friends and family not to distract you by taking photos, but you may not be able to control the entire audience. If someone does start taking photos in the middle of your song, try to focus on an object in front of you so you aren't looking right into the flashing light. Blinking lights from camcorders can also be mesmerizing or maddening. Television cameras have a red light to indicate recording and the cameras may move around a lot to get different angles.

- ✔ **Other performers:** In the wings, you may see many people milling around waiting for their entrance. Focus on your task and ignore them. In a smaller cast, you can ask them to not move around the sides while you sing, but you may just have to figure out how to ignore them if they forget or if you're in a large production with a lot of stage crew.

Handling Those Hands

Keeping your hands at your sides is safest. It may not be the most interesting place for them, but you won't go too wrong by erring on the side of calm and still. If you choose to gesture, make it a complete gesture and make sure that your elbows move out, away from your body. You may look like you're flipping burgers if you move just your hands and not your arms. Of course, if you're using a hand-held microphone, your gestures need to accommodate it. (See the "Using the Mic" section, coming up next in this chapter.)

Another option for your hands is to clasp them in front of you. Clasping your hands at your waistline is cool, but wringing your hands isn't. Being nervous at a performance is okay, but try not to show it. Don't let 'em see you sweat, as they say. Pretend that performing is the easiest thing in the world. Your hands can also rest on the piano, if it's near enough to you and if the lid is closed. If the lid is open on a baby grand or grand piano, don't put your hand on the lid or inside the lid: It makes your audience nervous to see your hand right where the lid may fall. You can also check out Chapter 18 for some suggestions on gesturing.

You don't want to put your hands behind you and wiggle them or clasp them right in front of your zipper. Little kids usually put their hands at their zipper when they have to go to the bathroom, so you don't want your audience to make that assumption. Little kids also put their hands behind them to pick their seat before the show.

Using the Mic

Microphones (*mics,* for short; pronounced like the name *Mike*) can be secured on a stand, held by hand, set on the floor, or hooked onto your body. Knowing how to handle this bundle of electronic wizardry takes a little practice. Ask if you can practice with the mic before the instruments start playing. That way, you can hear the difference between too close and too far. Consider the following list of microphones and how you're going to work with the particular type you'll be using:

- ✔ **Body mic:** You may have seen body microphones on TV: A microphone cord goes through your clothing, and you wear a small box under your clothes or on your belt. If you don't get a chance to use one before the show, just visualize the sensation of having the box attached to you so that you aren't shocked to feel something hanging on your back.

- ✔ **Floor level:** If the microphones are on the floor, the audience is going to hear the sound of you walking across the stage. You want to practice walking in your performance shoes to know how much noise you make as you enter the stage. You may be tempted to tighten your legs or toes so you don't make so much sound. Instead, try walking without pushing down into the floor; connect with the floor but don't push your feet into the floor. This allows you to walk with ease and without too much noise.

✔ **Hand-held:** If you're using a hand-held mic, hold it far enough away from your mouth that you don't touch it with your lips, but close enough that the sound of your voice reaches the microphone. Consider these rules for mic use:

- Don't blow into the mic or tap on it to determine whether it's on. Instead, speak into it. Blowing into the mic or tapping on it may damage the internal parts.

- Place your hand on the mic but away from the head. Performers like to cup the mic. Placing your hand around the head of the mic totally changes the way your voice is amplified. Note the sound of your voice in the mic when you put your hand on the head and cover part of the head, and then compare the sound when you don't. You can talk to the sound engineer about the differences in the sound and what you need for your performance. You may have to explain that you want to cup the mic and that you need help to get the sound amplified to the audience.

✔ **Stationary:** If your mic is on a stand, you can move around to adjust the sound. Check out the stand before the concert. The height of most microphone stands is adjustable. Look at the middle of the stand, and you'll probably see a ring that you can twist to adjust the height. If you have to turn on the microphone, practice walking to the stand and finding the button so that you feel confident you can turn it on with your hands shaking. It's okay if your hands shake. You just have to know that it's going to happen and adjust your movements to feel confident.

If you don't sing with a microphone, use your knowledge of resonance from Chapter 7 to help your voice carry over the instruments.

Taking Your Bow and Leaving the Stage

The manner in which you take your bow depends on the concert. If you're a famous diva, you may curtsy, but I think it's better to wait on that until you arrive at one of the big opera houses. Until then, use the tried-and-true standard bow: Bend from the waist and bow your head to the audience.

✔ After you find your spot on the stage, stop in place (with your feet close together) and lean forward from the waist. You want your head down, looking at the floor momentarily. Otherwise, it looks like you're looking up to make sure that everyone is clapping. Remember that you have to lean forward in your performance attire. If that's a gown or tuxedo, make sure that it isn't so tight that you can't bend over at all or without revealing too much cleavage when you bow.

✔ Your hands can be along the sides of your legs or clasped in front. Allow your hands to slide down your leg as you bend over. Remember not to put your hands in front of your zipper if you choose to clasp them.

✔ Slowly count to two and raise your torso again. After you bow, acknowledge your accompanist. If the piece was a huge ensemble number, you may bow with your accompanist. You want to make that decision in advance and plan who bows when and after whom. Some people like to turn and extend their arm to acknowledge the accompanist. If the pianist isn't leaving the stage with you, that's appropriate. But if you're a team, plan bows separately and then together.

Exiting the stage is also an art. When you finish singing and take your bow, head toward the exit. Look at your audience again and smile as you exit the stage. If the audience just loved what they heard, they may continue clapping, so you can take another bow. Wait for the peak of the applause and then go back onto the stage. If you had an accompanist playing for you, ask the accompanist to bow with you again or bow with you at the next curtain call.

Depending on the situation, you may want to prepare an encore. How will you know when to sing the encore? Finish your last number, hear the applause, and exit the stage; return to the stage for your bow and exit the stage again; and return to the stage and sing the encore, or return for another bow and then come back out to sing the encore. An encore is appropriate for a recital where you are the main attraction or for a performance with a group such as a band or symphony. When you do more performing, you'll figure out when an encore is appropriate and what to prepare for the encore.

Part VI
Appendixes

In this part . . .

A helpful list arranges songs according to voice type. I also tell you whether the song is upbeat or slow before you even hear it. Singing songs for fun may not challenge your technique. This list of well-known songs is not only fun to sing but also helps you polish your technique.

You can also find out more about how you can use the super CD that comes with this book. Various singers recorded the exercises that you see next to the CD icon throughout the book; you can hear them demonstrate the sounds for you and then sing along yourself. Some of the sounds and ideas in the book may be new to you, and it's helpful to hear someone making the correct sounds for you.

Appendix A

Suggested Songs to Advance Your Singing Technique

· ·

This list of suggested songs is designed to advance your singing technique. As you practice the exercises and techniques in the book, you can use this list of songs to apply your new skills.

A beginner song is one with easy rhythms, narrow range, and melody that often moves in stepwise motion with the piano accompaniment at a comfortable tempo.

An intermediate song has more difficult rhythm, wider range, and melody that skips in larger intervals. It's somewhat independent of the piano accompaniment and moves at a faster pace.

Belt songs are typically much more difficult because of technique demands, big stories to tell, and difficult music. Work with the exercises in Chapter 13 until you feel confident that your belt is healthy.

The classical songs show a label of *slow, medium,* or *fast.* The musical theater songs are marked as a ballad or an up-tempo.

Classical: Ten Songs for Soprano

Five beginner songs for soprano:

- "Evening Prayer," from *Hänsel und Gretal,* by Engelbert Humperdinck (slow)

- "Sandmännchen" (The Little Sandman), by Johannes Brahms (slow)

- "My Mother Bids Me Bind My Hair," by Joseph Haydn (medium)

- "Clair de Lune" (Moonlight), by Camille Saint-Saëns (medium)

- "The Lass from the Low Countree," by John Jacob Niles (medium)

Five intermediate songs for soprano:

- ✔ "Auf ein altes Bild" (To an Old Picture), by Hugo Wolf (slow)

- ✔ "A Kiss in the Dark," by Victor Herbert (medium)

- ✔ "La Procession" (The Procession), by César Franck (slow)

- ✔ "Nina," by Giovanni Pergolesi (medium)

- ✔ "Con amores, la mi madre" (With Love, O My Mother), by Juan de Anchieta and Fernando J. Obradors (medium)

Classical: Ten Songs for Mezzo

Five beginner songs for mezzo:

- ✔ "The Ash Grove," folksong (medium)

- ✔ "Heidenröslein" (Hedge-roses), by Franz Schubert (medium)

- ✔ "Spring Sorrow," by John Ireland (medium)

- ✔ "Lied der Braut" (Song of the Betrothed), by Robert Schumann (slow)

- ✔ "Lasciatemi morire!" (Let Death Now Come), by Claudio Monteverdi (slow)

Five intermediate songs for mezzo:

- ✔ "Joshua Fit the Battle of Jericho," spiritual (medium)

- ✔ "If Music Be the Food of Love," by Henry Purcell (medium)

- ✔ "Aimons-nous" (Let Us Love Each Other), by Camille Saint-Saëns (medium)

- ✔ "El tra la la y el punteado" (The Tra La La and the Guitar-Strum), by Enrique Granados (fast)

- ✔ "Liebst du um Schönheit" (If You Love for Beauty), by Gustav Mahler (slow)

Classical: Ten Songs for Tenor

Five beginner songs for tenor

- ✔ "Sehnsucht nach dem Frühling" (Longing for Spring), by Wolfgang Mozart (fast)

- ✔ "The Gypsy Rover," traditional Irish ballad (medium)

- ✔ "Volkslied" (At Parting), by Felix Mendelssohn (slow)

- ✔ "Gia il sole dal Gange" (The Sun O'er the Ganges), by Alessandro Scarlatti (fast)
- ✔ "Amarilli, mia bella" (Amarilli, My Fair One), by Guilio Caccini (slow)

Five intermediate songs for tenor

- ✔ "Psyché," by Emile Paladilhe (medium)
- ✔ "I'll Sail upon the Dog Star," by Henry Purcell (fast)
- ✔ "Vittoria, mio core!" (Victorious My Heart), by Giacomo Carissimi (fast)
- ✔ "Ich liebe dich" (I Love Thee), by Edvard Grieg (slow)
- ✔ "Selve, voi, che le speranze" (Forest, Thy Green Arbors), by Salvator Rosa (slow)

Classical: Ten Songs for Baritone or Bass

Five beginner songs for baritone or bass

- ✔ "Red River Valley," by Celius Dougherty (medium)
- ✔ "Für music" (For Music), by Robert Franz (medium)
- ✔ "The Water Is Wide," English folksong (medium)
- ✔ "Silent Noon," by Ralph Vaughn Williams (slow)
- ✔ "Virgin, tutta amor" (Virgin, Full of Grace), by Francesco Durante (slow)

Five intermediate songs for baritone or bass

- ✔ "Now Sleeps the Crimson Petal," by Roger Quilter (medium)
- ✔ "The Roadside Fire," by Ralph Vaughn Williams (medium)
- ✔ "Kein Hälmlein wächst auf Erden" (Soft Dews from Heaven Falling), by W. F. Bach (slow)
- ✔ "Madrigal," by Vincent D'Indy (medium)
- ✔ "What Shall I Do," by Henry Purcell (medium)

Musical Theater: Ten Songs for Soprano

Five beginner songs for soprano

- ✔ "Goodnight My Someone," from *The Music Man*, by Meredith Willson (ballad)

- ✔ "Getting to Know You," from *The King and I*, by Richard Rodgers and Oscar Hammerstein (ballad)

- ✔ "Wouldn't It Be Loverly," from *My Fair Lady*, by Alan Jay Lerner and Frederick Loewe (up-tempo)

- ✔ "So Many People," from *Saturday Night*, by Stephen Sondheim (ballad)

- ✔ "Something Good," from *The Sound of Music*, by Richard Rodgers (ballad)

Five intermediate songs for soprano

- ✔ "Lovely," from *A Funny Thing Happened on the Way to the Forum*, by Stephen Sondheim (ballad)

- ✔ "Never Never Land," from *Peter Pan*, by Betty Comden and Adolph Green (ballad)

- ✔ "A Lovely Night," from *Cinderella*, by Richard Rodgers and Oscar Hammerstein (up-tempo)

- ✔ "Home," from *Phantom*, by Maury Yeston (ballad)

- ✔ "It Wonders Me," from *Plain and Fancy*, by Arnold Horwitt and Albert Hague (ballad)

Musical Theater: Ten Songs for Mezzo

Five beginner songs for mezzo

- ✔ "I'm Old Fashioned," by Johnny Mercer and Jerome Kern (ballad)

- ✔ "It's a Lovely Day Today," by Irving Berlin (up-tempo)

- ✔ "Anywhere I Wander," by Frank Loesser (ballad)

- ✔ "Feed the Birds," from *Mary Poppins*, by Robert Sherman (ballad)

- ✔ "Give My Regards to Broadway," by George Cohan (up-tempo)

Five intermediate songs for mezzo

- ✔ "The Party's Over," from *Bells Are Ringing*, by Betty Comden, Adolph Green, and Jule Styne (ballad)

- ✔ "If He Really Knew Me," from *They're Playing Our Song*, by Carole Bayer Sager and Marvin Hamlisch (ballad)

- ✔ "I'd Be Surprisingly Good for You," from *Evita*, by Tim Rice and Andrew Lloyd Webber (up-tempo)

- ✔ "A Cockeyed Optimist," from *South Pacific*, by Richard Rodgers and Oscar Hammerstein (up-tempo)

- ✔ "There's a Fine, Fine Line," from *Avenue Q*, by Robert Lopez and Jeff Marz (ballad)

Musical Theater: Ten Belt Songs for Women

Five belt songs for soprano

- ✔ "Gimme Gimme," from *Thoroughly Modern Millie*, by Jeanine Tesori and Dick Scanlan (up-tempo)

- ✔ "Wherever He Ain't," from *Mack and Mabel*, by Jerry Herman (up-tempo)

- ✔ "There's No Man Left for Me," from *Will Rogers Follies*, by Cy Colman, Betty Comden, and Adolph Green (up-tempo)

- ✔ "Waiting for Life," from *Once On This Island*, by Lynn Ahrens and Stephen Flaherty (up-tempo)

- ✔ "On the Other Side of the Tracks," from *Little Me*, by Cy Coleman and Carolyn Leigh (up-tempo)

Five belt songs for mezzo

- ✔ "West End Avenue," from *The Magic Show*, by Stephen Schwartz (up-tempo)

- ✔ "I'm Going Back," from *Bells Are Ringing*, by Betty Comden, Adolph Green, and Jule Styne (ballad)

- ✔ "Maybe This Time," from *Cabaret*, by Fred Ebb and John Kander (ballad)

- ✔ "Honey Bun," from *South Pacific*, by Richard Rodgers and Oscar Hammerstein (up-tempo)

- ✔ "I Resolve," from *She Loves Me*, by Jerry Bock and Sheldon Harnick (up-tempo)

Musical Theater: Ten Songs for Tenor

Five beginner songs for tenor

- "Anywhere I Wander," from *Hans Christian Anderson,* by Frank Loesser (ballad)

- "I've Got My Eyes on You," from *Broadway Medley of 1940,* by Cole Porter (ballad)

- "Long Ago," from *Cover Girl,* by Ira Gershwin and Jerome Kern (ballad)

- "'Til Him," from *The Producers,* by Mel Brooks (ballad)

- "Young and Foolish," from *Plain and Fancy,* by Arnold Horwitt and Albert Hogue (ballad)

Five intermediate songs for tenor

- "Old Devil Moon," from *Finian's Rainbow,* by E. Y. Harburg and Burton Lane (up-tempo)

- "Stranger in Paradise," from *Kismet,* by Robert Wright and George Forrest (ballad)

- "A Wonderful Day Like Today," from *The Roar of the Greasepaint — The Smell of the Crowd,* by Leslie Bricusse and Anthony Newly (up-tempo)

- "Geraniums in the Winder," from *Carousel,* by Richard Rodgers and Oscar Hammerstein (ballad)

- "I Believe in You," from *How to Succeed,* by Frank Loesser (ballad)

Musical Theater: Ten Songs for Baritenor

Five beginner songs for baritenor

- "On the Street Where You Live," from *My Fair Lady,* by Alan Jay Lerner and Frederick Loewe (ballad)

- "Waitin' for the Light to Shine," from *Big River,* by Roger Millel (ballad)

- "Lonely Room," from *Oklahoma,* by Richard Rodgers and Oscar Hammerstein (ballad)

- "Les Poisson," from *The Little Mermaid,* by Howard Ashman and Alan Menken (up-tempo)

- "There She Is," from *Titanic,* by Maury Yeston and Peter Stone (up-tempo)

Five intermediate songs for baritenor

✔ "Soon It's Gonna Rain," from *The Fantasticks,* by Tom Jones and Harvey Schmidt (ballad)

✔ "When I'm Not Near the Girl," by E. Y. Harburg and Burton Lane (up-tempo)

✔ "Santa Fe," from *Newsies,* by Alan Menken and Jack Feldman (up-tempo)

✔ "Steppin' Out with My Baby," from the film *Easter Parade,* by Irving Berlin (up-tempo)

✔ "Lucky in Love," from *Good News,* by B.G. DeSylva, Lew Brown, and Ray Henderson.

Musical Theater: Ten Belt Songs for Men

Five belt songs for tenor

✔ "Sit Down, You're Rockin' the Boat," from *Guys and Dolls,* by Frank Loesser (up-tempo)

✔ "This is the Moment," from *Jekyll and Hyde,* by Leslie Bricusse and Frank Wildhorn (ballad)

✔ "Moving Too Fast," from *The Last Five Years,* from Jason Robert Brown (up-tempo)

✔ "Mama Says," from *Footloose,* by Dean Pitchford and Tom Snow (up-tempo)

✔ "One Song Glory," from *Rent,* by Jonathan Larson (up-tempo)

Five belt songs for baritenor

✔ "This Is Not Over Yet," from *Parade,* by Jason Robert Brown (up-tempo)

✔ "Stars," from *Les Misérables,* by Claude-Michel Schönberg, Herbert Krutmer, and Alain Boublil (ballad)

✔ "Private Conversation," from *Side Show,* by Bill Russell and Henry Kreiger (ballad)

✔ "What Am I Doin'?" from *Closer Than Ever,* by Richard Maltby and David Shire (up-tempo)

✔ "Justice Will Be Done," from *Martin Guerre,* by Claude-Michel Schönberg, Alain Boublil, and Stephen Clark (ballad)

Country: Ten Songs for Women

- ✔ "Walkin' After Midnight," by Alan Bock and Donn Hecht, as sung by Patsy Cline

- ✔ "Redneck Woman," by John Rich and Gretchen Wilson

- ✔ "Sweet Dreams," by Don Gibson, as sung by Patsy Cline

- ✔ "Ring of Fire," by June Carter Cash

- ✔ "Deep in the Heart of Texas," by June Hershey and Don Swander

- ✔ "This Kiss," by Beth Nielsen, as sung by Faith Hill

- ✔ "How Do I Live," by Diane Warren

- ✔ "Blue," by Bill Mack, as sung by LeAnn Rimes

- ✔ "Backwoods Barbie," as sung by Dolly Parton

- ✔ "My Valentine," by Jim Brickman and Jack David Kugell, as sung by Martina McBride

Country: Ten Songs for Men

- ✔ "Your Cheatin' Heart," by Hank Williams

- ✔ "I Walk the Line," by Johnny Cash

- ✔ "The Gambler," by Don Schlitz, as sung by Kris Kristofferson

- ✔ "Friends in Low Places," by Dewayne Blackwell and Bud Lee, as sung by Garth Brooks

- ✔ "For the Good Times," by Kris Kristofferson

- ✔ "Who's Your Daddy?" by Toby Keith

- ✔ "The Thunder Rolls," by Pat Alger and Garth Brooks

- ✔ "When Love Fades," by Chuck Cannon and Toby Keith

- ✔ "Gettin' You Home," by Cory Batten, Kent Blazy, and Chris Young

- ✔ "It Did," by Brad Paisley

Pop-Rock: Ten Songs for Women

- "Downtown," by Tony Hatch, as sung by Petula Clark
- "It's Too Late," by Toni Stern, as sung by Carole King
- "Somewhere out There," by James Horner, Barry Mann, and Cynthia Weil, as sung by Linda Ronstad and James Ingram
- "Where the Boys Are," by Howard Greenfield and Neil Sedaka, as sung by Connie Francis
- "My Heart Will Go On," by James Horner and Will Jennings, as sung by Celine Dion
- "Do You Know Where You're Going To?" by Gerry Goffin and Mike Masser
- "When I Fall in Love," by Edward Heyman and Victor Young
- "Band of Gold," by Ronald Dunbar and Edith Wayne
- "Walk On By," by Hal David and Burt Bacharach, as sung by Dionne Warwick
- "River Deep, Mountain High," by Ellie Greenwich, Jeff Barry, and Phil Spector, as sung by Ike and Tina Turner

Pop-Rock: Ten Songs for Men

- "Georgia on My Mind," by Stuart Gorrell and Hoagy Carmichael
- "My Cherie Amour," by Stevie Wonder, Sylvia Moy, and Jenry Cosby
- "My Girl," by Smokey Robinson and Ronald White
- "Hurt So Good," by John Mellancamp and Georg Green
- "Good Night," by John Lennon and Paul McCartney
- "Wake Me Up Before You Go-Go," by George Michael
- "Shot Through the Heart," by Bon Jovi
- "Desperado," by Don Henley and Glen Frey, as sung by Eagles
- "She's Got a Way," by Billy Joel
- "Bridge over Troubled Water," by Simon and Garfunkel

Appendix B

About the CD

A ll the musical examples included in *Singing For Dummies,* 2nd Edition, are recorded on the CD that comes with this book. On the CD, you can find 63 exercises to improve your singing. In the chapters, next to the "On the CD" icon, you can find an explanation and helpful instructions for each of the tracks on the CD.

No singing experience is necessary to enjoy this book or the CD. Just follow the suggestions in the chapters to make consistent progress with your singing technique.

Be sure to keep the CD with the book. The suggestions and instructions in the chapters add helpful information to go with your listening pleasure as you sing along. The plastic envelope protects the CD surface to keep it in tip-top shape. Finding the CD in the book is also easier than hunting through your CD collection each time you want to listen to the exercises.

System Requirements

Note that this is an audio-only CD — just pop it into your CD player (or whatever you use to listen to music CDs). Use the CD as a cool tool to sing with at home, in your car, or wherever you find space to practice.

If you're listening to the CD on your computer, make sure that your computer meets the minimum system requirements shown in the following list. If your computer doesn't meet most of these requirements, you may have problems using the CD.

- A PC with a Pentium or faster processor, or a Mac OS computer with a 68040 or faster processor.

- Microsoft Windows 95 or later, or Mac OS system software 7.6.1 or later.

- At least 32MB of total RAM installed on your computer. For best performance, I recommend at least 64MB.

- A CD-ROM drive.

- A sound card for PCs. Mac OS computers have built-in sound support.

- Media Player, such as Windows Media Player or Real Player.

If you need more information on the basics, check out these books published by Wiley:

- *PCs For Dummies,* by Dan Gookin

- *PCs All-in-One Desk Reference For Dummies,* by Mark L. Chambers

- *Macs For Dummies,* by David Pogue

- *The Flat-Screen iMac For Dummies,* by David Pogue

- *The iMac For Dummies Quick Reference,* by Jennifer Watson

- *Mac OS X For Dummies,* by Bob LeVitus

- *Windows 95 For Dummies, Windows 98 For Dummies, Windows 2000 Professional For Dummies, Windows XP For Dummies,* or *Microsoft Windows ME Millennium Edition For Dummies,* all by Andy Rathbone

- *Windows XP All-in-One Desk Reference For Dummies,* by Woody Leonhard

Track Listings

Each track begins with the piano playing the melody or musical pattern you see printed on the page. After the piano plays the pattern, you hear a singer demonstrate the sounds of the pattern. The first time through, listen to the singer; then sing by yourself during the following repetitions of the pattern. Each pattern is repeated several times in several different keys, so you can practice extending your range. The CD features both male and female singers. Feel free to sing along with any of the tracks. If the demonstration is a male voice, look at the text in the chapter that corresponds with that track for tips on how to make the pattern work for a female voice.

If some of the patterns are too high for you, read the text in the corresponding chapter for help on getting your voice ready for the higher notes or other technical skills being addressed. You can also find suggestions on singing the pattern lower until you're ready for the higher notes.

As you listen to the CD, you may notice that the patterns gradually get harder. You don't have to sing every track today. You can work on the first few tracks until you're comfortable applying all the suggestions in the text. When you're really cooking, move on to the next group of exercises. You can also check out Chapter 10 for help designing a practice routine. Skipping some of the information you already know is always an option. If you're an advanced singer with some experience, you may want to skip to some of the harder patterns in the latter chapters. Go for it! If you find yourself struggling with some of the later patterns, back up and work on some of the earlier patterns a little longer. The CD is designed to keep you singing and practicing for quite some time.

After inserting the CD, you can use the track skip control button on your CD player to move between tracks. The cue/review function is also a fast-forward or rewind feature, which allows you to fast-forward through a specific track to get to just the right repetition of the patterns. The chart in this chapter gives you the exact timing of each track.

Following is a list of tracks on the CD, along with the timing of each track and figure number within the chapter. A figure number has two numbers; the first is the chapter number, which helps you locate the chapter that corresponds with the track. (The second number, if you're curious, indicates the order of the figures within the chapter.) Some of the tracks don't have a musical example printed in the chapter. On these tracks, singers demonstrate specific skills that you can work within that chapter.

Track	(Time)	Figure Number	Pattern Description
1	1:31	N/A	Introduction to *Singing For Dummies,* 2nd Edition
2	1:13	4-1	Lip and tongue trills
3	0:38	N/A	Sliding on pitch (Chapter 5)
4	1:34	5-1	Bouncing the tongue and jaw
5	1:06	6-1	Creating a legato line
6	1:02	6-2	Trilling a long, legato line
7	1:30	6-3	Managing long phrases
8	0:41	N/A	Straight tone and vibrato (Chapter 6)
9	1:18	8-2	Alternating vowels for precise lip shapes
10	1:06	8-4	Arching the tongue while alternating vowels
11	1:43	9-1	Singing tip consonants
12	1:30	9-2	Singing soft palate consonants
13	1:24	9-3	Singing lip consonants

(continued)

Track	(Time)	Figure Number	Pattern Description
14	1:00	9-4	Combining your consonants
15	1:09	11-3	Taking it down
16	1:43	11-4	Descending by step
17	1:16	11-5	Gliding through the middle
18	0:55	11-6	Moving along the four in middle voice
19	1:18	11-9	Singing fourth
20	1:10	11-10	Bringing up chest voice
21	1:17	11-13	Working with closed vowels
22	1:06	11-14	Spinning out in head voice
23	0:17	N/A	Demonstration of falsetto (Chapter 11)
24	0:50	11-15	Checking out your falsetto
25	0:51	11-16	Flipping out of falsetto
26	1:02	11-17	Gliding down out of falsetto
27	1:14	11-18	Sliding up to falsetto
28	1:23	11-19	Smoothing the transitions
29	1:28	11-20	Creating a legato line in and out of chest voice
30	1:22	11-21	Working from middle voice up to head voice
31	0:56	11-22	Spinning down
32	1:03	11-23	Sliding into a mix
33	1:29	11-24	Mixing it up
34	1:36	11-25	Alternating between chest and head dominated mix
35	1:24	12-1	Skipping around on staccato
36	1:18	12-2	*Messa di voce*
37	2:27	12-3	Descending
38	1:15	12-4	Stepping between registers
39	1:04	12-5	Flexing on five notes
40	1:16	12-6	Sliding up the scale
41	0:56	12-7	Tripping along the scale

Track	(Time)	Figure Number	Pattern Description
42	1:13	12-8	Spicing it up with syncopation
43	1:46	12-9	Bouncing on thirds
44	0:42	12-10	Checking out pop riffs
45	0:38	12-11	Descending pop riff
46	1:43	N/A	Improvising with chords on the piano (Chapter 12)
47	0:59	N/A	Improvising with a pop tune (Chapter 12)
48	0:49	N/A	Improvising by yourself on a pop tune (Chapter 12)
49	0:53	N/A	Speaking up the scale: Give That Back! (Chapter 13)
50	0:21	N/A	Demonstration of chest voice and belt (Chapter 13)
51	0:15	N/A	Male belting demonstration (Chapter 13)
52	0:58	N/A	Speaking in a mix: I Wanna Know! (Chapter 13)
53	0:26	N/A	High-energy speaking sounds (Chapter 13)
54	0:29	N/A	Three types of resonance: Back, middle, and front (Chapter 13)
55	0:39	N/A	Nya (Chapter 13)
56	0:55	13-1	Belt tune: "That Ain't It Man"
57	035	13-2	Belting Up the Scale: Not Now
58	0:35	N/A	Belt tune: "Take Shelter, I'm a Belter" (Chapter 13)
59	1:06	13-3	Sustaining belt sounds: That's mine! That's mine!
60	0:39	N/A	Belt tune: "Let's Celebrate" (Chapter 13)
61	1:13	17-1	Speaking through the rhythms of "Simple Things" (Chapter 17)
62	1:18	17-1	Singing the melody of "Simple Things" on *ah*
63	2:27	17-1	"Simple Things," by Martha Sullivan © 2003

Troubleshooting

If you have trouble with the CD, please call the Wiley Product Technical Support phone number at 800-762-2974. Outside the United States, call 317-572-3994. You can also contact Wiley Product Technical Support at www.wiley.com/techsupport. Wiley will provide technical support only for installation and other general quality control items. For technical support on the applications themselves, consult the program's vendor or author.

To place additional orders or to request information about other Wiley products, please call 877-762-2974.

Index

• *N* •

• *O* •

Wiley Publishing, Inc.
End-User License Agreement

READ THIS. You should carefully read these terms and conditions before opening the software packet(s) included with this book "Book". This is a license agreement "Agreement" between you and Wiley Publishing, Inc. "WPI". By opening the accompanying software packet(s), you acknowledge that you have read and accept the following terms and conditions. If you do not agree and do not want to be bound by such terms and conditions, promptly return the Book and the unopened software packet(s) to the place you obtained them for a full refund.

1. **License Grant.** WPI grants to you (either an individual or entity) a nonexclusive license to use one copy of the enclosed software program(s) (collectively, the "Software") solely for your own personal or business purposes on a single computer (whether a standard computer or a workstation component of a multi-user network). The Software is in use on a computer when it is loaded into temporary memory (RAM) or installed into permanent memory (hard disk, CD-ROM, or other storage device). WPI reserves all rights not expressly granted herein.

2. **Ownership.** WPI is the owner of all right, title, and interest, including copyright, in and to the compilation of the Software recorded on the physical packet included with this Book "Software Media". Copyright to the individual programs recorded on the Software Media is owned by the author or other authorized copyright owner of each program. Ownership of the Software and all proprietary rights relating thereto remain with WPI and its licensers.

3. **Restrictions on Use and Transfer.**

   (a) You may only (i) make one copy of the Software for backup or archival purposes, or (ii) transfer the Software to a single hard disk, provided that you keep the original for backup or archival purposes. You may not (i) rent or lease the Software, (ii) copy or reproduce the Software through a LAN or other network system or through any computer subscriber system or bulletin-board system, or (iii) modify, adapt, or create derivative works based on the Software.

   (b) You may not reverse engineer, decompile, or disassemble the Software. You may transfer the Software and user documentation on a permanent basis, provided that the transferee agrees to accept the terms and conditions of this Agreement and you retain no copies. If the Software is an update or has been updated, any transfer must include the most recent update and all prior versions.

4. **Restrictions on Use of Individual Programs.** You must follow the individual requirements and restrictions detailed for each individual program in the "About the CD" appendix of this Book or on the Software Media. These limitations are also contained in the individual license agreements recorded on the Software Media. These limitations may include a requirement that after using the program for a specified period of time, the user must pay a registration fee or discontinue use. By opening the Software packet(s), you agree to abide by the licenses and restrictions for these individual programs that are detailed in the "About the CD" appendix and/or on the Software Media. None of the material on this Software Media or listed in this Book may ever be redistributed, in original or modified form, for commercial purposes.

5. **Limited Warranty.**

   (a) WPI warrants that the Software and Software Media are free from defects in materials and workmanship under normal use for a period of sixty (60) days from the date of purchase of this Book. If WPI receives notification within the warranty period of defects in materials or workmanship, WPI will replace the defective Software Media.

   (b) **WPI AND THE AUTHOR(S) OF THE BOOK DISCLAIM ALL OTHER WARRANTIES, EXPRESS OR IMPLIED, INCLUDING WITHOUT LIMITATION IMPLIED WARRANTIES OF MERCHANTABILITY AND FITNESS FOR A PARTICULAR PURPOSE, WITH RESPECT TO THE SOFTWARE, THE PROGRAMS, THE SOURCE CODE CONTAINED THEREIN, AND/OR THE TECHNIQUES DESCRIBED IN THIS BOOK. WPI DOES NOT WARRANT THAT THE FUNCTIONS CONTAINED IN THE SOFTWARE WILL MEET YOUR REQUIREMENTS OR THAT THE OPERATION OF THE SOFTWARE WILL BE ERROR FREE.**

   (c) This limited warranty gives you specific legal rights, and you may have other rights that vary from jurisdiction to jurisdiction.

6. **Remedies.**

   (a) WPI's entire liability and your exclusive remedy for defects in materials and workmanship shall be limited to replacement of the Software Media, which may be returned to WPI with a copy of your receipt at the following address: Software Media Fulfillment Department, Attn.: *Singing For Dummies,* 2nd Edition, Wiley Publishing, Inc., 10475 Crosspoint Blvd., Indianapolis, IN 46256, or call 1-877-762-2974. Please allow four to six weeks for delivery. This Limited Warranty is void if failure of the Software Media has resulted from accident, abuse, or misapplication. Any replacement Software Media will be warranted for the remainder of the original warranty period or thirty (30) days, whichever is longer.

   (b) In no event shall WPI or the author be liable for any damages whatsoever (including without limitation damages for loss of business profits, business interruption, loss of business information, or any other pecuniary loss) arising from the use of or inability to use the Book or the Software, even if WPI has been advised of the possibility of such damages.

   (c) Because some jurisdictions do not allow the exclusion or limitation of liability for consequential or incidental damages, the above limitation or exclusion may not apply to you.

7. **U.S. Government Restricted Rights.** Use, duplication, or disclosure of the Software for or on behalf of the United States of America, its agencies and/or instrumentalities "U.S. Government" is subject to restrictions as stated in paragraph (c)(1)(ii) of the Rights in Technical Data and Computer Software clause of DFARS 252.227-7013, or subparagraphs (c) (1) and (2) of the Commercial Computer Software - Restricted Rights clause at FAR 52.227-19, and in similar clauses in the NASA FAR supplement, as applicable.

8. **General.** This Agreement constitutes the entire understanding of the parties and revokes and supersedes all prior agreements, oral or written, between them and may not be modified or amended except in a writing signed by both parties hereto that specifically refers to this Agreement. This Agreement shall take precedence over any other documents that may be in conflict herewith. If any one or more provisions contained in this Agreement are held by any court or tribunal to be invalid, illegal, or otherwise unenforceable, each and every other provision shall remain in full force and effect.